Everything is Grace:
The Diary of a Global International Immigrant Parish Priest

Fr. George Aranha Ed.D

With much affection
and sincere appreciation

Goa 1556

2013

$25

Goa 1556

First published in 2013 by Goa,1556 – an endeavor to promote the written word in Goa and beyond.

784, Near Lourdes Convent, Sonarbhat, Saligao 403511

Bardez Goa India. Ph +91-832-2409490 or +91-9822122436.

Email goa1556@gmail.com http://goa1556.goa-india.org

10 9 8 7 6 5 4 3 2 1

ISBN 978-93-80739-54-0

Typeset using LyX http://www.lyx.org by Goa,1556.

Printed in Bangalore by Brilliant Printers Pvt. Ltd

http://www.brilliantprinters.com

Project coordinated by Frederick Noronha, for Goa,1556.

Cover design by Russel Gonsalves

Contents

Contents

These memoirs are dedicated
to my father and mother
Eric and Cecilia

2013

Acknowledgements

I AM GRATEFUL to my parents, Eric and Cecilia, for being storytellers. In the tradition of the Indian countryside in which they were raised, they orally and constantly shared their wisdom and faith stories with me and my siblings.

We have always been a close family. So, I am thankful to my siblings for reminding me of some of the stories and details that I needed to prepare these memoirs. I am proud of them for their constant support.

A special word of thanks goes to Karen Gilleland, who edited the very first draft and encouraged me to tell the story.

I am thankful to my brother-in-law, Franklin Gonsalves, for offering helpful editorial recommendations.

My nephew, Russell Gonsalves, designed the cover.

I am grateful to God for everything.

Introduction

T HE IMMIGRANT Catholic priest in the United States of America since the seventies has been somewhat of an enigma. There are those who welcome him with open arms because there is a shortage of priests. Others believe that the Church in the United States will never face her own challenges as long as there is a steady stream of immigrant priests coming from all over the world. The number of Catholics in America keeps growing year after year fueled by people arriving from densely populated and overwhelmingly 'Catholic' countries (where Catholics form the majority). Yet, several parishes have been closed down all across the United States due to the lack of clergy and vocations.

The United States has always had missionaries to serve the needs of immigrants from European nations in the last two centuries. Although there were Italian, French, Spanish and Portuguese clergy and religious, the vast majority that came to this country was from Ireland. There were many Irish vocations to the priesthood and the religious life in the past and their Bishops and religious Superiors either commissioned young men to serve abroad or they themselves opted to serve in the missions of America.

In the last century, from the forties to the sixties, there were many homegrown diocesan and religious vocations, so much so that some older Americans even today wonder why foreign missionaries are needed at all.

In 1965 the United States Congress passed legislation changing the international law favoring immigration from parts of the world other than Western Europe. This legislation allowed for people from Asian and Latin American countries to enter the United States in unprecedented numbers. As the number of Catholics increased substantially, there was an even greater need for Catholic priests and religious to meet the laity's sacramental and spiritual demands.

Some want to know why these immigrant priests are coming here when they are needed more urgently in their own mission lands. Are economic and better living conditions the reasons why so many yearn to work in parishes and institutions in this country rather than in their countries of origin or in other poorer nations? Some believe that it is a fair exchange due to historical circumstances. At one time priests from the United States went to other countries to evangelize; so it's only fair, they say, that immigrants now come in this direction to spread the Gospel.

According to Rev. Anthony McGuire, former director of Pastoral Care for Migrants and Refugees of the National Conference of Catholic Bishops, the Second Vatican Council declared that every local church is not only a 'sending church' but also a 'receiving church.' With global communications and travel, to be a missionary church in these times, every nation with abundance or even a shortage of vocations to the priesthood should both send as well as receive. Today, some claim, this is the reality that the Church in the United States is facing.

Many Christians agree that the United States of America now has the characteristics of a mission land, where millions don't know or acknowledge Jesus Christ as Savior; even among baptized believers a large number do not go to church regularly to worship and celebrate the sacraments. The second largest 'denomination' of Christians in America is former Catholics who don't practice their faith anymore. This land is ripe for evangelization and for many devout American Catholics, the color or the country of origin of the evangelizer does not matter, as long as the missionary is Catholic.

A few liberal, 'angry' Catholics would like to see the Church in the United States end up in the same difficult and challenging situation as the Church in Europe, where there are very few priests, and very few Catholics attend church on a regular basis. They conclude that if the American Church looked like the European Church, the Pope and the Church hierarchy would panic and take some much-needed and urgent steps towards renewal and change. The steady supply of immigrant priests makes it look like everything is normal and thus these 'foreigners' unwittingly are slowing down or impeding the process and possibility of radical change in the structure and future of the institutional Church in America. According to them, Catholics in general and the current hierarchy in particular will not face the problem of the shortage of vocations to the priesthood and will not welcome radical solutions to the problem if immigrant priests and religious keep pouring steadily into the United States.

At a presentation I attended entitled "The Dutch Church's Response to the Vocation Crisis," organized by some of the liberal laity of one of my previous parishes, I was asked by a woman pointblank why I had come for the talk. I told her that the topic had attracted me and I was hoping that the speaker would have some solutions to the problem of shortage of priests and religious in the world. The presenter, a reporter for a liberal Catholic newspaper, referred to a visit he had made to the Netherlands and while attending Mass there he saw both laity and clergy 'concelebrating' the Eucharist. His conclusion was that this Dutch model could be the answer to the American problem of shortage of sufficient number of vocations and eliminate the need for foreign missionaries. No wonder, as an international immigrant priest in clerical attire, my presence at the talk was tolerated at best.

According to John Allen of the *National Catholic Reporter*, who has written about American Catholic demographics and the future of ministry, already one-sixth of the roughly 40,000 priests serving in the United States are from abroad, and the American Church adds about 300 new international priests every year.

An official of the Chicago Archdiocese said during a conference of Church Personnel Administrators that there would be no priests doing sacramental ministry in Catholic hospitals in Chicago were it not for these "international externs," meaning, priests from abroad. In 2009 one out of every four ordained men in the United States came from foreign lands or was born in the United States to immigrant families.

What are the underlying reasons for the steady decline in priestly vocations in Western nations? Some say the first reason could be the Second Vatican Council itself. This ecumenical council that took place from 1962-1965 called and challenged **all** the lay faithful to action and thus provided Catholics a different inclusive perspective on the path to holiness.

Vatican I, which had taken place a hundred years before Vatican II, had proclaimed that the main task of the Church was to teach, to govern and to sanctify. And who, according to that Council, was supposed to teach, govern and sanctify? Bishops and priests or simply, the Ordained! This meant that less than 1% of the Catholic population was called to ministry. The rest of the 99% and more of the laity were expected simply to pray, pay and obey!

Vatican II changed all that. It made us accept the fact that an ontological change does take place at ordination. But it reminded us also that there is a deeper ontological change that occurs in all Christians at their baptism. So, Vatican II taught that while only some men are called to ordination, everyone, children, youth, women and men, because of their baptism, are called to holiness and to participation in ministry and service. The Sunday Eucharistic gathering of the people of God today is referred to as the ministry of the entire assembly, not just of the Ordained.

It is not only priests or the ordained that have a calling. Everyone has a baptismal call to holiness. Catholics today are invited to participate in a variety of ministries and thus see more than one way to follow the footsteps of Jesus and to become his disciples. Paradoxically, this may have led to less of a desire for the priesthood and religious life.

The second reason may be the decline in religiosity in Western nations. Blessed Pope John Paul II and the current Pope Benedict XVI have often commented on the secular and humanistic culture of our times, even referring to it as 'the culture of death.' The media and modern technological advances have flooded the Western mind-set with secular influences, rather than with the religious impact the Church had on all its members before the modern era. A secular, worldly way of thinking and acting naturally affects the spiritual nature of priestly vocations and ministry. Today you can 'Google' many of the answers, topics and issues that may have seemed to be mysterious and mystifying in the past to the average lay person. Does one still need the Church and the priesthood today for solutions and guidance? In a recent newspaper headline, regarding the sacrament of reconciliation, the question was asked: "With a smart phone, does one still need a priest?"

The third reason may be a lack of desire for long-term commitment. The modern culture of instant foods, quick fixes and multiple choices abhors permanency in relationships.

Finally, there is a decline in the respect given to celibacy, which today in our secular world is seen more as a negative than a positive (which would be a way of loving many people freely and deeply, not just one's own family). In the Western world families have fewer children than their ancestors. Parents today might be more interested in having grandchildren through their only child rather than ending the family line by having their only child become a celibate priest or nun.

This makes a priest an endangered species. The story is told of a mother, on a Sunday morning, who knocks on the bathroom door, urging her son to finish quickly so that he can make it to church on time. From inside he loudly complains that he does not want to go to church either because people don't like him or because he can't stand anybody. Finally, his mother insists on him making it to church immediately by shouting loudly: "Hurry up, son; you're the only priest they got!"

Statistics can change like the weather or the economy. Although there was a steady decline in the number of men being ordained priests in the beginning of the third millennium, in 2009 the number has gradually gone up. Has the trend been reversed?

What is characteristic of vocations today is that many men who join the seminary have already had an earlier professional career. They have seen and experienced the world as engineers, lawyers, computer scientists, teachers, men of the Armed Forces and

5

so on. Today's vocation scene is radically different from my beginnings when I entered the seminary at the tender age of sixteen, right out of high school.

Still one finds priests to be a precious commodity. Even the slight increase in vocations cannot keep up with the growing Catholic population in the world and the need for more priests and religious (to fill up the vacuum created by retired and deceased clergy). Without them there is no celebration of the Eucharist. This is the situation not only in Western countries but also in many densely populated 'Catholic' nations. Some villages and small, remote towns in countries of South America, for instance, may see a priest and have the celebration of Eucharist only once a month, if they are lucky.

Nations like Ireland, Spain, France, Portugal and Italy that sent a lot of missionaries to the United States for several decades presently don't have enough vocations for themselves. Ireland that sent so many missionaries to America in the past now does not even have enough priests for its own needs and currently has only a couple of seminaries in the entire nation. Meanwhile, the number of Catholics has increased especially through immigration (both legal and illegal) in the United States. Thus, Northern America that used to send as many missionaries as possible all across the world has now become **the** mission land destination for priests from every other continent.

Most of the immigrants to the United States come from Spanish speaking countries that have huge Catholic populations. The United States Conference of Catholic Bishop's Secretariat of Hispanic Affairs reports that more than thirty-five percent of the current (as of 2009) United States Catholic population is Hispanic. Since 1960 Hispanics have contributed seventy-one percent to the growth of the Church. More than fifty percent of all United States Catholics, younger than age twenty-five, are of Hispanic heritage. More than two-thirds (sixty-eight percent) of all Hispanics in the United States (forty-six million) consider themselves Catholic. By 2050 it is estimated that the Hispanic population will exceed one hundred million.

The Catholic Church has allowed Protestant clergy members who have converted to Catholicism to stay married as ordained Catholic priests. Recently there has been a move to welcome not only individual Anglicans into the Catholic Church, but entire communities and dioceses of Anglicans. They are being welcomed together with their married spiritual leaders, both priests and bishops, and even allowed to bring in their traditions of prayer and worship. But because of the law of celibacy, Catholic priests who leave ministry to get married are not allowed to continue to minister as priests of the Catholic Church. This situation has eliminated thousands of good men who still wish to work in parishes and institutions as Catholic priests, while they stay married and have families. If this situation is made possible for converting Protestant clergy, why not, some argue, give the option to Catholic priests to marry or stay celibate? This is the Catholic Church's Achilles' heel.

Immigrant Catholic priests, like me, who have found our way to the shores of the United States of America, are filling the vacuum created by the shortage of priests and religious vocations.

Generally speaking we have been warmly received and deeply appreciated for the spiritual services and sacraments we provide and celebrate. We are welcomed with open arms into the homes and hearts of many parishioners and families.

I must emphatically add at the very beginning that an immigrant priest like me also receives a great deal from the people I minister to in this country. My life is abundantly blessed and enriched, just as I bless, serve and enrich the lives of those who welcome my presence and priestly ministry.

This then is my story...

I AM WHERE GOD WANTS ME TO BE

I F HOME is where you belong, then my home as a global, international, immigrant, Catholic parish priest from Bombay (Mumbai, as the city is known today), India, is the United States of America.

I once gave a workshop to the "Divorced, Remarried and Widowed" of our diocese. After the presentation, a woman came up to me and told me that she had never heard a priest before say openly the simple, spontaneous words that came from my mouth, namely, that "I love being a priest." Yes, even after thirty-five years of continuous, active, sacerdotal ministry, I love being a Catholic priest.

Recently, in my prayer and meditation I had a personal revelation, namely, that *I am where God wants me to be.* I consider this "ah-ha" moment to be the defining statement of my life.

As I look back at my entire life story, I truly believe that my vocation and journey of priesthood are the cause of my deep joy and inner peace. I have sensed that the Holy Spirit has had a hand in all the significant aspects, decisions and transitions of my life, thus making me conclude that *everything is grace.*

I consider my life as a Catholic priest to be a gift from God; as a matter of fact, I believe that my entire life is 'graced' (meaning that the Holy Spirit constantly works within us). The God who called me from the beginning of my life will also lead me through his Holy Spirit to wherever He wants me to go. Therefore, I am at this moment in time and in this place exactly where God wants me to be. Because of this, I believe that everything that has happened in my life, despite my best intentions and plans, is a part of the Divine Mystery and of Grace.

St. Paul reminds us that "in God we live and move and have our being."

"God has created me," Blessed Cardinal Newman wrote, "to do Him some definite service. He has committed some work to me, which He has not committed to any other. I have a mission; if I am in sickness, my sickness will serve Him; in perplexity, my perplexity will serve Him; if I am in sorrow, my sorrow will serve Him."

As I will describe later in detail, I arrived in Santa Clara, California, as an immigrant, some twenty-eight years ago, and presently, I find myself back in the Mission City of Santa Clara as a Pastor, thus coming full circle in my journey of priesthood in the United States. This historic parish of mine, named after St. Clare, the co-patroness of the Diocese of San Jose, is right across the street from the Jesuit University of Santa Clara, which takes me back to my first mentors and professors in the seminary of Bombay who were also Jesuits. Yet another circle of life!

Recently also the family that invited me to the East Coast of the United States and the family that eventually got me to come live here on the West Coast met for the first time, since I arrived in America in 1983.

Santa Clara is known as the 'Mission City,' an appropriate setting and possible final assignment for my ministerial life as a global, international, immigrant parish priest. One of twenty-one Missions founded by the Franciscans, the best known among the Friars being Fr. Junipero Serra, and a Mission Church dedicated to a woman saint of Assisi, St. Clare Parish has a unique missionary and global feel to it because Masses are celebrated here in seven different languages: English, Portuguese, Spanish, Cantonese, Mandarin, Japanese and Tigrinya (a language of African Eritrea)!

God is symbolically represented as a circle that has no beginning or ending. My life is a series of circles that are touches of the divine and of grace. The smaller life circles I have experienced and lived are part of the larger circle "in whom we live and move and have our being." As I look back, in every smaller life circle, I have nestled within the graced and blessed presence of God, who has promised us that He will be with us till the end of the age.

In the marriage rite, during the exchange of rings, I like to tell couples that the blest rings they will wear for the rest of their married lives will remind them externally of God's presence because the rings have no beginning and no ending. It is God's mysterious providence and love that brought them together in the first place. I also like to add that the inside of the rings touches their skin and fingers and are linked to their hearts. What touches their hearts through these rings are the presence and love of all the people God has brought into their lives and will be there for them in their journey of marriage.

These circles of life that are part of my journey of priesthood are not coincidences; rather, they are God moments.

Coincidences, someone said, are God's way of remaining anonymous.

This is what motivates me to share my memoirs. I believe that many Catholics will find themselves in one or other aspect of my life journey even though they may not have received and chosen to follow a religious or priestly vocation.

Grace happens! Some of us go through life without a dramatic, defining moment that could happen, for instance, because of an accident, a birth or death in the family, a significant achievement, a tragedy, a long journey or a major spiritual conversion or crisis. I truly believe that my life's journey will resonate with many who have tried to understand the nature of God's voice and how God speaks to us and calls us through our simple, ordinary, daily lives. Every sincere person wishes to do God's will and yet, very often, they do not know for sure whether it is really God who is calling them.

All of us, without exception, have inner struggles and are filled with concerns, regrets and anxieties. We either wrestle with the past or live fearfully concerned about what might happen in the future.

A friend of mine concludes his e-mail messages with the words: "Be kinder than necessary, for everyone you meet is fighting some kind of battle."

For me, it is a profound act of faith to say with conviction: "I am where God wants me to be." When I consciously make this acknowledgment of God's protective and leading hand in my life, it usually removes all major debilitating forms of regrets and anxieties in me. It does not mean that I will never be tempted again to live in the regrets of the past or to be worried and anxious about the future. It simply means that when my life is overwhelmed by regrets and anxieties, whenever I have questions about the purpose and meaning of life, when I am either struggling and in pain or when I am intensely joyful and successful, I will gently remind myself that where I am in my life at this moment in time and in this place is exactly where God wants me to be.

If you constantly seek to do God's Will, you will never be alone, you will never be abandoned.

In the here and now, the present, the past and the future come together as one celebration of grace.

In the understanding and profound insight of Blessed Cardinal Newman's inspirational words, even my sorrows and perplexities will serve the God who has called me; the one who has entrusted a specific mission only to me.

This is how I perceive, whether we are laity or clergy, our common baptismal call to holiness.

When I remember that "I am where God wants me to be," then I can make the Blessed Virgin Mary's response to the Archangel Gabriel my own: "Let it be done to me according to your Word."

Jesus' words, both in the 'Our Father' as well as in the Garden of Gethsemane, where he sweated blood, resonate with my personal and priestly experiences and the faith response of Mary and all holy women and men: "Thy Will be done."

This spiritual attitude can make me vulnerable. But to be vulnerable is to know the paradoxical power in surrendering ourselves to God, as Mary did, and to God's will for us in all circumstances. It is to allow the power of God's Spirit to take over and to move through our being. It is to know that by ourselves we can do nothing, but with a surrendered heart we can do all things through the Spirit who gives us strength. With a surrendered heart we can have the power in us to do infinitely more than we can imagine or accomplish ourselves.

The powerful symbol of surrender for a priest is experienced at his ordination when he lies prostrate on the floor surrendering his person and his future to God's Will and to the service of all God's people.

For several decades there has been a shortage of clergy in the Roman Catholic Church. Although I have been ordained a Catholic priest for thirty-five years, I have always been considered to be a 'young priest.' That is not simply because of my good genes but also because there are not too many young and fresh faces to replace the retired ones, the ones who have quit active ministry to get married, and the ones who have gone to greener pastures (I am not referring to the clergy on golf courses).

This shortage of priests has created many challenges for the Catholic Church and has increased the load and burden of ministry on the few remaining elderly American priests as well as the international immigrant clergy who are here to fill the vacuum. Yet I have never been overly stressed or burdened. I have consistently enjoyed doing what a priest does, even though the burdens of ministry and service have increased tremendously over the years.

Even after so many years of ordination I love being a Catholic priest because I am where God wants me to be.

*****

I was born and raised in the city of Bombay (Mumbai), India. My mother reminds me that I came into this world on a Saturday at 6:30 in the morning. I have several siblings. My mother, even till today in her early nineties, remembers the day of the week each one of us was born and also the time of the birth. In India, if you were born close to the time for breakfast, lunch or dinner, you were considered to be a 'full pot' of food and drink, a favorable sign of prosperity. My life has been richly blessed, and in many ways, I have been a full pot of strength, joy and inspiration for my family, friends and parishioners.

My entry into this life, my birthday, happened to occur on the Muslim feast of '*Bakri Eid*.' We had Muslim neighbors, who rejoiced with my Catholic family, to welcome a newborn baby boy born on an auspicious feast day for them. If we had Jewish neighbors, they, too, would have rejoiced because '*Bakri Eid*' is really the celebration of the faith test that Abraham went through, first of all, to show his fidelity to the One God, who had called him out of his comfort zone and led him to an unknown and distant land and then, most importantly, even to the point of his willingness and faith to sacrifice his only son.

This Biblical connection reminds me that even the day of my birth was important in the mind of God. We are all created unique and we are all special and precious in the eyes of God. One day I, too, would be called out of my family centered comfort zone and led to a distant land, not on the backs of camels and caravans, but inside a gigantic 747 Boeing Jet!

God had promised Abraham a child in his old age, through whom would be born many, many generations, as numerous as the stars in the sky and the grains of sand on the seashore. Jews believe that the promised son was Isaac born as a promise to elderly parents, Abraham and Sarah. Christianity has carried on this Judaic tradition. On the other hand, Muslims believe that the promised son was Ishmael, born of Abraham and his concubine, Hagar. Even though these important players in the history of salvation are different for the Jewish, the Christian and the Muslim faiths, the story unfolds the same way for all three monotheistic religions. Because of Abraham's deep, abiding faith and his willingness to sacrifice his only son, because God demanded it, an animal is provided by an Angel of God for the sacrifice to replace Abraham's only son. That is what '*Bakri Eid*' is all about, and on that auspicious day I was born.

By calling and by vocation, I am a Roman Catholic priest. Many parishes in all the dioceses of the United States presently have a strong representation of foreign-born clergy like me. My vocation story, journey and life transitions will be helpful for lay people, clergy and religious in the United States and in the Mission world to understand the presence, the need and the unique contribution of an international immigrant Catholic parish priest today.

In Jerusalem the early Christian Church first showed signs of being Catholic, according to the late German Jesuit theologian, Karl Rahner, when Gentiles were allowed to belong to the first Jewish Christian communities as converts to the Christian faith. The second time the Church showed a major sign of universality and Catholic identity happened during the Second Vatican Council (1962-1965), where bishops came and participated not mainly from Europe as at the First Vatican Council a hundred years earlier, but from all corners of the globe representing almost all nations and peoples of the world.

I personally like this definition of the word 'Catholic': "here comes everybody."

In the year 2007 I was visiting Rome and the Vatican with several laypeople from our northern California parishes. It was a very moving experience for me and for all of us who love the Church and are involved in it through so many lay ministries, to see the relics and what through the glass appears to be the almost well-preserved body of Blessed Pope John XXIII, who moved by the Holy Spirit, opened a window to what he called, 'aggiornamento' or renewal in the Catholic Church.

For four hundred years before Vatican II the doors and windows of the Church seemed to be closed to outside and secular influences. Since the Second Vatican Council that Blessed Pope John XXIII convened in the early sixties, the Catholic Church has never been the same.

It is also very interesting to note co-incidentally that in 1965 when the Second Vatican Council ended and opened the doors of the Church to the modern world, the Congress of the United States of America opened the doors to immigrants from parts of the world other than Western Europe. This secular act of Congress coincided with the global, Catholic understanding of mission work ushered in by the Second Vatican Council.

Bishop Kenneth Untener, of Saginaw, Michigan, who has inspired my life and ministry, and who died recently, once conducted a clergy study week for us. He sat down at a piano and proceeded to sing and play a familiar hymn. When he finished his solo performance he looked in our direction and asked us to sing along with him the words of the same hymn. When the singing was over, he asked, "What do you think of the first version when I sang alone?" We told him that it was enjoyable. Then he asked, "And what do you think about the second version?" We all agreed that it was fun to sing along. Then, with a smile, he said: "The first version is the priesthood *before* Vatican II; the second version is the priesthood *after* Vatican II."

In a fun and simple way the Bishop helped us understand that the priest before Vatican II, especially in Worship and Liturgy, was a solo performer, making everybody else spectators of the Sacred, but after Vatican II all the baptized join together in creating Spirit filled harmony between the human and the divine in, with and through Jesus Christ.

Since the Second Vatican Council the Catholic Church celebrates liturgy and the sacraments in the vernacular, in the language of the people. Lay people are invited to full, active and conscious participation in the liturgy, which today is correctly understood as the work of the people and not just of the priest alone. There is no separation of the sacred and the secular spaces as indicated by the removal of communion railings in many churches. The Word of God is integral to the celebration of Eucharist and the people are nourished at the table of the Word as they are at the table of the Meal and Sacrifice when they partake of the Body and Blood of Jesus Christ. Moreover, more and more Catholics are relishing today and participating in the historical study and the prayerful meditation of the Bible.

In one of my previous parishes, which were a merging of several Catholic communities, one of the churches was sold to a conservative Anglican community. The first thing these Anglicans did was to reinstall the communion railing that had been removed several years earlier by the Catholic parish community following the directions of Vatican II. From a Catholic modern point of view since the Second Vatican Council, the Anglican community regressed into a past model of church where the 'secular' and the 'sacred' were separated by the symbolic communion railing.

All kinds of ministries have flourished since the Second Vatican Council. Ministry is not restricted anymore to ordained priests. There are lectors, Eucharistic ministers, hospitality greeters, ushers, altar servers, commentators, musicians and singers, art and environment ministers, sacristans, *et cetera*. This sense of participation and ministry has flowed also into leadership involvement where lay people bring their expertise into the fields of finance, buildings and grounds, ministry and administrative staffs, and especially, parish councils that set parish policies and advise pastors on how to effectively run parishes today. The Second Vatican Council opened the avenues of dialog with other denominations, other religions, with science and technology and above all, with the modern world.

For four hundred years prior to the nineteen sixties the Church appeared to look the same everywhere in the world. But in this last generation, the Catholic Church appears to be like Joseph's coat of many colors!

Global, international immigrant clergy and religious seem to be an outgrowth of this very Catholic, universal mentality that was generated by the Second Vatican Council and the gathering of bishops and their consulters who traveled to Rome in the sixties from all parts of the Catholic and modern world.

Not only in a financial sense, but also from a religious perspective, the earth today is flat. It's a global economy whether we like it or not; similarly, it's a global Church whether we like it or not.

The United States has outsourced most of its call centers to countries like India and the Philippines. We might say that the Catholic Church in India and the Philippines has outsourced many priests, nuns and religious to cater to the spiritual needs and to staff the spiritual call centers (parishes) of the United States.

One of the major problems of outsourcing, whether financial or spiritual, is effective communications. Just as some Americans don't understand some of the men and women that respond to them from the call centers of the world because of their heavy accents or lack of knowledge of Americana and Americanisms, so also some immigrant and international priests with heavy accents, lack of knowledge of the English language or of

American culture cause a lot of frustration among American Catholics, especially among the elderly and the hard of hearing.

After the sixties the Catholic Church in the United States with the new waves of immigrants was sometimes so desperate for ordained clergy that it did not always require and mandate that international immigrant clergy, even those from non-English speaking nations, should be fluent in English and well trained in the art of effective communications. Today programs that help immigrant clergy to understand American culture and the American language rectify this situation.

There are languages and communications programs today to help foreign priests speak English correctly and to support them with 'accent reduction' or 'accent acquisition.'

The problem of foreign clergy adapting to American life is not new to the Church in the United States. Some of the priests and religious who were brought in by needy and desperate Bishops as Catholic life was being established in the American colonies in the last two centuries were generally deemed to be misfits. Several missionaries, especially from Ireland, were not used to the democratic way of life in the United States and exercised a dictatorial and hierarchical style of leadership. Many elderly priests and parishioners remember that they had a difficult time understanding the brogue of Irish missionaries and the heavy accents of Italian, German, French, Spanish and Portuguese priests and nuns. One particular Archbishop in San Francisco would send his newly arrived Irish seminarians and priests to the local seminary to learn to speak American English during their first six months in the United States.

*****

A friend of mine used to be a Presbyterian minister and was recently received into the Catholic Church by our parish community. Needless to say, he took a major step in his journey of faith to become a Catholic, since he came from several generations of Presbyterians. Our Catholic parish received him on 'Gaudete' (Rejoice) Sunday in Advent. Now, every Advent, on the third Sunday, he accompanies me to all the churches where I celebrate Sunday Masses and he shares his ongoing journey and conversion story with the assembly. His reflections are always well received because they strike a resonant chord in our hearts. They remind us of our own story and journey of faith.

A couple of years ago, in his reflection he added that on the day he was received into the Catholic Church he was a Protestant who became a Catholic. The following year he felt that he was a Catholic who used to be a Protestant. Now, he states simply: "I am a Catholic." Then he adds with a smile and repeats for emphasis: "Did I tell you that I love being a Catholic?"

His words echo my own regarding priestly ministry: "I still love being a priest."

In his most recent public faith reflection, he confessed that his conversion to Catholicism did not start only a few years ago on the day he was received into the Catholic Church. Several years earlier, he had read Thomas Merton's '*The Seven Storey Mountain*.' He was inspired by Merton's writings, faith journey and conversion, but he was not ready to make a personal commitment to the Catholic Church. Even though God kept calling him, he admitted that he had delayed his response to God's invitation as long as he could. What intrigued me in his public faith sharing was his honest confession that God had been calling him from the very beginning of his spiritual awareness, but he was the one who was not ready to shout the final 'Yes' to God's invitation and to conversion.

What I realized from his reflections was that the Spirit of God is always there from the very beginning of our lives nudging us and inspiring us to go down the spiritual path of conversion; but either our lives are so busy and noisy that we cannot hear God's voice, or we are simply not ready and courageous enough to respond to God's invitation. Fortunately God, as the hound of heaven, does not give up on us and when we are able to stop and look back, we realize that God's Spirit was always there calling and guiding us and being always patient with us.

I can accept the fact that I am where God wants me to be because I truly believe that God was always there in my life from the very beginning, even when I was too young, too busy or too self-centered to notice.

God does not call us once but several times. We might say that God's initial call into being and life is sanctified by the call to Baptism. At each stage of our development as persons and as believers, there are calls that challenge our growth. For a Catholic the sacraments continue to be calls to healing, nourishment, wholeness and service. In between these sacramental calls, there are other calls and echoes of calls that come from the situations and circumstances of life itself.

It is as if God is saying to us: "There is a need here and I need you to freely respond."

In spiritual life there are no accidents or coincidences. If we are in tune with the Spirit, we will see the hand of God everywhere. At a recent staff Christmas party, when it came to my turn, I picked up my secret gift from under the Christmas tree. It was a book entitled *The Language of God*, by Francis S. Collins, one of the country's leading geneticists and the long time head of the International Human Genome Project. The subtitle of the book was: 'A Scientist Presents Evidence for Belief.'

More than the scientific nature of the book itself, I was drawn by the title that reminded me that God is always speaking to us. God's voice is an energy that brings new challenges for growth when we respond to it. President Clinton invited the author to the White House and in his speech began comparing the human DNA sequence map to the map that Meriwether Lewis had unfolded in front of Thomas Jefferson in that very same East Room of the White House nearly two hundred years earlier. Clinton said that day: "We are learning the language in which God created life. We are gaining ever more awe for the complexity, the beauty, and the wonder of God's most divine and sacred gift." To which Collins responded: "It's a happy day for the world. It is humbling for me, and awe-inspiring, to realize that we have caught the first glimpse of our own instruction book, previously known only to God."

Those who have heard God's call and responded generously to it with their lives, like Abraham, Moses, Samuel, Elijah, Isaiah, Ezekiel, Ruth, Judith, Esther, Mary (the mother of Jesus), Mary Magdalene, Joseph, John the Baptist, the Apostles, the many saints and holy men and women and children of our faith tradition, have known the language that God speaks. Each of us today, whether we are scientists, astronauts, politicians, homemakers, accountants, teachers, lawyers, physicians or priests can come to our own realization that God is constantly conversing with us and calling us by name.

Faith, which is a gift, is the interface that helps us to read and to recognize the language of God.

My life today is not the realization of the 'American Dream' (a reason given by many immigrants who come to the United States of America to improve their financial situation). I am not wealthy and successful in the worldly sense of making it big, of moving from rags to riches. And my priestly life is also not the realization of the 'Ecclesiastical Dream.' I am not an Archbishop or Cardinal of the Catholic Church as is the case with some of my companions from my years of study in Rome. I am simply a pastor, a shepherd, to whom the Good News has been given somewhat like to the shepherds by angels at the birth of the Savior, and to whom the service of God's people has been entrusted.

Blessed Mother Teresa of Calcutta reminded us that only some of us are called to be successful in this life; but all of us, without exception, are called to be faithful. We are not all called to do great deeds, but we are all called to do little things with great love.

I believe that each person who came into my life was sent on my path to teach me what is truly spiritual, human and life giving.

In the spiritual journey with God, wherever you find yourself, that's where God intends for you to be if and when you truly seek God's Will. It's a mystery, not to be solved, but to be enjoyed, appreciated and lived.

And I intend to do just that for the rest of my life.

CHAPTER 2

GROWING UP CATHOLIC IN INDIA

I WAS BORN in Bombay, India, in the year 1950. On January 26th, 1950 India became a Republic. It may not have been a significant year for most people in the world but it was definitely an important year for the Catholic Church. Since 1300 A.D., first every fiftieth, then every twenty-fifth year has been declared a Holy Year in the Catholic Church, a year of Jubilee, a year of favor from the Lord. The Jewish people celebrated such Jubilees, when prisoners would be freed, debts would be forgiven, and the poor could help themselves to whatever was not harvested. Thus, 1950, the year of my birth, was a holy year for the Catholic Church.

In spiritual life, as I've stated earlier, there are no coincidences or accidents, only God-moments and God-encounters. While 1950 was a Holy Year, so was 1975, the year I was ordained first a deacon in Reinsfeld, Germany, and then a priest in Bombay, India. Blessed Pope John Paul II declared 1983 a special Holy Year, being 1950 years since the birth of Jesus. And that happened to be the year I left India permanently to live and work as an international immigrant priest in the United States. In the year 2000, another Holy Year, I was back in Rome at the North American College Seminary on a sabbatical to celebrate my twenty-fifth anniversary of priesthood. During those three and a half months of relaxation and renewal, I lived right next door to the International Seminary and University of the Propagation of Faith, on the Via Urbano, where I had done my final year of theological seminary studies twenty-five years earlier. In that year 2000, it felt like I completed a full circle in my journey of priesthood: from India to Rome, then to the United States and finally back to the heart of Roman Catholicism.

The Cardinal of Vienna, Austria, whom I met in that Jubilee year, and who offered me hospitality in his 'palace,' gave me a picture of himself with a hand written message: "In celebration of 25 years as a Priest and 50 years as a Pilgrim."

To our neighbors I may have appeared to be just another child and an extra mouth to feed in the Aranha household since I was the ninth sibling in my family. But not so to my parents who welcomed each one of us as a gift from God. Much before I was born, three of my older siblings had already died as babies and hence I never had the joy of knowing them and growing up with them. I sometimes wonder what life would have been for me if they had survived. Their names were Epiphany, Joseph and Rose. After my birth, my parents, Eric and Cecilia, had three more children, bringing our grand total to a complete dozen.

The nine surviving siblings were divided into thirds: representing the head, the body and the tail. Of course, the oldest three, Charles, Teresa and Rita, took their responsibility of being the head very seriously handing down sometimes a variety of loving, disciplinary measures to the body and the tail. The tail of the family, Ronald, Sandra and Alan, wagged a great deal, freely and happily, apparently without too many cares and concerns in childhood. It is easy to be free and happy when you as the youngest ones are generally pampered and spoilt. With Plassey and Nancy, I belonged to the body, the middle, and the delicious and succulent portion of any sandwich. The middle members of the body felt they were in the best position because while they had to respect the head, they could also have fun with the tail.

One's birth order does influence one's attitudes to life. I have always seen myself as being both responsible as well as playful. Life from childhood has always been interesting and exciting for me due largely to being born closer to the center of the surviving Aranha clan!

From the Indian cultural point of view, my birth as a boy born after three girls could have been considered a lucky omen for the family. My native language is Konkani. We have a word for my birth order, which is '*Tiklo*,' (a boy born after three girls) a word that could be synonymous with 'Lucky.' This cultural superstition would bring a quick smile to anyone in our neighborhood who was informed that I was born after three girls. I definitely felt very lucky all my life not because of my birth order, but because I was loved and spoilt rotten by my older sisters.

My older brother, Joseph, was also a '*Tiklo*,' but he wasn't lucky enough to survive infancy. Why did I survive? Why was I the really lucky one to live this long? I guess we will never know. That is why life is not a problem to be solved but a mystery to be lived.

Charles was my oldest brother and he died at the age of 30. Then three girls were born in the Aranha family: Teresa, Rita and Epiphany (who passed away when she was a baby). The first '*Tiklo*' in our family, Joseph, only survived three months. After him were born another three girls: Rose (who died as an infant), Plassey and Nancy. The Lord shut off the flow of female abundance by welcoming me as the next '*Tiklo*' in the Aranha family. Finally, the mold of a boy's birth followed by the birth of three girls was broken with the birth of a girl between two boys: Ronald, Sandra and Alan.

My mother confessed to us once that in the hospital after giving birth to so many children, her doctor insisted that her tubes be tied. My mother being a very devout Catholic adamantly rejected the doctor's suggestions. When my youngest brother heard this story, he quickly added: "I just made it!"

India has many languages and dialects. There could be as many as eight hundred of them and out of these, at least twenty-five languages are widely spoken. That includes Konkani which my parents always spoke at home. It is one of those widely spoken languages that do not have their own written script. It can be phonetically written in the Indian 'Devnagiri' alphabet, which we later studied in school, or the one we were familiar with growing up, namely, the Latin alphabet. Because of the richness of Indian languages, one grows up familiar with many more sounds and letters than those one finds in the English language. While English has twenty-six letters with five vowels; Hindi, India's national language, has twice as many letters and twelve vowel sounds.

Language affects us in many ways. One example that comes to mind from my childhood speaking Konkani at home is that there were no literal words or expressions to say 'thank you.' There is a Konkani equivalent, albeit not a literal one: '*Dev borem korum*', meaning, 'may God do good to you' or 'may God bless you', a phrase used in both directions, younger to older people and older to younger people.

Much later in my travels when I found myself in Germany during summer vacations, my elderly German foster parents would wonder why I would not say 'thank you' for every delicious meal they prepared for me.

The first time I was surprised that they even asked me such a question. Then I tried to explain to them that the words 'thank you' were not said or spoken in my family, like the words 'Danke schoen' in German, because we used Konkani to communicate with each other; but I also added that the way we lived our lives caringly and obediently expressed in action the gratitude we felt for everything our parents or siblings did for us.

Even today when I give a gift to one of my siblings or to my mother, or I receive a gift from any of them, usually there is no 'thank you' expressed or expected. We are expected to live by concrete actions the gratitude we feel in our hearts towards each other.

We grew up speaking several languages. While we conversed with our mother in Konkani, we spoke Hindi (the national language) and Marathi (the regional language of the state of Maharashtra, of which Bombay is the capital) with our friends and neighbors and, finally, English with dad, my siblings, our fellow parishioners and our classmates in school. This rich linguistic environment in which I was raised gave me, later on, a strong desire to learn several other European languages and to be acquainted with many other cultures of the world.

An international immigrant priest brings with him a richness of languages and cultures to his ministry. My linguistic background prepared me for the rich multicultural environment of California. It did not take very long for me to make America my home.

I weighed just a tad over six pounds at birth. At St. George Hospital where I was born (and I understand from my family that my dad chose to give me the name 'George' to reflect British Royalty) there were English nurses still working in various capacities even though the British had given up control of their Indian colony in 1947. In those days women spent at least ten days in the hospital after giving birth. It was a brief respite, a sort of mini-vacation, for my mother, for the effort made to carry each of us within her womb for nine months.

It was said that the time spent in the hospital after giving birth would be possibly the only 'vacation' away from the difficult chores of family responsibilities a poor Indian mother would ever get in her life!

I never really put on much weight in my early years. Still I maintained quite a macho, tough-guy attitude in our closely-knit neighborhood. I believed that my mission was to protect all my five sisters, even though four of them were older than me, from some of the 'rowdy' elements of our community. I grew tall very quickly, but I was always just skin and bones. In Hindi, the kids around had a name for me: *'Haddi Pahelwan,'* which means, 'Bony Wrestler.'

*****

Ironically, even though India gives great importance to the presence, role and influence of women, many traditional Hindu parents prefer boys to girls. Because of the dowry system, girls are considered to be a financial liability to the family. A girl born after three boys is considered unlucky. My parents, however, as good and devout Catholics, did not care much about or believe in this aspect of Indian culture because each of us, sons and daughters, was important to the whole family. In fact, as my sisters did, I, too, as a boy, had to seek attention from my parents intensely, competitively and aggressively. We were all treated as equals in our family.

I believe we were a model Christian family to our Hindu and Muslim neighbors.

As reported in the *San Jose Mercury News* under the title: 'The Plight of India's Women,' (a weekly quiz provided by *The Globalist*, a daily online service that covers issues and trends in globalization) generally speaking, it is tough to be born a female in India. At more than 600 million, the number of females in India is about 100 million larger than the populations of the United States, Russia and Canada combined. Despite the country's rapid economic growth, women in India still face a vast array of challenges.

Girls suffer from very low levels of education and literacy. Even though Indian laws require a woman to be at least eighteen years old at the time of marriage, fifty-six percent of girls in rural India are married before the age of eighteen – and that despite the legal threat of fines and imprisonment. As a result of factors such as these, of every one hundred girls who begin primary education in India, only thirty actually complete school. Around half of all Indian women are illiterate, compared with a ratio of around one to seven among women in China and one to four among men in India.

Females face economic discrimination. Boys are preferred because they do not require the enormous dowry payments that can bankrupt poor families in India when daughters marry. Even though dowries have been illegal in India since the year 1961, every year about 6,000 women are killed – often doused with kerosene and set on fire in staged kitchen accidents by husbands and in-laws angered by unmet dowry demands.

Women face discrimination even before birth. Since inexpensive ultrasounds are more readily available, the number of abortions of female fetuses in India's major cities like Bombay and Calcutta has risen significantly. Even though India's 'Prohibition of Sex Selection Act' has outlawed the use of ultrasound examinations to determine the sex of a fetus, since February of 2003, the practice has become so prevalent that the sex ratio at birth in certain prosperous neighborhoods has fallen to as low as 762 girls for every 1,000 boys. In comparison, the national average is 927 girls for every 1,000 boys. Other factors causing the decline in the number of girls include neglect of the girl child, high maternal mortality, and female infanticide. Countrywide, there are 107 males per every 100 females.

The caste system is still prevalent in India. Even though this system is not anti-female in itself, it does make life very difficult for girls and women of lower castes. The only work they might get, since they have no access to education, is menial construction jobs, carrying stones and bricks balanced on their heads and frail bodies. Others end up as street and garbage sweepers, cleaning public toilets and doing back breaking jobs for a pittance.

Loan sharks add to the misery of the poor and of some women in rural India. Powerful people give loans to the poor backed by clothes, tools, land and sometimes women as collateral, figuring they can sleep with them if they're not repaid. By charging exorbitant interest rates (often as high as sixty percent), moneylenders take the land, the livelihood and the women of poor farmers, when they are unable to pay back their loans. An estimated 200,000 Indian farmers have committed suicide since the end of the last century, largely because of debt.

India's huge population has only two and a half percent Christians. Most Indians are Hindus (about eighty four percent) and then there is a sizable Muslim population (about eleven percent). Finally, there is an almost equal mix of Sikhs, Buddhists and other religions combined.

Even though I was born and raised in India, my family name: 'Aranha,' is Portuguese in origin. My Portuguese friends today in Santa Clara remind me that *Aranha* means 'Spider.' Therefore, I playfully call myself 'Spiderman.' Portugal's sailors and traders found their way to India at the end of the fifteenth century with the help of the well-renowned navigational skills and sense of adventure of Vasco da Gama. When I visited Lisbon, Portugal, for the first time, I made it a point to go visit the area, called Belem, from which all the famous Portuguese sailors and navigators set out to discover the sea routes of the world. In the Monastery of St. Jerome, Vasco da Gama is buried and honored.

The Portuguese came to trade and to spread Christianity. Thus, many Catholics in India have Portuguese last names. My ancestors, converted several generations ago possibly from Hinduism, had always been aware of the highest Brahmin caste to which it previously belonged. My Hindu ancestors may have had the last name of 'Shenoy.'

Christianity brought a sense of equality among its members. We were all aware as Catholics that thanks to our baptism we became brothers and sisters, children of God. Mahatma Gandhi, the father of modern India, who was familiar with the Bible and its teachings, especially the Beatitudes and the Sermon on the Mount in Matthew's gospel, tried to share this same belief in parallel terms when he called the untouchables (the lowest in the caste hierarchy), 'Harijans', or the people of God.

My dad's baptismal name was Emmanuel and he was born in 1901. As on Ellis Island when officials depending on how they heard them pronounced changed a lot of names, the British converted Emmanuel to Eric Manuel. My dad was neither British nor Scandinavian but Eric suited him well. He was relatively tall, fair skinned and sported a moustache most of his life. He worked for a British textile company and continued to work at their head office even when the Indian government took over and the textile company became 'India United Mills.' Dad's office was close by and so he either walked to work or took the bus. The office had a 'canteen' (cafeteria) for the employees. Once in a while Dad would take me or one of my siblings in turn with him to work and we always enjoyed some wonderful treats at the cafeteria.

In a large family you are lucky if you get any attention at all. Yet, my dad was an expert at the personal touch. Just as he took us individually to his place of work for a sumptuous treat, for many years as a child and later as a teenager, I thought I was the only fortunate sibling to receive an extra coin for after school snacks, until I embarrassingly discovered later on in life that every sibling of mine also received the same personal and concrete monetary sign of love from dad.

All my siblings were equally encouraged by my parents to become nuns or priests, if they so desired. However, I am the only one who entered the seminary and religious life in my immediate family. Sometimes I jokingly say that having become a priest, I am the only fool in the family.

Thanks to my dad, I always had a positive and strong image of a 'father.' Today when people of all ages address me as 'Father,' it reminds me of the nurturing paternal influence with which I grew up. I am grateful to my dad for being such a powerful father figure in my life.

I would experience dad's personal attention and love if for some reason I was late coming home from school. Since we lived on the ground floor of our apartment building, like the father in the parable of the Prodigal Son, my dad would pace up and down outside the building until the moment I would return home. Then I recall his beautiful smile and his sense of relief as the two of us embraced. Dad would not sit down for supper with the rest of the family, until I was safely home. I knew I was missed; I knew I was always loved.

In my pastoral ministry I have met people who have not been able to forgive themselves. It's as if they were fearful of returning home. In this sense I have rarely been afraid. Spiritually speaking, even at times when I have sinned and I feel I don't deserve to be loved or forgiven, I have always imagined our heavenly Father, like my own dad, pacing up and down, even in the dark of the night, eagerly awaiting my return. My image of God is that of a loving, forgiving and comforting presence because I experienced my own dad to be always encouraging, caring, and never distant.

I was never made to feel bad or guilty upon my return. My dad was simply happy to see me home and in his strong arms. It's sad that there are many children today in the world who do not have a healthy and strong fatherly influence in their lives. As a consequence, their image of God, too, can get skewed and distorted. Sometimes when people say they don't believe in God it may be because they have had a difficult parent-child relationship or they don't want to believe in a heavenly God who resembles their earthly father.

For a long time as a child and even as a teenager I believed that we children came directly from God because three of our neighboring older married couples had no children. And the explanation we were given by our parents was that God chooses to give or not to give children to a specific married couple. I wasn't yet privy to the knowledge of the birds and the bees, so I strongly and innocently believed even into my teenage years that our family with so many children was abundantly blessed and loved by God, and that there was no sex involved between my parents!

One day, out of the blue, a childhood buddy and neighbor revealed to me the secret of how children are conceived. I was shocked! Deciding that offense was a stronger form of defense, I told my scandalizing classmate and friend that his parents may have been doing what he said needs to be done in order to have a child, but definitely this was not the case with my parents because they were gifted with children directly from God.

I grew up in a world of blissful innocence and simplicity. It was a happy and playful world where you lived your childhood to the fullest. We played in the dirt and in the hot sun, never concerned or worried about getting sick.

I must have been a very good kid or at least a very quiet, well-behaved child. My mother would speak well of me to the neighbors by saying: "Georgy is such a good kid that compared to his siblings we hardly knew he was born!"

There is a saying that "still waters run deep." This serenity I exhibited to the outside world would hide the deep well of ideas, passions and dreams that constantly stirred up within me.

When I was three years old, my grandmother's sister, a nun by the name of Sister Crispina, held me in her arms and 'prophesied' that one day I would become a priest.

She passed away a few years ago but she did attend my ordination ceremonies to the priesthood in the year 1975. At first her regional Superior refused to let her travel to Bombay to attend the ceremony, but she was adamant, even threatening to leave the convent if refused permission.

After all, she was the 'prophetess' to whom God had revealed that the child she held in her arms many years earlier would finally make it to ordination and priesthood.

During the reception that followed the ordination ceremony, she smilingly whispered to us that even though she had threatened her Mother Superior about leaving the convent if refused permission, she would have still joined another religious order, after returning home from the ceremony and reception. Her plans were never to give up her life and ministry as a nun.

I wonder sometimes if I have benefited both from Sister Crispina's prophetic role as well as her feisty spirit.

Convent rules and mores were very strict in those days. Sister Crispina told us that if a wedding procession passed in front of their convent house, they were not allowed to say the word, "wedding" in their conversation with each other. Since they were sworn to chastity and celibacy, the nuns were strongly urged to leave all marriage terminology outside the convent walls. So, instead of saying, "Wedding," they had to refer to this prohibited activity with words like, "dum, dum," sounds that imitated the drums played in the wedding procession.

She would make us laugh with these stories. Sister Crispina's prayers, sacrifices, anecdotes and angelic smiles accompanied me all the way on my seminary and priesthood journey. I am grateful to Sr. Crispina for the important role she played in my formative years.

She served as a model for me of the religious life that does not deny or sacrifice one's humanity. While she enjoyed being a nun, she also expressed her true thoughts and feelings, whenever and wherever they mattered. Nuns or priests are called to wholesome living. They are called to be in the world, and not of the world. It was St. Irenaeus, a bishop of the second century, who said: "The glory of God is a human being fully alive." Even with the vow of celibacy, priests and nuns, like all the baptized, are called to live fuller lives.

My father reminded me one day that when I was a little child about four years of age, even though he wanted me to sleep in longer, I would jump out of bed instinctively to accompany him daily to the early morning Mass. Dad had the gift and peaceful conscience of falling asleep when his head touched the pillow. He slept soundly (and snored louder than a hibernating bear) and would wake up early every morning to make coffee and breakfast for the family so that my mother, who was not a good sleeper, could rest a little longer in bed. By the time all the children went to sleep, my mother would be totally exhausted. Being married to my dad for fifty years, my mother came up with a new beatitude: "Blessed are they who fall asleep first, for they will not have to stay awake to listen to the snoring of their spouse or of the other family members." I was barely four years old, but since I was up anyway, my father would dress me and take me to church.

Oddly enough later on in the seminary, only one thing bothered me about becoming a priest, and that was getting up early every day to celebrate Mass. In a big city like Bombay, several middle class and wealthy families had domestic servants and maids. The Catholic parishes of this metropolis would have a Sunday Mass as early as five in the morning to give these servants and maids an opportunity to fulfill their religious obligation. Although I woke up instinctively as a child early in the morning so that my dad would take me to church, as I grew older, I realized that my sleeping habits were more like my mother's than my father's. The only sleeping habit I inherited from my dad was the snoring. I wish I had also got his peaceful conscience and the gift of falling asleep at once. My mother slept late and slept in longer because she had to prepare so many children for bed. What was my excuse?

Fortunately we change and we grow. If I have to get up early for a round of golf or to celebrate Sunday or daily Mass today, I do so promptly. Blessed Cardinal Newman once said: "To live is to change. And to be perfect is to have changed often."

*****

The whole family, all eleven of us that included my parents and nine siblings, lived in one large room. Room Number Eight, our home, was on the ground floor of a five storied building on one of the main streets of downtown Bombay. In one corner of the room was a tiny kitchen and adjacent to that a small shower area enclosed by a curtain. The shower area had a good sized metal drum to store fresh water because the water supply in the crowded city of Bombay was always rationed. We quickly took our showers during the hours we had water flowing through the only faucet in the house; we also filled the metal drum to the brim for daily use, especially for drinking and cooking. Drinking water had to be boiled to be safe, but that did not prevent us from drinking straight from the faucet. Our immune system could withstand just about any waterborne illness or disease. Poverty and exposure to the elements in childhood can be good partners to strengthen the immune system and resistance to diseases and illnesses.

On the other hand, every time I have visited India since coming to the United States, I have been sicker than a dog. It's partly my fault because I like to try everything, including the childhood delicacies prepared under the open polluted skies in the streets of Bombay.

The plumbing in our building was basic and there was no water tank on the roof, as there are today in high rise multistoried buildings, for the people who lived on the floors above us. The water pressure in the ground was very low due to which the upper floors did not get sufficient supply of water. Water was rationed so the municipality supplied only a couple of hours of flowing water in the evenings. During the hours when water was piped into our building, a long rubber hose was run from our kitchen faucet to the outside of our building, so that our neighbors could fill their pots with water and then carry them upstairs to their 'flats' or apartments.

My parents were caring and generous neighbors to all, never self-centered or insisting on privacy for our family. What awesome role models I had in my childhood!

In our one room home there was a huge bed right in the middle, against the wall. My parents slept on this bed and included any of the children that needed special attention before falling asleep. The rest of us slept on the floor on mattresses and pillows lined up next to each other. There is no way you can dislike or hate your siblings when you have to share space and prepare your sleeping arrangements so closely and as tightly as we had to growing up. Yet we did find some golden opportunities for pillow fights. They did not last very long because the only fluorescent light would be switched off and that was a clear summons to be quiet and to go to sleep.

My eldest brother, Charles, would sleep on a cot outside the door of our house. As I grew older, I was allowed occasionally to join him and sometimes with some of my peers I would sleep outside the building and enjoy the cool, tropical nights under the open skies.

I still feel uncomfortable to talk about the lavatories in our building. There were two stalls on every floor and because they were common public toilets, the traditional old models with the big hole in the ground, they were rarely kept clean. They did have doors for privacy. Even now I shudder when I think about how scary it was to do your routine at these, what seemed to me as a child, gigantic holes that could swallow you up if you misbehaved during the day or at night. One of our older siblings would reluctantly accompany us and wait patiently till we were done.

Just outside the building walls were deep gutters and huge rats. I still have occasional nightmares and rat phobias from living in this poor section of the city. Every aspect of your life influences your thoughts, your attitudes and your future relationships. I feel that in my pastoral ministry as a priest I have great empathy for the poor and for those who lack the basic amenities of life. It's not that I lacked anything essential as a child. It's only later on when I had experienced and witnessed different and more decent middle class styles of living; it was then that I began to truly understand the plight of those who are deprived of human dignity even in the twentieth and twenty first centuries.

Yet, this living arrangement of my childhood and its location were very convenient for many reasons. This was a building that was teeming with families and activities. Just a block away was St. George's Hospital, where I was born and where medical treatment and hospitalizations were free. With so many siblings we had many reasons to spend a lot of time in this public hospital. During the time of the British, it was, according to my parents, an efficiently run and a wonderfully clean hospital.

A few blocks away was our parish church, called St. John the Evangelist, where I was baptized exactly two weeks after I was born. In those days because of higher mortality rates or simply because of religious customs and traditions, a child was baptized very soon after birth, while the mother was still recuperating in the hospital.

My dad worked close by. He walked to work every day or took the bus when it rained. Public transportation, that included trams, buses, trains and taxis, was right at our doorstep. The General Post Office was round the corner. And everywhere there were shops, stores, schools, street vendors, fish, meat and vegetable markets and movie houses. As a family we may have been financially poor, but our environment and surroundings were rich in services and benefits beyond measure, all within walking distance.

I have fond memories of going often to the movies with my friends and my siblings. The movie house closest to our home was called 'Rex Talkies.' Before there were individual seats, they had benches. Some of us, who stood in line early to get tickets, would rush in and lie on the benches to reserve the best spaces for family and friends. As a child I only watched Indian Bollywood movies. The very first movie experience I had in the English language was the foot thumping musical: 'Seven Brides for Seven Brothers.' We were on the edge of our seats (or benches) throughout the entire movie.

My dad was the sole breadwinner while my mom was the homemaker. Responsibilities were shared equally. Early each morning dressed in a proper suit, tie and a hat, my father would leave for work. He worked for a British textile company at their Main Office as the Head Clerk. My dad was light skinned and handsome and fit in perfectly both with his Indian co-workers as well as the British staff and owners of this textile company. In fact he got along so well that he stayed with the same company for thirty-seven continuous years, even after it changed ownership and passed into the hands of the Indian government, where the company's name was changed to 'India United Textile Mills.' He retired from this company when he was in his sixties and was highly respected for his ethical standards and hard work.

Although my parents grew up speaking Konkani and also taught us to speak this language from childhood, yet, very often, we spoke English with my dad because of his professional work with a British company. He grew a stylish moustache and smoked smelly cigars. While my mom was responsible for our health, education and religious practices, dad provided some semblance of discipline when he returned home from work. If my mother told him that one of us had to be disciplined or reprimanded, dad would raise his voice and his right hand to show that he was upset and ready to punish us. But he never laid a hand on us. Corporal punishment was common and acceptable in those days. I knew of fathers in our neighborhood that would beat their children with canes and belts very often out of frustration and drunkenness. I also knew very early on that that kind of discipline had no positive effect. When my parents occasionally disciplined me, mainly through words, even though at that moment it was embarrassing, I always knew that it was done out of love and for my own good.

Either because of my dad's work in a British company or because my parents saw the good life that came from the British influence in Bombay, they had a very good opinion of the English. There was no dissatisfaction or anger expressed at the three hundred year old colonial presence of the British in India. Rather, the English language and English habits were strongly encouraged in my family.

Sometimes today an American might ask me: "But what is your *real* Indian name?" Americans are generally surprised that both my parents and all my siblings, including me, have strong English and Christian names.

Many Indians in Bombay did not think like my parents. These people were very anti-British; they would go on a rampage to disfigure the statues of British royalty in the city parks, by cutting off their noses, or simply chopping off their heads.

The city of Bombay was huge and very cosmopolitan. When my parents first moved into the city from Mangalore in the south of India where they were married, it was clean, beautiful and sparsely populated. Gradually the population increased and with it also the proliferation of slums. Today forty-two percent of the city is covered with slum pockets, like the human body covered with nauseating and disgusting sores all over.

For a lot of the simple, uneducated people who had immigrated to the city from the neighboring villages and towns, Bombay was one big spittoon. Some people would regularly spit on the city pavements and building walls, and the red saliva that came from chewing '*paan*,' which is a betel leaf substitute for tobacco, made this huge metropolis look like a war zone. It appeared from these red stained walls that murders and riots took place constantly on the streets of Bombay; which, of course, was not the case. Growing up in the city of Bombay was generally a safe and pleasant experience for all of us. We had all the benefits and very few hazards of living in this crowded and bustling city.

The Indian caste system did not have any direct effect on us. Although the caste system is still practiced in the villages of India (which comprise about eighty percent of the population), yet, in a metropolis like Bombay, which is so literate and over-populated at the same time, people constantly rub shoulders with members of other castes and have no possibility of living separately from each other.

My parents came from families that were possibly converts from Hinduism. In Christianity caste does not play a role but growing up in India one never forgets one's roots and origins. My parents did remind us from time to time, that even though we were Christians, we belonged to the highest caste, that of the Brahmin priests.

I wonder sometimes if my vocation to the priesthood was influenced by the Brahmin caste to which my ancestors belonged.

I loved to sit at the feet of my dad when he came home from work. Occasionally, in order to relax he would smoke a cigar. There was such a strong sense of paternal love and co-presence when he would pass his fingers through my then thick hair and move his hand gently over my eyes, my nose, my chin, my mouth and my forehead. I often reminisce about those caring moments and touching memories. I believe that I have received from my dad a sense of quiet strength and stability that has been the hallmark of my life as a priest. The fruit does not fall very far from the tree.

My dad had a persistent and strong leadership influence in my life. He was the President of the Men's Club in our parish and was called upon once to give the keynote speech in the presence of India's first Cardinal. The Cardinal himself was known all over the country as a distinguished orator. So, in his final words of gratitude, he praised my father for his well prepared memorized and effectively executed speech. I feel blessed to have received my dad's sense of leadership and public speaking skills.

The apartment building in which we lived had many good and devout Catholic families. In the corridors of each floor we would pray the Rosary in the months of May and October, which are dedicated to the Blessed Virgin Mary. When the statue of Our Lady of Fatima was brought to our homes, she would be taken from one family to the next every evening. Many of the neighborhood children and families would gather inside and outside the home which had welcomed the statue of Our Lady of Fatima, pray the Rosary, sing hymns and then share a treat of boiled garbanzo beans sprinkled with tiny pieces and shavings of coconut.

Recently when watching the 'International Rosary' on EWTN (Eternal Word Television Network), I was thankful for having this childhood memory of praying the family Rosary and meditating on the mysteries of our faith. I realized that just as we have the 'Lord's Prayer' in common with other Christian denominations, together with the celebration of the Eucharist we have the Rosary and its mysteries in common with Catholic people and families all over the world.

I was a fussy eater, so mom would distract me with the Sunday newspaper cartoons. Every day the widely read 'Times of India' newspaper would be delivered to our doorstep. This was the main source of news besides the radio because there was no television in India when I was growing up. The Sunday edition of the 'Times of India' was huge and also included several illustrated cartoon pages in color. I would be fascinated and distracted by the illustrations and cartoons not realizing that my mother had secretly and successfully stuffed me with enough nourishment and food for the day without any resistance from me, and without my knowledge.

Growing up in a large family with so many siblings, there was no dearth of babysitters. Since I was born after three girls, I was especially loved and spoilt by my older sisters, some of who were quite close in age to me. We never lacked for anything even though my dad f was the only breadwinner in the family or many years. We did not have much money in the house for extras and luxuries. I don't remember ever getting toys. Once a month, when my dad received his paycheck, the entire family went out to a special restaurant for tea, bread pudding and *'samosas'* (an Indian deep fried snack stuffed either with vegetables or meat) with loads of ketchup.

With so many mouths to feed there were no gourmet meals to be found at home, except on Sundays and special holidays like Christmas. Food courses and menus were quite predictable. Every morning for breakfast, several eggs were scrambled and mixed with tomatoes, onions and green peppers and served with 'rotis,' the Indian version of wheat tortillas. When we went to school, hot lunch was delivered to us by an amazing meal delivery system, in stainless steel containers called *'dabbas,'* straight from the family kitchen to the school playground or office cafeteria, as if mom had arrived in person to feed you her hot freshly prepared specialties. In India lunch is the main meal of the day and so this meal delivery system worked miracles to provide home-cooked food right where it was needed.

Those of us in India who were non-vegetarians ate fish several times a week. Being a tropical, hot and humid country, meat was not on the menu very often. Occasionally, we would eat chicken after witnessing how a live hen was killed and cooked. Dad always had the honor of conducting the ritual sacrifice, a maidservant always freshly ground the spices and the taste was to die for, even though the chicken was mainly bone with little meat left mostly to your imagination. Once in a while, for special occasions and feast days, one of my sisters who worked at a five star hotel, would bring some turkey breasts home and that was quite a delicious treat. Beef was cheaper than lamb but tasted terrible because it came from animals that were so skinny, so malnourished and almost so dead before they reached the slaughterhouse. Sundays were special because, for lunch after morning Mass, we would feast on pork (which my dad would personally shop for – the only time he did so) prepared in a delicious spicy sauce with moist, fluffy rice cakes and delicious rice pancakes.

It seemed like the proper thing to do, which is to have a big and spicy meal for lunch, so that you could burn off the calories during the day, and sleep better at night. No wonder Indians, in general, do not suffer from obesity. The only fast food we were familiar with was the hastily cooked meal at home always with fresh ingredients; not the unhealthy, saturated fat and calorie loaded 'happy meals' of today's fast food restaurants. Supper was light and late. After a full day at school or work, we would have a light dinner made up mainly of lunch leftovers before saying our night prayers and going to sleep. Due to the lack of refrigeration, all food items were consumed by dinnertime so that there were no stale leftovers the next day.

Before supper the whole family would gather in front of the family altar to pray the Rosary. All my siblings have fond memories of praying the family Rosary. If a family that prays together stays together, then the daily family Rosary played a big part in holding us together in good and difficult times. As children we had to return promptly from playing outside with friends at about seven each night to pray as a family. The tough part of the Rosary was not the recitation of the five decades, but the praying of the 'Five Our Fathers and Five Hail Mary's,' on our knees, raising our hands up high, in commemoration of the five wounds of Jesus on the Cross.

Even if you fought with your older siblings on the playground, at the end of the recitation of the Rosary, you had to approach your parents and then each of your older siblings for a blessing. Even though you did so reluctantly you humbly folded your hands and said to each one: "Please, bless me." After which, they would make the sign of the cross on your forehead or hold your folded hands and say: "God bless you." What a lesson in humility and in showing respect for elders, even for those just a year or two older than you! Being sandwiched between younger and older siblings, I had the joy of being blessed by older siblings and, at the same time, of blessing three younger, rather spoilt, family members, before they could complain to my parents about how they felt bullied by their older siblings and friends at play. My parents had the patience of Job to listen to all our playful complaints and sibling rivalries. One of the important lessons one learns in a large family is how to get along with those who are different from you, an invaluable lesson for priestly and parish ministry.

In our family every birthday was celebrated. Everyone was made to feel special at least one day in the year. The same sister who got us turkey meat from time to time would also order a special cake for the birthday person. In the evening when everyone was home, the birthday cake would be cut to the traditional tune of 'Happy Birthday' and to the special family tune of 'The Happy Birthday Polka,' a very joyous foot stomping melody. Then we would sing and dance for a while before partaking of a sumptuous home cooked dinner and more birthday cake. Having a lot of sisters, I had several partners for family dances and parties.

These happy family gatherings and memories have always inspired me to create joyful and vibrant events and sacramental celebrations for people of all ages in my parishes and communities.

*****

Although India is largely a Hindu country, we lived in an area with many Catholic families, who went to the same parish church and to the same Catholic coeducational school. It was our own Christian faith ghetto, like the ghettoes of the early immigrants to the United States. For this reason as a child I thought almost everyone in India was Catholic. Only in school did I experience the melting pot, which is India, and also the realization that Catholics are a small minority.

The apartment building we lived in was endearingly called by us 'The Last Building.' That may sound apocalyptic but it only meant that there were no houses or apartments behind or beyond where we lived. Surrounding us were giant government warehouses separating homes and buildings by huge walls and barbed wire fences. These walls and warehouses created a long corridor behind our 'Last Building' that was our play space for cricket, field hockey, soccer and other creative childhood sports. A huge net was tied between the Last Building and the neighboring one, named '*Tarvoti Bhavan*' (Sailors' Haven), where the youth and young adults of the neighborhood would gather to play volleyball on Sunday evenings. Everybody in the neighborhood, both young and old, watched us play from his or her windows. It takes a village, they say, to raise a child. I was certain that besides my family, everyone in the neighborhood knew where I was at all times.

We also played other games like 'Seven Tiles,' 'Spinning Tops,' 'Marbles,' and '*Gilli Danda*' (a game with a long stick that is used to hit a smaller sharpened piece of wood, while your opponents try to catch it with their bare hands). While this last game caused a lot of hurts and bruises, there was another dangerous game where kids jumped on the backs of other kids who, with their faces down, had to guess correctly how many fingers were raised by the leader of the jumping group. We could easily have hurt our backs or the backs of our friends, but in those carefree years of childhood playing and winning was all that mattered. In our fantasy world, we thought our play space was beyond the known world. We had a sense of freedom and boundless joy. We only hurried home and left our freedom corridor when threatened by these ominous words: "If you don't come home right now, you will go hungry to bed."

With my peers and my family I attended the parish of St. John the Evangelist, where I was also baptized. With the British and Christian influences my parents and older siblings gave us English and saints' names. All the males in my family have middle names starting with the letter 'A' (Anthony, Augustine, Aloysius, Alfred and Andrew). The women have the letter 'M' for their middle names (Maria, Marceline, Matilda, Monica and Maize).

As a child, as with everything else, our parish church appeared to look like a great big edifice for me. In the center of the main wall was a huge crucifix. On either side of Jesus hanging on the cross were his mother, Mary, and his beloved disciple, John the Evangelist. Among all his chosen apostles, John was the disciple Jesus loved the most. He and his brother, James, were fishermen and were referred to as the sons of Zebedee. Sometimes, they were called the sons of thunder because of their explosive personalities. Even their mother had ambitions for them asking Jesus to honor them in his kingdom, one on his right and the other on his left. John is called the Evangelist because he is the author of the Fourth Gospel. He also wrote the letters of John and the Book of Revelation, on the island of Patmos where he was exiled, and the latter is the last book of the New Testament and of the Bible. From the Cross, it was to John, the beloved disciple, that Jesus entrusted his mother.

That closeness and intimacy that John, the beloved, had with Jesus and later with his mother, Mary, in my baptismal parish may have also influenced my vocation to the priesthood. Every Sunday as a child I gazed upon these gigantic figures on the wall of our parish church and somehow felt included within their triangle of Spirit, Love and Mystery. I wanted to be the beloved of Jesus my Savior, like John the Evangelist, and to be close to his mother as well. Those images of Jesus Christ and the significant disciples (Mary is known as the First Disciple) at the foot of the Cross, have never left my imagination, my memory and my vision.

One may feel called by powerful images and representations as St. Francis of Assisi felt called when he heard Jesus speak to him from his special Cross, which can be found today in the Basilica of St. Clare in Assisi, Italy. From that Cross, Jesus asked Francis to rebuild his church, which in the beginning St. Francis misunderstood as Jesus asking him to fix the broken-down church of San Damiano. Later, he saw clearly that God was calling him to be a prophet and a radical disciple to renew the whole Catholic Church, which had in many ways moved away from living and following the life and the teachings of the Christ of the Gospels.

The word 'vocation' comes from the Latin, '*vocare*,' which means to call. Yet, a vocation cannot be limited to a one-time call. A vocation is a call that starts a journey. One is challenged not only to answer the call, but also to take on a new direction in life, to embark on a new way of living and to persevere in one's new spiritual journey. The Apostles Jesus first called on the shores of Galilee lived with Jesus for three years before they even understood what Jesus was all about. No wonder that several times in the New Testament, Jesus says to his disciples: "Don't you understand? Don't you understand?"

In one of Giotto's frescoes in the Upper Basilica of St. Francis of Assisi, we see the face of his earthly father turn green with anger, his fist clenched to strike Francis (fortunately the fist is held back by someone in the crowd), yet Francis, who is naked (fortunately his body is covered by the bishop's cape), is smilingly looking up at the skies, where there is the open hand of his heavenly Father blessing him for his obedience to the call. When one has answered the call, one is not concerned about what one wears or what other people think. Thanks to the call and to the response, one is simply aware of being abundantly and constantly blessed.

In the church of St. John the Evangelist in Bombay, I learned to pray as a child and I celebrated the sacraments of Baptism, Eucharist, Reconciliation and Confirmation. I learned to be a faithful Catholic and to grow in my faith. But my priesthood vocation journey was only just beginning. The seeds of priesthood were already planted in me through the example of my family and the nurturing sacramental life of my parish.

This vocation journey was strongly influenced by the priests of the parish. They always seemed to be happy. They smiled and always had time to talk with you. I don't remember ever seeing them grumpy, sad or angry. They had an aura of simple holiness and humanity about them. They were approachable, yet highly respected. Not once did I hear anyone speak ill of each other. At home my parents spoke of their parish priests with love and respect. The journey that begins with a call, even sometimes in our mother's womb, was being intensified with this priestly contact and early impressions. First impressions are lasting impressions. Why would I **not** want to be like someone who is happy and content with his life and ministry? Why would I **not** want to be a priest like these 'guys?'

Another happy experience and adventure I had as a teenager was going to a beautiful hill station, just outside Bombay, called Lonavla. A very popular priest, Fr. Rodney Esperance, would organize a summer camp where young people played together, worked side-by-side and participated in daily Mass and communion. His enthusiasm and inspirational talks kept us returning to the summer camp. Seeing his happy and youthful demeanor I wanted to become a priest like him. Several years later, soon after my ordination, I was appointed to a parish where he was also the associate and the principal of the school.

On 'Priesthood Sunday,' during a discussion on Vocation and Ministry in one of my parishes, a parishioner reminded everyone that many years ago, when there were several children in a family, at least one son would be given to the land, one to the military and one to the church. This parishioner added that since he had only one son, he wanted to hold on to him so that he could have grandchildren someday! He added that he could not sacrifice his only son to the priesthood. He wanted to make sure that the family name was carried on.

This was not the case with my family. Although we were a large family, no one had as yet become a nun or a priest. I was going to be the first and the only one in the family. There was absolute joy and celebration in the hearts of my parents and siblings when I announced on my graduation day from high school, at the age of sixteen, that I wanted to become a priest.

But I am getting ahead of myself!

*****

Before the call to priesthood deepened in my soul at the ripe 'old age' of sixteen, there was still elementary and high school to finish. In India there is no separation of Church and State. Every parish in Bombay, where I grew up, tried to build a school next to the parish church, so that most of the Catholics in the area could attend a parochial school. Most parishes were poor, so a school could bring added revenue and prestige to the parish community.

Tuition in Indian schools was very low. When Indira Gandhi, the first Indian woman (and no relative of Mahatma Gandhi), became Prime Minister of India, she eliminated school fees for all girls so that girls would not be forced to remain illiterate by their parents or extended families. Many Indian families do not send girls to get an education because the purpose of a girl's life, according to them, is to get married as soon as possible and to start a family. Only boys are encouraged to pursue higher education and their life ambitions. Although there were good Church-run, same-sex schools for boys and for girls, my parents decided to send us brothers and sisters to the same co-ed parochial Holy Name High School.

In 2010 President Barack Obama on his first major trip to India, with his family and his entourage, visited my school, during 'Diwali,' an important Indian festival of light.

In my childhood days, Holy Name High School was just one huge rickety wooden building that housed both the elementary as well as the middle and high school classrooms. As a result, we did not have any special elementary or middle school graduation ceremonies. We went all the way for eleven years from one grade to the next till we arrived at the Secondary School Certificate public examinations in order to receive our high school diploma, and for the grand finale of a long school career, we had our one and only high school graduation celebration.

'Hand me downs' were common in my family. One of my older sisters would buy cheaper second-hand textbooks, which were then passed on to the first younger sibling and then to the next, till I finally inherited them. I had such a phenomenal memory as a child that I would rarely open those textbooks. At the end of the year, they would be sold to the local bookstore as second-hand books, still in pretty good shape. I had enough older sisters to make sure that I did my homework each day and prepared for my tests and annual examinations.

Being good at school and getting good grades led me to being chosen for leadership roles. One such role was to be a school monitor and enforce discipline while the kids went to their classrooms after morning general assembly. We were part of a disciplinary outfit called 'Road Side Patrol' or R.S.P. Those who did not like us referred to us as R.S.P. – *'Ragada, Samosa, Pattice'* (names for delicious Indian snacks)!

A priest is called to be the leader of faith communities. I believe that every experience of leadership I had as a teenager provided the skills I would need one day to be in charge of parishes and special ministries.

I may have been thirteen then, and experiencing the stirrings of puberty, because I suddenly felt drawn to a beautiful, petite Muslim girl in my school called Shabnam. She was my first teen infatuation. I made sure that I glanced at her every morning on the way to class. One day we talked. I remember being very nervous when she slipped me a note and asked me for a written reply. In a moment of weakness, I wrote her a personal note and asked her to destroy it after reading. Very soon I forgot about the note. One day, one of my sisters confronted me about this love-note I had written. How did my sister find out? Apparently, Shabnam had not destroyed the note as I had explicitly asked her to do. Instead, she had carefully preserved it in her Hindi language textbook. Her Hindi language teacher found the note. Popularity has a price and, being in a variety of leadership roles, everybody knew me; and they were also familiar with some of the members of my family. That's how my older sister was informed and that's how also that brief infatuation with Shabnam ended. I wonder sometimes what this relationship with Shabnam would have meant for Catholic-Muslim dialog, if we weren't found out!

One thing Shabnam made me realize was that I was a normal teenager attracted to the opposite sex. More than half of the school was comprised of girls. Being educated and growing up even in a Catholic parochial school meant shorter uniform skirts for the girls and shorter navy blue half pants for the boys. Although the school required that skirts and shorts should hang just a little over the knees, many of the girls would shorten their skirts to attract the boys and the boys would fold their shorts to show off more of their skinny legs.

It's hard to imagine and somewhat embarrassing to remember what teenagers in those days did for forbidden love!

Indian feature movies are now famously referred to as Bollywood hits, after Hollywood, where most American movies are made, coupled with the name of the city of Bombay where most of the Indian films are produced. Yet, even though India produces more feature films than any other country in the world, kissing in public, even among married couples, is considered illegal and obscene. So, a lot of romantic flirting goes on in Bollywood movies but no lips-to-lips or mouth-to-mouth kissing is allowed. In my youth, to kiss or not to kiss, was the question and dilemma for Indian films.

One can imagine the scandal that took place in our revered Catholic school grounds one day, when a high school senior kissed a high school junior during recess on the lips and publicly in the sight of all. They made history that day even though they did not graduate from our school.

One of my upper grade class women teachers, according to an older sister of mine, would beckon me to her desk as if to reprimand me. I had no idea what was going on. In reality she just wanted to get a close up of my eyes and of my smile! Luckily for me, I was told about this 'teacher's pet' attraction much later, after I had finished school and entered the seminary.

Holy Name Proto Cathedral Church was right next to our school. During recess and lunch break some of us would visit this beautiful neo-gothic church for a quick prayer. Outside the church, we would often run into the many parish priests who resided there. We knew some of them because they taught religion in our school.

Just like the priests in my baptismal parish, I also found the priests in our school to be happy and contended with their lives and their vocations. This included the school principal, who was himself a priest. They would take the time to say 'hello' to you, and if they knew your family, they would ask about them. Even as children we were never afraid of priests. There was a certain attraction to their lifestyle, yet their cassocks reminded you that they had another life different from the one of other adults. They were approachable, yet they kept their distance. They were kind and they were intelligent. They played games with you and they were funny. Their words and actions were fertile grounds for the nurturing of the seeds of vocation sown by my family and my childhood experiences; to deepen and to solidify my sense of the call and the journey of vocation to the priesthood.

Oliver Wendell Holmes once said, "I might have entered the ministry if certain clergymen I knew had not looked and acted so much like undertakers."

There are priests who make ministry attractive and there are those who take the flavor out of the priesthood.

There was one clergy encounter that was best forgotten. When I was in high school, we went to the nearby public school grounds for our annual sports and athletics event. Since three of my friends and I had already participated in our sporting events and had no more interest in the rest of the proceedings, we decided to go home early. As we were about to leave these public grounds, we saw a fruit tree. My friends could not resist the temptation, so two of the bold ones climbed the tree while two of us stayed below and picked the fruit they threw down at us.

Suddenly we heard an unusual sound of a thousand running feet pounding the ground; we looked around and noticed with great trepidation and fear that the entire school was coming in our direction led by an angry reverend school Principal. Since my friends and I had encroached on public property and were caught stealing (I always claimed that I was innocent because all I did was collect the fruit which fell to the ground), we were given a horrendous and humiliating public flogging by – what appeared to me from the perspective of an innocent, frightened boy – a mad, mad monster of a priest.

How can one forget the humiliation and pain of such a public scourging? I was reminded that day that in every profession, including the priesthood, there are some very bad apples. Every priest is human. Not every priest is holy; not every priest's life is worth emulating. Fortunately, this school Principal lasted only a year in office in our school.

In high school as a senior I took part in the annual final debate. Our class teacher prepared us for the event where the entire school would be present. The teacher went so far as to also manipulate my classmates' applause to our key debate points. He told them when they were expected to clap. I had memorized my entire speech and was looking forward to a spirited and successful confrontation with the opposing side. When I came to an important point in the debate, I raised my voice for emphasis and expected the students from my class to applaud as planned. No one clapped. There was this eerie silence that was deafening. I forgot my lines and had to revert to my notes for help.

Fortunately, I did not take this embarrassment to heart and give up public speaking. Otherwise I might never have become a priest, considering that a priest is frequently called upon to speak to large audiences in a variety of situations and gatherings.

Apart from the debate debacle my senior year of high school ended on a very positive note. On one day of the year, the school Principal and the faculty would leave the school premises to go for an all-day relaxing picnic. That day the senior graduating class would be in charge of the whole school, from the general assembly in the morning to classroom teaching and administration. During the day parents and grandparents would come and walk around the school and see how responsible the seniors had become.

I got the most important leadership role. I became the school Principal for a whole day! And in a Catholic school, the school principal is usually a priest or a nun, so I was, once again, through another unique sign, being helped and prepared for my vocation and priestly ministry. The suit and tie I wore that day for the first time in my life would soon be replaced with a white cassock, and eventually with a clerical suit and clergy vestments.

I may not have consciously thought about it that momentous day, but I was firmly on the road to priesthood.

CHAPTER 3

SEMINARY LIFE

T HE YEAR 1967 was a banner year for Holy Name High School. Six seniors from my class, including me, decided to become Catholic priests. One entered the Jesuit novitiate, and the others joined St. Pius X College Seminary, in the suburban town of Goregaon, Bombay.

By our decision to become priests, we made history that year. We were told (and I'm not sure that it was totally true) that the year we decided to join the seminary, there was not a single vocation to the priesthood in the entire city of Rome! The unbelievable and impressive fact was that four out of the six were born and raised in the same apartment complex, the one we lovingly remembered and cherished as: 'The Last Building.' There was, literally, one prospective candidate to the priesthood on every floor.

Sometimes I wonder why there were so many vocations in one neighborhood and possibly none in the Eternal City. It takes a village not only to raise a child but also to nurture the seeds of vocation to the priesthood and the religious life. Our family life, our life in the neighborhood, our parish life at St. John the Evangelist and our Holy Name School experience – all together had a cumulative and definitive role to play in our being called to the priesthood.

We were all about sixteen years old, fresh out of high school. The implications of leaving home and family forever for the Lord had not crossed our minds.

The day we left to go to the Seminary, which was located about twenty five miles from our homes, our families decided to rent a huge school bus. It was going to be a neighborhood sendoff. Many neighbors wanted to come along and so we traveled as one big extended family. Once the bus was on its way we sang picnic songs, laughed and joked with each other and enjoyed the ride. Nobody seemed to experience any sadness on this journey and if they did it was undetectable. Only when the bus was preparing to exit the beautifully manicured Seminary grounds, and we were waving goodbye to our families as we stood on the side of the driveway, did I suddenly feel alone and sad. I felt like crying but I managed to hold back the tears.

Spanish Jesuit professors and administrators ran the Seminary. India currently has the second largest number of Jesuit priests and brothers in the world. In my Seminary days, American Jesuits worked in Northern India, while Spaniards focused on the western regions of India that included the city of Bombay. At sixteen this was my first contact with European missionaries. They were pleasant to work with. And I got along very well with them. Surrounded only by Indians as a child, I was not aware that English could be spoken with surprisingly different accents. I suddenly realized that English could sound quite funny and mysterious coming from Spanish-speaking mouths. Even though we could not understand them at times, we respected them because of their White complexion. Indians had always respected (and continue to do so to this very day) the fair skinned strangers and foreigners who lived and worked among them. However, that did not prevent us from mimicking their cute accents.

Since for over three hundred years the British had refused to mix and mingle with the local Indian population, except to trade with them and to exploit their natural resources, this sense of distance and 'splendid isolation' introduced by them gave Europeans in general, in our eyes, an air of superiority. The Spanish missionaries benefited from this colonial edge. They occupied an entire floor by themselves and never joined the

Indian seminarians for meals and games. Although pleasant and generally approachable, they kept to themselves because of the demands of their religious community life. I was too excited by my new life to be troubled or bothered by any of this.

We lived dormitory style, three or four seminarians to a room. Each of us was given a single mattress bed, generally lumpy and hard, surrounded by a mosquito net. Mosquitoes plagued the town of Goregaon, like most of the suburban areas of Bombay. Even a single one of these critters, flapping its wings faster than a humming bird over my ear, could keep me awake all night. To add to it, I had, what everybody called, 'sweet blood,' that served as an open invitation to every blood sucking thirsty mosquito.

Every night before going to bed, there was a ritual massacre of those clever bugs that had somehow made their way to the inside of the net waiting patiently for their human victim to enter the sacrificial battle ground. Before falling asleep, we would do battle with both hands in a clapping motion with these few unfortunate mosquitoes that had the audacity to enter the net uninvited, so that in the morning we could count the bloodstains on the mosquito net as our victory trophies.

I knew I was becoming a soldier of Christ, but was this the fighting I was going to do for the rest of my life? I felt untrained for this nightly battle in the suburbs because growing up in downtown Bombay, we had no mosquitoes to contend with, just flies, crows and rats!

We were also each given a simple wooden cupboard to store our personal belongings and a small table and chair for reading and study. The lighting was inadequate but young eyes can penetrate every level of darkness.

For the first six months we participated in a very intense and rigorous spiritual program of formation. In India young Hindu kids who want to become disciples and Buddhist boys who want to become monks, leave home and spend several years often alone with a spiritual master. Our program was different because it involved an entire community of young men. A loud bell awakened us every morning at 5:15 followed by a half-hour to wash up and dress. My fears of waking early were coming true and I hated the sound of that bell. So did everybody else.

Then we went to meditate within the beautiful, marble floors and walls and stained glass windows that adorned the imposing Seminary chapel. Our prayer space was clean and shiny, because every evening, after supper, some of us would be assigned to wipe the pews and mop the floors.

Every night, before going to bed, we received an end-of-the-day spiritual talk for about half an hour, and then we were given, in Jesuit Ignatian spirituality style, three points to ponder in our beds and in our sleep. Thus we always retired with spiritual thoughts and reflections. The morning chapel meditation was a continuation of deepening our understanding and spirituality on the reflection insights of the night before. Most of us carried a piece of paper to the chapel with the three meditation points. But within a few minutes many of us would fall asleep like the disciples in the Garden of Gethsemane.

The pieces of meditation paper would gently leave our laps and fingers and fall all over the marble floor of the chapel sounding like a lullaby. Our spiritual formation made us define sleep as 'horizontal meditation.'

The Seminary building and property were like an oasis in the quaint town of Goregaon. The only other well-known landmark there was the Aarey Milk Colony. As a child I was brought here on a field trip to see how milk was pasteurized, bottled and distributed all over the city of Bombay.

About two hundred seminarians lived in community style on this spacious gated hill, not too far from the railway station. On the road from the station, as anywhere else in Bombay, you took your life in your own hands. This road between the Seminary and the railway station was shared by B.E.S.T. (Bombay Electric Supply and Transport) red and white, both single and double-decked buses, pedestrians, chickens, rickshaws, hundreds of honking yellow and black taxis, handcarts, trucks (also known as lorries), and the occasional, carefree sacred cow!

The Seminary was an impressive structure built in the late fifties, with a beautiful marble chapel and its nine side altars, situated right in the center of the seminary, with living quarters on either side of it. There was a huge library and an even bigger dining hall, that we called 'the refectory.' Outside on twenty-five acres, there was a soccer field, cricket grounds and some volleyball and basketball courts. A grotto area made for a quiet and meditative place to pray alone or with others. The grounds were improved upon by the seminarians themselves. Everyone had to take an hour each evening for outdoor games and recreation. If for some reason, you preferred not to play, then the option you were given was to take part in a program called 'CAW.' or 'Campaign against Weeds.' This was a clever way devised by one of our Jesuits to get us to do some physical exercise and at the same time to rid the property of unwanted and ugly weeds.

The huge dining hall was run and staffed by the 'P.S.O.L.' (Poor Sisters of Our Lady) nuns, in their immaculate white habits and blue sashes. Because of India's gigantic population, labor was cheap. The sisters themselves did not do the cooking. They supervised the kitchen help and regularly fed this small army of God's foot soldiers in formation.

The Seminary looked wealthy but it really wasn't. Since we all came from relatively poor families, no fixed tuition was expected, just whatever the family could afford to donate. I remember one year taking in cash the offering my family made for my lodgings and tuition to the Jesuit finance minister of the Seminary. It amounted to four hundred rupees, which of course was a lot of money in those days, but in today's inflationary exchange rate it would be equal to about ten dollars.

I recall standing by the minister's desk and softly whistling to myself, while he entered the amount in his ledger. I either hummed or softly whistled popular tunes often during the day. It was just a habit to fill silent moments. The finance minister priest was a small man with a round chubby face, like a valentine cherub. He looked up at me, stopped what he was doing and proceeded to ask me in a squeaky nasal tone whether I would whistle if I were in the presence of the Pope!

So, for what we paid into the system, the food was relatively good and kept us alive. We never went to bed hungry. And we always knew what was being served every week from Monday to Saturday. As a matter of fact, we presumed that the menu for the meals was mimeographed for each day of the week and for the entire year (except Sundays and feast days). Mondays was rice and lentils, Tuesdays, vegetable soup, beans and rice, Wednesdays, beef curry and rice, Thursdays, noodles and chicken, Fridays, fish and rice and Saturdays, mixed leftover surprises with rice! Rice is the staple food of India.

The Jesuits were founded by St. Ignatius of Loyola, who as a wounded soldier, read the lives of the saints in his hospital bed and then said to himself: "If they can be saints, so can I." His followers became educators and missionaries and they became a strong Counter Reformation to the growing protestant influence in Europe, doing everything, as St. Ignatius insisted, "*Ad Maiorem Dei Gloriam*" – for the greater glory of God.

In fact the patron of the missions is none other than St. Francis Xavier, a very early companion of St. Ignatius, and whose body is still preserved today in a church in Goa, India. The remains of St. Francis Xavier are gradually shrinking, and it is said that when his remains disappear, the world will end.

July 31st, the feast day of St. Ignatius Loyola, was a good day for all of us because we were always treated to a sumptuous dinner by the Spanish Jesuits in celebration of their patron saint's feast day.

On the other hand, the patron saint of diocesan priests like me is a French cleric by the name of Jean Marie Vianney of Ars, near Lyons in France. In the recently concluded 'Year of the Priest' the Church celebrated the 150th Anniversary of this humble and dedicated patron of diocesan clergy. St. John Vianney as a parish priest was known to hear confessions sometimes for fourteen hours a day and to be very ascetic, living on just bread and water and potatoes. Well, on his feast day, August 4th, we were treated to just that: bread and water and potatoes! This made us conclude that the Jesuits take the vows, but we diocesan parish priests practice them!

Right after we joined the Seminary, we were allowed to return home one day a month. Instead of a lot of family members traveling a long distance to visit each seminarian at the Seminary, the authorities decided it was more practical for us to go home once a month. On our first visit our childhood friends and neighbors were surprised that we returned home so quickly, especially since they had said goodbye to us only a month before. They jokingly reminded us that they were hoping never to see us again. After all, it was understood in those days that when one leaves to join the Seminary, one gives up family, friends and home forever. But we were so happy to be home among loved ones and, boy, those home cooked meals never tasted so yummy! It got to be more and more difficult to leave our family and friends every month and return to Seminary life.

One of our seminarians would get food cravings even after lights were out for everyone at 10 p.m. He did not survive in the Seminary. Not that he died of hunger. It was simply determined that he did not have a vocation to the priesthood because he lacked self-control. Discipline was constantly enforced. After all, the Jesuit superiors needed to know very early in our formation whether we truly had a vocation to the priesthood. Two Jesuits were assigned to this task of 'discernment': a Spiritual Director and a disciplinarian, called 'Father Minister.' While all the other professors and administrators lived on a separate floor by themselves, with their own private dining facilities and recreation area, these two men lived on the same floor with us, one at each corner, and constantly watched our comings and goings. From time to time we had to have meetings with both men, who would then discern together whether we had a vocation or not.

The Rector or Superior of the entire seminary, too, would keep a close watch on the seminarians. After hours when we were all supposed to be in bed asleep, the Rector would sometimes pace up and down the corridor apparently praying the Rosary. Brother Alex was our resident cartoonist. One day we all had a good laugh as we stood around the bulletin board looking at Alex's recent humorous observation of seminary life. He showed the Rector walking down our bedroom corridor presumably passing his fingers over the beads of a huge Rosary behind his back and below were the words: The second Joyful Mystery – 'The Visitation.'

When we started our first year of seminary life in 1967, there were twenty-three seminarians in my class. At the end of ten years of formation and study, only nine were ordained to the priesthood. This was not bad considering the statistic that only one-third of any class would normally persevere to the end to ordination.

I still remember how shocked I was when I heard about the first seminarian to leave the Seminary mysteriously and permanently.

I couldn't believe that the loving God who called a young man to service would renege on His invitation a few months or a few years later. But who was really saying 'No' to the call? Was it even possible to say 'No', once the 'Yes' was spoken? Blessed Pope John Paul II refused laicization to priests after the exodus of the sixties and the seventies because he said that the strong 'Yes' they had spoken in response to God's call, should sustain them even when they are weak and want to quit the priesthood.

Towards the end of his life, this saintly Pope when asked whether he would retire for reasons of health turned the question around by asking whether Jesus would have retired from his mission to save the world or come down from the Cross because the suffering was too much for him.

I was beginning to have doubts about how the Holy Spirit really works in our lives. But in this intense, rigorous spiritual formation period, our Spiritual Director urged us to eliminate doubts from our minds as bad thoughts and did not permit them even in conversation. The only safe place to express doubt was in the confessional.

Those were the days when we were trained to measure the length of our thoughts. If we entertained a fleeting temptation mentally, according to one of our retreat directors, for more than ten seconds, then it would become a bad thought, a sin and it would have to be confessed as such in the sacrament of penance. It was so easy to make the shift from such a literal and meticulous measurement of thought processes to the realm of guilt trips.

I am reminded about what the theologian, Paul Tillich, said concerning doubt: "Doubt is not the opposite of faith; it is one element of faith."

*****

On September 3rd, a few months after we joined the Seminary, we were given white cassocks to wear with blue sashes (ordained priests in India used to wear white cassocks with white sashes): marks of our initiation and identity. The full length of the cassock was a sign of complete commitment. When we wore them, we knew that we now had a calling that was different from other young men our age in the world.

For some, grasping one's true identity takes an entire lifetime. When would I understand what the priesthood really meant in my life?

When we noticed some of our Spanish Jesuit professors and administrators wearing short cassocks, several inches above their ankles, the joke went around that they were not fully dedicated.

Subconsciously, we were already learning to portray an external image of priesthood, whether it was true or false. We had a saying that 'a cassock covers many sins.' What we wore underneath our cassocks, torn or soiled, as long as it was not visible, did not really matter. No one saw the real '**you**.' By wearing cassocks, we could, if we wanted, camouflage and hide our true authentic selves from the rest of the world.

The clothes you wear affect your thinking and your behavior. To others, what you wear may either be a mirror of your authentic self or a mask to hide the person you really are. I felt sometimes that I lived in two worlds: one, when I had my cassock on me during the day, and another, when I returned to my room in the evening and removed it. Even our tone of voice and the choice of words were different in and out of our clerical dress. In our cassocks we were representing the hierarchy of the Church, therefore we had to mortify our true selves and behave ourselves in public in order not to give the wrong impression to outsiders, especially non-Catholics; or to scandalize the simple minded in the church.

This form of spirituality was intensely applied in the first rigorous months of spiritual training. It eased somewhat, with more freedoms during the next two and a half years that I spent at St. Pius X College Seminary.

Those first six months of formation were so intense and rigorous that even after thirty-five years of priesthood, I can still sense the effects of that priestly training.

I remembered how important it was to always wear the cassock in public whenever we had our monthly 'Home Visitation' days. Once, I went with some friends to see the movie: 'The Graduate,' starring Dustin Hoffman and Anne Bancroft. Being tall and skinny, and not quite eighteen, I was still able to go watch the

'R' rated movies of those days (nothing compared to what is acceptable and passed on as 'R' rated movies today), but, of course, I would walk into the theater without my cassock. What would people think if they saw a seminarian sneaking into an 'R' rated movie theater!

In this classic film, an older married woman seduces a young graduate. After watching the movie, even though I had not worn my cassock, I felt reassured in the thought that we were given a protective garb to ward off the seductions and the evils surrounding us. I said to myself that as long as I continue to wear my symbol of vocation and commitment in public, I would never allow myself to be seduced or to do any wrong to others. I arrived at the same conclusion when I later saw 'Superman II,' where he loses his superpowers (divine calling?) and his indestructible cape (cassock?), while falling in love with his sweetheart, Lois Lane.

Recent sexual scandals in the Church all over the world have proved that some bishops and priests (including some popes in our long Church history) have lived two lives: one which they externally and publicly portrayed by the habits and clerical collars they wore, and the other by what they scandalously did privately and secretly. A habit, cassock or clerical collar can cover many things, but one's true personality and devious inclinations cannot be forever hidden.

If there was one thing Jesus could not tolerate, it was hypocrisy. He welcomed sinners, even dining with them in public. He taught that repentant tax collectors and prostitutes would be the first to enter the heavenly courts before the Scribes and the Pharisees. For Jesus, hypocrisy had no place in God's kingdom. He wanted his disciples' holiness to surpass that of the Scribes and Pharisees.

Today people treat their priests differently. With the exception of some elderly Catholics, most parishioners call their clergy by their first names. Some priests insist on this informality, if people have doubts about how to address them.

Sometimes Church members have difficulty accepting the style of ministry of certain priests. In today's environment of warmth and hospitality, some priests like to hug their parishioners as they leave church. Such behavior is frowned upon especially by those who see the church only as a sacred space to pray and to be close to God, and not for socialization and community building. Other introverted priests will not even step outside the church facility, so that they don't have to make any physical or social contact with members of the assembly. Such cold and distant beings are unappreciated and criticized by the 'reach out and touch' younger socially conscious generation of churchgoers.

Problems such as these of behavior and attitudes existed also during the time of Jesus and John the Baptizer. There were those who couldn't accept John's ascetic lifestyle, and others who freely criticized and condemned the dinner party welcoming and celebrating style of Jesus. While some people thought that John the Baptizer was wild and unsophisticated, others labeled Jesus as a sinner and a glutton for hanging out with tax collectors and public sinners. People did not really understand what Jesus and John were really about. There is nothing worse than having people say things about us that are not true, whether it is to neighbors or to news reporters. Both Jesus and John knew the sting of slander.

The important thing I learned from the examples of both Jesus and John was to be true to yourself and to your identity, despite what others think about you. Jesus taught his disciples to respond with love not bitterness and hatred towards those who might label and judge you falsely.

*****

In the year I joined the seminary, a very significant family situation affected my newly established identity of being an individual called by God. In September of that year, just three months after I joined the Seminary, on the day I received my cassock, the family member who was present for this event was my oldest brother, Charles. Out of respect, we younger siblings called him in my parents' language of Konkani, 'Charlibaba.' He was thirteen years older than I was. I was so happy that Charlibaba could be present for this important spiritual-identity celebration in my life to represent my parents and the rest of my many siblings. After one's parents, the oldest son in the family has the same responsibility and authority placed on his shoulders to represent and to speak on behalf of the entire family in the hierarchical society of India.

Charles was an engineer by profession. When my father retired after working for the same company for well over thirty-seven years, Charles decided, with the help of my dad's retirement and pension funds, to start his own business. This career move gave me a tremendous amount of appreciation both for my brother as well as my father. My brother was ahead of his time and was one of the first in our neighborhood to start an independent family business. My dad was always open-minded even if it meant risking his entire life savings. He trusted his children and believed in them and in their ideas.

Charles invested in some lathe machines and started making small precision metal parts for naval ships. Since the Indian Navy ships were increasing in numbers and growing in strength, size and tonnage, my brother did extremely well for himself and for the family within a few years of starting his business.

In the beginning it was truly a family business. After these metal parts were assembled at the factory, they were brought home where we cleaned them, counted them and prepared them for delivery. It was a messy job. After long evenings of work, the floor and our hands would be covered with dirty oil and some sharp metal filings. But there was a deep sense of family pride as we saw the business grow from its humble beginnings to government recognition.

I remember the day when a bright, white refrigerator was wheeled into the house and we actually were able to produce our own ice. Prior to that slabs of ice would be delivered to the house by vendors pushing handcarts in the neighborhood. Our little one room home seemed so much bigger with this new addition. Our family was moving on up.

Who would not be proud of such a successful and hardworking brother? In the year 1967 when he attended my cassock ceremony, he began to have swelling of some glands around his throat and neck. Very soon after that we were shocked to find out that he had developed an acute form of leukemia. The shock was great because his condition was totally unexpected. My brother was the picture of health. I still remember his daily narcissistic pose in front of the family mirror, checking frequently his biceps and triceps. He worshipped his body with regular exercise and grooming. After working hard all day, he would faithfully do some body building exercises for about an hour.

If today I work out and exercise real hard, I feel that it's my brother, Charles, who still inspires me. I only wish I had his consistency and courage.

From September to the end of November of that year he was given several blood transfusions because of his low blood cell count. Every time he was administered a pint of blood, there would be some healthy, rosy color in his cheeks. But a little time after the transfusion, all that flush redness would drain from his face and he would begin to look deathly pale.

I had never experienced the agony of death and dying in my immediate family. At the bedside of my brother, I could see my mother and my sisters holding back their tears, and then, when they would walk away from him, they would simply cry and cry all the time out of a sense of helplessness. Even at death's door my brother was amazing. He refused to believe that he was dying, and from time to time when he had some strength left in him, he would make personal and business plans for the future. The thought of death never crossed his mind.

For a while, the doctors kept him alive by trying injections, still in the experimental stage, from Europe and the United States, but nothing seemed to help. These shots were very painful for my brother and very expensive for my family. But nothing was more precious to us than my brother's life. Even in the midst of these tragic circumstances, I felt a great sense of closeness and intimacy with my family. On December 1st of that same year, less than three months after I received my cassock, my beloved brother, Charlibaba, died at the young age of thirty.

Just when you think that your life has come together, an event occurs that makes you reassess everything and reorganize your priorities. For my family, it seemed as if we had lost our anchor and our foundation. Without exception, everyone in my family and in the neighborhood was devastated.

I wasn't by my brother's hospital bedside when he passed away. I got a call at the Seminary to come home. When I arrived I remember breaking down in tears in the presence of my family and friends. One of the senior seminarians that lived in our 'Last Building' took me aside and told me that I should not cry because seminarians one day become priests whose main role is to comfort others. Crying exposed weakness. He reminded me that as a cleric I should remain strong and refrain from crying. But that did not stop my tears. I was feeling sad and helpless. As I look back I am glad I was able to express my feelings.

As a priest today, when people are grieving or confronted by the death of a loved one, you may not know what to say to them to ease their sorrow and sadness. Sometimes all you can do is to listen, empathize and to allow yourself to be moved to tears.

I recall the story of a little boy who went across to his neighbor's house through the back door. The neighbor Joe had recently lost his wife of many years, and used to sit alone on his sofa quietly and with great sadness for hours on end. When the little boy returned home, his mother asked him where he had been. "I went to see Uncle Joe," the little boy said. "And what did you say to him?" his mother gently asked. "Nothing," the little boy answered. "I just sat on his lap and let him cry."

In India children also accompany their parents to bury the dead. With its huge population, you see funeral processions in a big city like Bombay almost every day. Due to limited means, most families go on foot to the local cemetery or crematorium.

India is largely Hindu by religion and culture and Hindus cremate their dead. If a parent dies, the oldest son is expected to light the pyre. Christians and Muslims generally bury their dead. There are hardly any morgues to keep bodies for very long after death in hot, humid, tropical situations. Usually Catholics will have their beloved dead brought either to church or to the family living room. It is there that family members, relatives and neighbors gather to pray the Rosary and to console one another. As soon as the parish priest is able to come to the house, the final prayers of commendation are said, and the procession to the cemetery begins. If families can afford it, buses are hired to transport anyone who wishes to go to the cemetery for the burial. Due to tropical heat and humidity, the funeral usually takes place the very next day, if not the same day of death.

Sometimes photographs are taken by professionals both of the dead body as well as of grieving family members, and later, are shown to other family members and friends who could not be present on the day of the funeral. Due to huge crowds, photographs are also a way for family members to know who showed up for the funeral. They are also a way to indicate how much a deceased family member was loved.

Death and dying are a way of life in India and even children are exposed to them from the very beginning.

Because I was in the Seminary when my brother died, Charles got one of the biggest funerals in our parish and in our city. Dressed like me, there were about one hundred and seventy five seminarians in white cassocks and blue sashes. There were also many priests, dressed in white cassocks and white sashes, both from the city parishes as well as from the Seminary faculty. In addition there were many busloads of people that accompanied my family to the church and later to the cemetery.

The many people and clergy who showed up at my brother's funeral did not take away the pain and the emptiness we all felt as a result of this tremendous loss. My parents continued to miss Charles, and I could intensely feel their sadness. They say a parent's greatest sorrow is to bury their own child.

Since I was the oldest among the brothers after Charlibaba (I have several older sisters), I felt that from our Indian cultural standpoint, it was my duty to take over responsibility for the wellbeing of the family. Being so young in matters of life, I did not quite understand the ramifications of this manner of thinking, but I felt obliged to reason this way. I was barely seventeen years old.

I was maturing very quickly in life's classroom.

In India age is not the factor to determine responsibility within the family. It has to do with your birth order and with your gender. When daughters are married they leave the family and go to live with their in-laws. The oldest son may be barely ten years old, but if the parents cannot manage to earn a living, then this kid has to step forward and take the reins of responsibility for family life and survival. Even in my teens, I instinctively sensed this cultural expectation and demand in my heart.

Visiting home one day from the seminary, I went to my dad and told him that I was prepared to leave the seminary so that

I could help him, my mother and my siblings with the family business. I really did not know what I was saying as I had no interest either in engineering or in running a business.

My dad gently looked me in the eyes and said the words I have never forgotten to this day: "Son, you have chosen your vocation. Don't worry about us. God will provide. We will manage somehow." Although I did not know the consequences of my own statements to my dad, I don't think that even he knew what he was saying. My dad was always a man of few words and that day, I realized, that he was also a man of deep faith. He was sure of one thing and that was the call or vocation I had received from above to become a priest. Nothing should come in its way, not even urgent family needs. His voice and defining words that day became for me the voice and the defining Will of God.

Sometimes we know that the words that come from our mouth are not our own, but it is the Holy Spirit who speaks on our behalf. My father's words were not logical or reasonable in this family situation. Rather, they were words and expressions of faith for me; they revealed God's Will.

In my thirty-five years of priesthood, I have learned to believe that God can speak to us in many ways. We can know the Will of God through our senses, our imagination, our dreams, nature, the Scriptures, the Sacraments, the guiding voices of elders and in many other human ways. The Catholic faith is very incarnational. God, in Jesus Christ, is Emmanuel, meaning, God with us. In Jesus, God became human so that we could more easily understand and follow the ways and the voice of the Divine.

After all, Jesus himself said: "Unless you are ready to give up parents and brothers and sisters and homes and belongings, you cannot be my disciple." In that short exchange between my father and me, there was such an intense and divine co-presence, that it has left an indelible mark in my soul and in my life as a priest.

It is my strong belief that God calls us from childhood. The first call, about which we may not be conscious, starts a journey of faith. On this sacred and mysterious path, there will be significant and defining moments that affirm us in our call and vocation. My dad's faith-filled and emotional response to me actually came, as I looked at it from a spiritual perspective, from God. It was the only language I could understand, and it confirmed me in my journey to the priesthood.

Henceforth, even if challenges came my way, including disappointments and hurts, I would not falter. That day I felt the same confidence and reassurance expressed by the Psalmist in the 23rd Psalm: "The Lord is my Shepherd. There is nothing I shall want."

I remembered the words of Martin Luther King, Jr.: "The ultimate measure of a man is not where he stands in moments of comfort and convenience, but where he stands in times of challenge and controversy."

My brother's death was a time of challenge for me, but God showed me that a vocation is an irreversible path. There are many moments when and reasons why you want to quit. But God sends angels, His messengers, like my dad, for instance, when I thought I should leave the seminary, to gently remind us that He has other plans for us. Of course, we can still insist on following our own plans and end up going our own way, but God will not abandon or desert us. God remains faithful to every call He makes. His invitation is a two-way street because it demands a constant and generous response from us as well. Although I did not have that spiritual maturity at the age of seventeen to recognize the hand of God working through my father, I did trust my father's words spoken with faith and conviction:

"Don't worry about us. God will provide." It was as if Jesus were calming the storm and saying to me: "Do not be afraid."

A friend of mine tells me that when he thinks of quitting, he is reminded about his childhood when his mother would ask him to look at a crucifix. Then she would say to him: "If He could remain on the Cross for three agonizing hours and die for us, then you have no reason to quit."

If I know about someone leaving the seminary or quitting the priesthood, I simply say to myself: "There go I but for the grace of God."

God's call is the beginning of a faith journey. It is important to move forward despite challenges and difficulties, because the Lord is in front of us, constantly and gently saying: "Come, follow me. Do not be afraid. I will be with you always."

CHAPTER 4

ALL ROADS LEAD TO ROME

G OD'S CALL is intensely experienced by all the prophets in the Bible. The prophet Jeremiah's call, for instance, reaffirms the fact that God can choose us from the very beginning:

> "Before I formed you in the womb, I knew you;
> before you were born I dedicated you."

The prophet Isaiah hears these personal words:

> "Fear not, for I have redeemed you; I have called you
> by name; you are mine."

> "I will never forget you. See, upon the palm of my
> hand, I have written your name."

> God is constantly speaking to us but we fail to hear God's
> voice because of all the noisy chatter in and around us.

Elijah, the prophet, hiding in a cave, heard God's voice not in the thunder or the earthquake, but rather in a tiny whisper.

The St. Pius X College Seminary in Bombay continued to be a wonderful place for prayer, meditation, listening and growing. Just as my elementary and high school education took place on the same campus, the intense spiritual formation of the minor seminary occurred on the same premises as my soon to come study of Philosophy and Theology. The Minor and the Major Seminary of Bombay were located in the same place.

The Major Seminary was a house of formation where one focused on the study of Philosophy and Theology, basic course requirements for the priesthood. The Minor Seminary, on the other hand, was the equivalent of college studies to broaden our minds to embrace the world with subjects like World History and Geography, Latin, Homiletics, Introduction to Scripture, Methodology, Spiritual Exercises, Logic and so on.

But a smooth, logical and linear flow of seminary education and formation in the same location was not in God's plan for me. After all, God's plans are not our plans and God's ways are not our ways.

They say that if you want to hear God laugh, just tell Him your plans.

Life happens when we are making other plans. A journey with God is always an adventure filled with unknowns and surprises.

Unbeknownst to me, changes were under foot. In the minor seminary, I had three years of Latin and I was one of the better students in my class. At first, the seminary professors and administrators had decided to send me to Poona (now known as Pune), a satellite city, located about a hundred miles south of Bombay, which housed a papal seminary, for the study of Philosophy and Theology.

But God works in mysterious ways. The Spanish Jesuits administered St. Pius X College Seminary during my time. They were wonderful professors and spiritual directors but with the dwindling number of foreign missionaries allowed to work in India, they were now looking to hand over the running of the seminary to the diocesan clergy of the Archdiocese. Foreign clergy were allowed into the country strictly as skilled professionals but were denied visas if they chose to come to India as priests, religious and missionaries.

Diocesan priests like me needed training and preparation to become future professors and administrators of the Major Seminary of Bombay, which was in the process of becoming a national college of religious studies and priestly formation. The first Indian Cardinal had a vision. He wanted the church of India, especially the seminaries and houses of religious formation to look less colonial and more as an authentic reflection of the people of India. There was a time and a place for foreign missionaries to spread the gospel across this Indian subcontinent; but now the Church in India needed to be sustained and nurtured in the Christian faith with the help of her own sons and daughters.

India's first Cardinal had a towering personality. He was an excellent orator and an admired administrator. He told us once that people in the West were not familiar with the Indian sub-continent and were generally ignorant of the long-standing presence of the Catholic Church and the British Empire in Indian society. A woman from an English-speaking Western nation once said to him: "You speak so well. Where did you learn to speak English?"

India at one time was comprised of over four hundred independent kingdoms, ruled by Maharajahs and Maharanis. Gradually under British rule and after independence in 1947, India became politically one united nation.

There is an ancient, undocumented tradition that St. Thomas, the Apostle, came to India to spread Christianity. This could very well have happened because even two thousand years ago, there existed a very ancient Jewish community along the southern Indian shores, and even today, one may find historical traces of synagogues that date back to the time of Christ. Like St. Paul, the original Apostles too, who were themselves Jewish, would start preaching Christianity wherever they could find established Jewish communities and synagogues. Going way back to the doubting Apostle Thomas of the New Testament, these devout believers, especially in the southern region of India, refer to themselves as 'Thomas Christians.' The Apostle is said to be buried in Mylapore, in the Indian state of Tamil Nadu. Most Thomas Christians in India can thus be found in the two southernmost states of Kerala and Tamil Nadu. Today they are scattered across the country and all over the world.

With Vasco da Gama, who, unlike Christopher Columbus, discovered the quicker trade route to India after he set sail from Belem, in Portugal, at the end of the fifteenth century,

Portuguese missionaries came with the dual purpose of trading and of spreading Christianity.

One of the most prolific evangelizers of India, Sri Lanka, China and Japan was a Spanish Jesuit by the name of St. Francis Xavier. His body is still preserved in the Basilica of Bom Jesus in the Old City of Goa, India, and seems to be in great condition even after being exhumed four hundred years ago.

For almost five hundred years, European missionaries did their evangelizing work selflessly and courageously. Most Catholics like me have Portuguese last names. Upon conversion, a family would adopt the last name of the sponsor or of the priest himself who celebrated their baptism and entry into the church. Unlike the British, who almost never mingled with the local population, the Portuguese would marry the locals and create mixed families wherever they settled.

The Cardinal was grateful to these wonderful European missionaries but his new vision for the Church of India was to make her look like India itself and not a foreign, colonial entity.

Most countries that have been under colonial rule and domination seem to want to discard all the signs and shackles of the past. After three hundred years of British rule, the names of almost all the streets of Bombay were changed from English royalty and heroic figures to Indian names of local heroes, politicians and deities.

I remember once in the Minor Seminary being invited to sing in our seminary choir together with other Indian and religious groups. When it came to our turn to sing, we had planned to sing songs with an Indian flavor and in local languages. We were shocked when the organizers told us that the local languages of India do not reflect Christianity or the Church itself. The best musical way to express the heritage of the Catholic Church was for us to sing in Latin! What a shock for us and what a misperception of the identity of the Catholic Church in India.

To implement his larger vision for the Church in India, the Cardinal decided to send me to Rome, Italy, instead of Poona, India, to pursue my seminary studies of Philosophy and Theology.

My family was excited when they heard the news. My eldest sister, after her marriage, was the only one in our large family to travel outside the country. None of my other siblings had lived away from home.

In India, unlike the West, one does not rent an apartment and live independently just because one has reached adulthood. In those days, you lived with your family till the day you were given in marriage, if you were a daughter, or as in the case of Catholic families like mine, you left home to become a priest or a nun.

I was almost nineteen years old, had never left the city alone and had never flown in a plane.

*****

The only traveling we did as children was to go on vacation with my parents (often with only my mother and some of my siblings) to our grandparents farm in Mangalore, about five hundred miles south of Bombay. Most of the times my dad stayed at home and could not accompany us because of his work. In those days, the exhausting and arduous trip by train and bus from Bombay to Mangalore took almost two whole days.

The trains had only two sections: Economy and First Class. We were too poor to afford the luxurious and air-conditioned first class carriage. Instead, we had to charge onto the incoming trains, while they were still moving slowly, and fight to reserve a tiny bit of space on a hard bench (there were no individual seats in economy) for the entire traveling family. For those who were not strong or courageous enough to jump onto a running train, there were red turbaned 'coolies' or attendants, who would gladly find some seating for you for a fee.

In much of life, the fun is more in the journey itself than in arriving at the destination. But these family train trips to Mangalore were uncomfortable and scary, especially to us children. You took your life in your hands and constantly counted the family members to be accurate, afraid that somebody may have been left behind in the rush from one means of transportation to the next. The economy section had its own version of air-conditioning and cooling: the windows were frequently left open and most people spent their time near the open doorways of the train compartments. The extremely bold and restless would climb on top of the train and enjoy the luxury of free, dangerous, ticketless travel!

Our slow and sooty locomotive would stop frequently and the train stations were a delight for us kids. That's when the hawkers would come to sell their wares. You could buy local fruit (like, papayas, mangoes, jackfruits, berries, watermelon etc.), tea, coffee, juices and all kinds of candy as well as spicy treats. During the day, if you were lucky to get a window seat, you could look outside at open fields and animals grazing lazily in the hot sun.

It was a different sensation from the one that comes from life in the big city, where there are thousands upon thousands of buses, taxis, auto rickshaws, lorries or trucks, handcarts, people and animals everywhere you turn. City life in Bombay is truly an assault on your senses: the smells, the noises, the honking, and the pollution — all seeking your trapped, undivided attention.

After two long train rides, the second one lasting a full twenty four hours, there was still the dangerous bus ride along and over the Western mountain range of the Indian coast. India has its own unique version of the Italian Amalfi Coast! Before buses started the climb up the steep sides of the mountains, the bus drivers would stop to pray at roadside shrines dedicated to Hindu Gods. There was also a widespread rumor that these same drivers hastily imbibed some strong spirits to have the courage to face the death-defying dangerous ride. For us kids it was always an adventure. I don't recall ever being afraid. But I would notice from time to time that a passenger here and another there would bow their heads in prayer, just in case the drivers had not prayed enough for the safety of all the passengers.

The story is told that when a priest and a bus driver from Bombay make it to heaven at the same time, the priest is given a small house while the bus driver is rewarded with a mansion. When the priest asks 'Why?' he is told that when he preached in church people slept; on the other hand, when the bus driver drove the bus, the people always prayed.

*****

Once we got to our destination safely and we were lovingly welcomed in the arms of our grandparents, we would cast aside our cares and concerns and enjoy the rest of our school vacation. Those were happy, carefree days in the countryside, with plenty of fruit, fish, food and fresh air.

My grandparents on my mother's side were farmers. They had a big farmhouse that had a large portico and the doors were never locked. People dropped in to visit all the time.

This same tradition continues even in a big city like Bombay. People still drop in whenever they wish. Hardly anybody calls ahead of time to ask whether it's okay to stop by for a visit. The only difference is that the city apartments are heavily padlocked for fear of thieves and burglars.

In rural Mangalore there were plenty of chickens, dogs and squealing pigs that ran around the house much to the delight of all my siblings. There was a fresh water well from which we would take turns to draw water for drinking, bathing and for the thirsty rice fields. Rice is the staple food of Indians and paddy fields need a lot of water. All kinds of tropical fruit could be found in my grandparents' farm. There were mangoes, bananas, jackfruit, papayas, sugarcane, guavas, cashews, coconuts and a variety of citrus fruits.

The most popular among the tropical fruits in India are mangoes. There are many varieties of them. My grandparents' farm had some of the best and the biggest and the juiciest mangoes. When they were almost ripe and ready for picking, they were plucked from the trees in large numbers and stored in a shed with hay strewn all over them to help them ripen to perfection. Our school vacations were always in the hot 'mango season,' from mid April to the beginning of June (when the south westerly monsoons would come and schools would reopen). As children we did not have the patience for perfection, so we would sneak into the mango shed and help ourselves to as many delicious mangoes as possible.

Mangoes have huge seeds in them. After licking and sucking a mango of all its succulent flesh and juices, we would call out the name of one of our siblings or our country cousins. If they responded, we would fling the seed as far as we could into the surrounding field, and say in Konkani the equivalent of: "Run after that seed." It was our playful way to treat a sibling or a cousin as a dog and to tease them into running after a stick or a bone or, in this instance, a large mango seed!

Growing up in the concrete jungle of the city, the only fruit we saw was at the local market. One day on my grandparents' farm not having any marbles to play with as we regularly did in the city, my brothers and I decided to take out practically all the small raw lemons on my grandfather's prized lemon tree and use them in place of marbles. When we heard that grandfather was coming home from a hard day's work in the fields, we innocently and hastily placed all the raw lemons at the foot of the tree, hoping that grandfather would not even notice the crime we had committed. Needless to say, we were caught and given a lesson about leaving alone unripe citrus fruit on the tree till they mature and can be safely plucked for food or cooking. As city slickers we learned the important farm lesson that fruit was not meant for playing.

I also learned from my devout and hardworking grandparents that food and the fruits of the earth should never be wasted. It took many hours every day from sunrise to sunset and a lot of backbreaking work to grow food on the farms and fields of India in those days.

Two very unusual experiences for us city kids on our grandparents' farm were: taking a bath away from the house and going to the bathroom after sunset. There was no plumbing or running water, so water was drawn from a well not only to quench the thirst of parched paddy fields, but also to fill a huge copper drum that was balanced over a fireplace in a neighboring shed for privacy. Here, our bath water was warmed and we bathed quickly in the flickering flames of the fireplace, and then ran as fast as we could back into the house. The only lights we had were in the house itself. After sunset the countryside was dark and scary.

Another reason for rushing into the house after a quick bath was the ghost stories that circulated in the countryside around the farm. Every family knew what was going on with everyone else. Since doctors and hospitals were not easily accessible, many medical needs and situations were taken to local healers. Prayers, incantations and superstitious practices would lead to further health complications, which then were associated with demonic possessions. These nightmarish ghost stories would reach our tender ears. The fireplace in the darkness of the shed filled us children with fear and trepidation. An adult always accompanied us and stood outside the shed while we took our baths.

Even today I take quick showers and occasionally look over my shoulders.

The fields around the farmhouse appeared to be one big outhouse. Depending on your age, you chose the appropriate distance from the house that would give you some relative privacy to relieve yourself. The squealing pigs would suddenly stop running and poke their noses in the spots we had chosen. For this reason, as kids we would have an adult accompany us and keep the pigs at a safe distance.

*****

My mother grew up in a large family of twelve children. That gave me many wonderful aunts and uncles to visit during our vacation in Mangalore. There were also many cousins to play with. Although my mother is the only one to survive in her entire family, she herself raised twelve children. Thus, my mother has never been alone.

My dad's side of the family lived in the midst of forests and mountainous territory. As you approached my father's ancestral home, bougainvilleas, betel nut palms, betel leaf vines and banana plantations welcomed you. The main crops were mangoes, cashews and the farming of betel nut trees. Together with some other exotic ingredients, these chopped betel nuts were then rolled into betel leaves and chewed by many Indians all day, if smoking and drinking alcohol were not their other preferred pastimes.

I observed that the adults on the farms had traditional addictive pastimes, because there was no city life or urban distractions around them. Many of them, after a hard day's back-breaking work, would sit around the front of the house smoking. India's version of cigarettes was known as *'beedis'*. A *'beedi'* is a thin, often flavored 'cigarette' made of tobacco wrapped in a 'tendu' leaf. Dental care was not available, so people would lose many of their teeth very early in life because of their smoking addiction. Many poor people drank cheap locally brewed alcohol. Some Indians had the habit of spitting in the fields and on walls, when chewing and eating *'paans'* (betel leaves) so much so that as I have mentioned before the streets of Bombay of my childhood looked like scenes of bloody battles!

Many Indian families in the countryside as well as in the big cities keep their homes very clean and tidy, but may not have the same civic sense for the areas outside their homes. Most of the discarded stuff is recycled, however, so very little goes to waste in the end.

My dad had two brothers, Marshall and Diego; and dad was the youngest of the three. They were all born in the span of just five years. My grandmother was seven months pregnant with my dad, when my paternal grandfather died in an accident. My grandmother never remarried. My dad and his two slightly older brothers grew up without a father figure. My appreciation and love of him was even greater because it never appeared that he did not know how to be a good father to all of us, his many children. My dad's mother lived to be eighty years old. I had never seen my father cry, but the day his mother died, he shed tears remembering how she had raised her three sons by herself working two or three jobs to put food on the table for her family. My uncle, Marshall fell from a tree, broke his spine, was paralyzed for a while and then died quite young. My uncle, Diego, on the other hand, lived to be almost one hundred years old. My dad was eighty-three when he passed away peacefully at home, as if he were taking a nap. He always prayed for a peaceful and happy death and God remembered his prayer.

Because of the forests surrounding my father's home, the regal, yet ferocious wild animal that roamed in that area was the tiger. Needless to say, we were exceptionally quiet and well behaved when visiting my dad's relatives. We would only spend a few days to make the long trek and pay our respects to my dad's side of the family tree. When I look back at those days, I am grateful for having both: the lush countryside and carefree, open experiences of my mother's side of the family, as well as the rugged mountains and reflective, contemplative hikes and meandering pathways of my father's ancestral home.

I wonder if this is the reason why I was, personality wise, in the middle: about fifty percent extroverted and about an equal fifty percent introverted (when I took the Myers-Briggs test several years ago). I would imagine that the extroverted side emerged from my mother's ancestral open fields where she grew up and where she returned to have her first child. To receive practical lessons in child rearing, you were expected as a new mother to return to your own mother to deliver and raise the first child in her presence and under her tutelage.

Whenever you walked out of my mother's ancestral home, you found yourself in the open fields, meeting people, swapping stories, and drinking many cups of hot tea.

The introverted side, it appears, came from my dad and his ancestral heritage. He generally spoke only when he had something important to say. He would remind us that because of the many tigers in his surrounding environment, he had to be alert and attentive all the time when he went to school, to church, to the market or to visit a neighbor's house. I never saw a live tiger when visiting my dad's relations. We weren't there long enough to have such a scary encounter. But dad would tell us stories of his childhood. He had seen tigers attacking and killing domestic animals like cows, pigs and goats. Although the tigers had never attacked human beings, my dad recounted how he had accompanied the adults from the village to capture these wild animals.

*****

It was in the month of September of the year 1967, that I first received my white cassock with a blue sash, a symbol of my priestly identity. Exactly three years later, also in the month of September, armed with just a few clothes and currency amounting to twenty-one British pounds (worth about thirty dollars today) I left for Rome, Italy, to study Philosophy and Theology.

The Indian Rupee was not considered hard currency, so there was no sense in carrying rupees to Italy, except as souvenirs.

They would be quite useless. In those days, the Indian government was lacking in hard foreign currency, so a young man going abroad for studies was only given twenty-one British pounds to survive in a foreign land. But mine was a full scholarship. I was not going to have any major expenses and I was not going to starve in Rome.

We had no relatives in Europe and I had no knowledge of the Italian language when I landed at the Fiumicino (currently known as Leonardo Da Vinci) airport of Rome. Two young Italians from my soon-to-be college residence came to pick me up at the airport. I thought they were driving too fast in their tiny Fiat on a two-lane road. In Bombay the traffic of my childhood was so bad that one could only travel most of the time during peak hours about five to ten miles an hour. And suddenly I panicked when I saw a huge tourist bus flying in our direction from the other side of this very long and narrow road. "Oh, no," I said to myself as I closed my eyes, "we are definitely going to crash." I felt an accident was inevitable because we were driving in the wrong lane.

That's when it hit me like a ton of bricks. I kept talking to myself because my hosts did not speak a word of English and I had no knowledge of the Italian language. I said to myself: "I'm no longer in India. I am in Italy, where they drive on the other side of the road! I am in a different world."

I realized that my journey had shifted to the other side. What did this mean? I remembered the words of a friend, who said: "Dreams don't end. They simply change direction."

I sensed that a radical and transformative shift was about to happen in my life.

A very symbolic and tragic event took place a few months after I left Bombay for Rome. A big portion of my beloved 'Last Building', where I was born and raised till I left home to join the seminary, came crashing down in the middle of the night taking the lives of many of our former neighbors. My own family had moved away a few years earlier to another larger apartment about twenty miles from the downtown area of the city of Bombay. Thus my family did not suffer any casualties, but for several months we mourned the loss of longtime neighbors and friends.

For me this crash was symbolic because living in Rome I was not physically close to the devastation. I just had this sense that my world as I knew it growing up was not there anymore. Like the beloved 'Last Building' of my childhood, much of my past had collapsed into the dust.

Would I ever be able to return 'home' again? Was that even possible?

When we were kids living in our beloved 'Last Building,' we would often go to the home of one Mr. Fernandes, who taught us the meditative poses of Yoga. He would ask us to close our eyes and repeat to ourselves often during the day: "I see the moon; I see the moon." The idea was to have concentration and mindless attention, free from distractions and anxieties. He would remind us that if we continued the practice of Yoga, we would be healthy and live a very long life. He boasted that he could and was definitely planning to live to be at least two hundred years old with the benefit of Yoga and proper breathing techniques. The 'Last Building' crash in the dead of night took the life of Mr. Fernandes, much earlier than he had expected, and much sooner than the couple of hundred years he had planned to live.

Here was another lesson for me, namely, that we are not in control of our destiny and our future. We cannot determine and decide how long we are going to live on this earth. We cannot anticipate where life is going to take us next. After all, God's time is not our time. Our lives are totally in God's hands.

That first morning in Rome, I suddenly woke up to the loud sound of Beethoven's Fifth Symphony. I was startled. I opened my eyes and groggily looked around. I was in my very own room, but for a few moments, I could not remember where I was. Jet lag can cause such disorientation. As consciousness began to set in, I realized that I was truly alone, far from my family, my friends, and my roots and from my country.

The year I was sent to Rome for studies also turned out to be the year that I was the only one selected from India in my entire class. I was truly alone confronting and protecting myself from the rest of the world.

83

A friend of mine told me that when he was a commanding naval officer during the Second World War, the Japanese sank his ship. For the next eight hours he swam and tried to stay alive in the deep, freezing waters. As he looked up at the full moon, he suddenly had this scary thought that no one, absolutely no one, in this entire world knew where he was at that moment. Later he was brought ashore and became a prisoner of the Japanese for three years. He said the prisoners did not get much to eat. But finally it was not hunger that killed some of his companions, but sheer despair. Even those who were eating relatively well, died from losing hope of survival and freedom. Even though he was only skin and bones when American troops came to rescue him and those who had survived this ordeal, he strongly believed that his faith had kept him alive; his faith had preserved him from despair and death.

My situation in Rome wasn't so dire and dreary and I certainly wasn't living in a prison camp. But loneliness anywhere and in any circumstance can corrode and destroy one's spirit, if one does not know how to live alone. Loneliness is a constant companion in a priest's life. Without faith and hope, all could be lost. Yes, like my friend, the prisoner of war, I, too, felt that I was alone in the world. Was I being taught to live the life of a priest by total immersion?

For a brief moment that morning I was awakened to the fact that it was in my hands to make or break my life. What a sense of responsibility in the final year of my teens, on the threshold of adulthood!

*****

The seminary in Rome was located on the Via di Torre Rossa, on the outskirts of the city. It was the residence for those who would be attending the Urban University of Propaganda Fide (Propagation of Faith). For me, Rome was turning out to be a new world in many ways. I now had the comfort of my own suite. In my home in Bombay we had only one big room for the entire family with one huge bed in the middle for my parents. At the St. Pius X College Seminary in Bombay, I shared a room dormitory-style with four other seminarians.

Here, in Rome, I had my own shower, my own bathroom, and my very own bedroom.

In the dining room and in the chapel, I saw young men for the first time belonging to many races and nationalities. Not growing up with television, I had never seen Africans before, or for that matter, any Arabs from the Middle East or Australians from down under. The universality of the Catholic Church was evident from the very beginning at this recently built college seminary.

'Propaganda Fide' which is the Latin for the Propagation of Faith arm of the Catholic Church, represents many nations in so-called 'mission lands.' In these countries, missionaries are still needed to spread Christianity. Its mission is based on the final exhortation of Jesus to his disciples: "Go, therefore, and make disciples of all the nations, baptizing them in the name of the Father, of the Son, and of the Holy Spirit."

Representatives of over seventy-five mission countries walked the corridors of this college seminary. There were students from almost all the countries of Africa and Asia, and there were young men from Australia, Micronesia, South America as well as the former Communist nations of Eastern Europe. North America, western European nations and a few other countries considered to be widely Christian had their own independent colleges and religious formation houses. As you walked the streets of Rome with all these thousands of young seminarians and priests and many nuns dressed in their unique habits, you knew for sure that you were in the heart of Catholicism.

Adjusting to races and colors for the first time in my life was not too difficult. The basic shades were black, white and brown. Soon, a story circulated among us that when God was making cookies one day, in his first attempt he burned the cookies and that is where we get the Black races; God tried again but this time the cookies were undercooked. The White races resulted from God's second attempt. Finally, God got it right the third time and the brownish races are the result of God's successful creative cooking attempts.

Stories like these are definitely racist, but they are also humorous attempts to deal with differences at an early stage of development. If one does not mature and go beyond such stories

85

and humor to explain differences, then one remains shackled by the chains of prejudice and racism.

In accepting, celebrating, tolerating, respecting and living with differences, I truly experienced the universality and globalism of the Catholic Church at her best.

Although some spoke English in our college seminary, there were many languages heard and spoken all around me. It was fascinating to hear the sounds of Spanish, French, Portuguese, Latin, Swahili, and Slavic tongues, dialects and other national languages. Even English was spoken with many interesting accents. I can understand why Professor Higgins, the phonetic expert in 'My Fair Lady,' asked himself why the English don't speak their language anymore. Even the Indian seminarians had their own special English accents and spoke other languages that I did not understand or recognize. Was I in a college seminary studying for the priesthood, or had I reached the top of the Tower of Babel? The confusion of sounds and languages in Rome eventually and positively inspired me to learn several new languages.

In Rome, because no one else spoke the language of my parents and grandparents, I had to make friends with the rest of the world and create a new international family of my own.

In India I had grown up speaking the language of my parents, which is called Konkani. The west coast of India includes a region called the Konkan and a rich language with its own literary tradition emerged, which had no written alphabet, but is spoken by millions of people today. Like Konkani, there are many widely spoken languages in India.

Since Bombay is a cosmopolitan city and the business capital of the nation, I was exposed to several Indian languages. Playing in the streets of Bombay with my friends and neighbors, I spoke Hindi, the national language. In the third grade, we were introduced to the language of the state of Maharashtra, which is Marathi. Bombay was also the economic hub of the country, so one would hear many other languages, like Gujarati, Bengali, Tamil, Malayalam *et cetera*, and of course, English, inherited from the British Raj. In the eighth grade, we were offered a choice either to continue with Marathi, or to start learning French. I studied French for four years in high school. We were not taught

French by immersion, so learning French grammar turned out to be a very boring task.

Later on I learned the art and science of linguistics, which I applied to the study of several western European languages.

Generally speaking, Indian languages have twice as many sounds and letters as the English alphabet. So, growing up in India, exposed to so many more sounds and languages, it was not very long before I could speak Italian fluently. Later on I applied the same immersion tools for the study of German, French, Spanish and Portuguese.

In Rome a new source of communications in my life was television. Since television was not introduced to India until the year 1971 (I left India a year earlier), the first programs in Rome seen and heard by me were in Italian. There were only two channels and television was still black and white in those early years. Italian news, called '*Telegiornale*,' was difficult to comprehend, because the language was spoken too fast, at least to our ears. In the beginning, a sentence sounded like one long unintelligible word. Although I hate watching television commercials today, in the seventies in Rome, Italian commercials were a lot of fun. There were dances and singing and melodious jingles that one could easily memorize and remember. This was a fun and quick way to learn a new language.

I am a visual person, so the television medium fascinated me. I could watch it for hours. Since there were two channels and most seminarians loved to watch soccer games, the college ended up investing in two television sets, to give everyone a choice to watch their favorite programs. Television had a mesmerizing effect on me. The images and the music had me glued and addicted almost every evening. Besides being able to learn Italian, I received a fascinating peek into the larger world outside the seminary walls.

Television brings the whole world into our living rooms. In those days there were no reality programs to remind me of the poverty and misery that I had left behind in India. Instead, vicariously through game shows and through other entertainment programs where everyone dressed well and life seemed fun I was able to travel to beautiful places all over the world.

Bringing two television sets into our recreation salons created peace and harmony among us. Would seminarians fight for their favorite programs? They sure did! I was not raised that way and so I expected them to act in a civil and understanding manner with each other because one day they would have to be good role models as priests and bishops.

The fact is that when we are in the company of our peers, we sometimes tend to insist upon our rights, act selfishly and if provoked push aside anyone who comes in the way. I saw that with seminarians in Rome, and I have experienced that with clergy at different gatherings. I also heard that that was the case even with bishops and cardinals who assembled from all over the world in Rome for the Second Vatican Council. When standing in line for coffee or meals, some of the bishops would make sure that no one else would sneak in and cut in the line when they were talking among themselves.

Only when we are in the presence of subordinates, we tend to monitor our words and actions, and also secretly live in the expectation that we are going to get preferential treatment.

Having a religious vocation does not imply that one is free of the herd mentality or that one behaves in a saintly manner all the time.

Since we seminarians were initially all foreign to the Italian language, an Italian missionary from Australia came to give us a one-month crash course in the language to prepare us for the study of Philosophy. What helped me most to learn the language quickly was not only television commercials or daily immersion into Italian culture and living, but also the opportunity to act in an annual college play. Memorizing the lines was a great way to increase the use and mastery of the Italian language. The religious play was entitled 'La Famiglia Cristiana,' (The Christian Family) and was a public performance for the families and donors who supported the college of 'Propaganda Fide' in Rome. It was also part of the annual cultural programs of the seminary.

In the center of the college residential seminary was a beautiful chapel on the upper floor and a large theater below. The acoustics were wonderful. Occasionally, the theater was used for the projection of movies. I had always enjoyed acting on stage. In school in Bombay I took part in several dramatic plays and musicals. At St. Pius X College Seminary, also in Bombay, I was chosen to act as 'Saul' who later became Paul, on the 'Road to Damascus.'

St. Paul was thrown off his horse and had a life-changing conversion experience on the road to Damascus. From persecuting Christians, he became after his conversion the fearless preacher of the Gospel of Jesus Christ. Such acting experiences led me to the stage several more times in my life. They also prepared me to be comfortable with crowds and to project my voice in order to become an effective presider and preacher later on in priestly ministry.

The stage experience in Bombay and in Rome was yet another reminder that whatever we do in life is worth doing well. Because one day, we will benefit from this past experience and our future will be enriched. Very few past experiences are isolated and insignificant and have little or no influence on our future.

*****

At the college seminary, the first year students were divided into four distinct dorms, or 'camarate,' as they were known. Each group had about twenty-five members selected at random, and who lived in suites close to each other. Your *'camarate'* became your prayer group, your study group, your support group and your extended family.

It was the responsibility of the dorm members to celebrate your Saint's name day, a common practice in Rome and Italy. So my group of new friends in the *'camarate'* took on the responsibility of celebrating the feast of St. George on April 23rd. For my *'onomastico'* or patron's feast day, I was simply expected to show up and enjoy myself. The rest brought the food, the drinks, and provided the entertainment. Your birthday celebration was your own responsibility. Since we did not have any family in this foreign land, it was wonderful to invite everybody from the *'camarate'* to your own suite, and to a party that you yourself had planned to celebrate 'you.'

Thus, I got introduced to new foods and new cultural habits. I began to notice some of the mannerisms and idiosyncrasies of my classmates. The Nigerians taught me to play tennis, and I also noticed that they would always laugh heartily, while bobbing their heads, when a new person was introduced to the group. The Sri Lankans were generally quiet and well mannered, almost to the point of being shy and reserved. The Australians were difficult to understand, at first, because they spoke English with a heavy 'down under' accent. I realized that many people spoke English but with many colorful accents. Besides India, there were representatives from other British colonies, like Ghana, Tanzania, Uganda, Liberia, Pakistan, Hong Kong, Australia, New Zealand and Sri Lanka and so on.

The Indians did not all speak English among themselves. As a matter of fact, I gradually distanced myself from the Indians, because even when I was invited to join them, they would speak to one another in their own tongue, which I did not understand. It was strange to hear the guttural sounds of Arabic coming from Palestinians, Lebanese and Syrians. The French-speaking Africans from Burundi, Togo, the Ivory Coast, Rwanda and Zaire were always soft-spoken, kindhearted and refined. The Romanians spoke fluent Latin. The Slavs generally came from the former Yugoslav republics, like Serbia, Croatia and Slovenia, and still understood each other and remained close friends. I learned songs in Swahili and other international languages and also learned to greet and dress in many ethnic and cultural ways.

I underwent a radical transformation in this global village. At first, I considered all of these world cultures to be outside of myself. As I found more and more opportunities to make contact with these strange and challenging 'alien' cultures, languages, nationalities, and exotic mannerisms, I began to discover that these cultures were not outside of me, but, in reality, existed within me, waiting to emerge.

The first contacts with other cultural differences brought forth an initial dislike and negative reaction of that which was different from my limited upbringing. Then gradually, the dislike turned to appreciation and acceptance. I could sense that I was slowly being transformed into a full human being.

I began to see how these cultures are really inside each of us, in as much as we share a common humanity. The less contact I have with other cultures, the more limited and the more incomplete human being I turn out to be.

A South American writer once remarked that when you reject a particular culture or language, you are really dying to a part of your own real self. When you cannot love what is different from yourself and your world, then you yourself are a lesser human being.

The more contact I had over five years in Rome with the rest of the world through food, music, language, dance, customs and behaviors, the more open and tolerant I became as a human being, and eventually as a priest.

Political and national boundaries are man made. Today's DNA research has proved that we all originally came and migrated from somewhere in the southern part of Africa, and that we developed a variety of traits, characteristics and physical complexions as we migrated and adapted to different parts of the world. Too much sun or the lack of sunshine can affect the pigmentation and color of our skins. Adaptation to intense cold or heat can shape our muscles, eating habits and even the size of our bodies.

Our human spirit is what we have in common, and that which brings us back to each other. My Roman sojourn not only opened up the world to me, it also expanded my spirit.

I would never be the same person again.

*****

For five years in Europe I traveled everywhere and whenever I could. Every summer, through immersion, I tried to learn a new language, starting, of course, with Italian and then shifting gears and changing tracks to study other languages like French, Spanish and German. My knowledge of Latin and English facilitated the study of neo-Latin and Romance languages. Rome fascinated me, as did the rest of Europe. In the very first year, my knowledge of Italian was so good that I was allowed, as an exception, to spend the summer with my eldest sister and her family in Scotland.

While the rest of my classmates went to Perugia, north of Rome during our first summer in Europe to improve their knowledge of Italian, I was allowed to travel with my sister's family through Scotland, Northern Ireland, notably Donegal and some areas, including the capital city of Dublin, of the Republic of Ireland. It was scary to drive through Belfast and Londonderry, especially because one of my little nephews carried a plastic toy gun with him in the car and he wanted to play with it while we were crossing the border very early in the morning. In Dublin, at a bed-and-breakfast place, a young Irish lad gave us an overview, over breakfast, of Ireland's history and the current Irish political landscape. It was definitely a hearty Irish breakfast!

The following summer I went to study French for three weeks at the University of Caen, in Normandy, France. The immersion experience and process of learning a foreign language was embarrassingly made clear to me on the first day of class.

The teacher asked us for the meaning of a word, expecting to receive a French synonym from us. I raised my hand and gave the response in English. The French teacher reminded all of us that he had a doctorate in English Literature and that he had traveled to every corner of Great Britain, and that he was not there with us to study English from us. Rather, we were in France to study French, and that we should raise our hands only when we could think in French and have a French synonym to offer! Needless to say, I was embarrassed. But I never forgot that lesson and gained valuable wisdom that day about what a language immersion program is all about.

Life is about learning lessons and gaining wisdom from the mistakes we make.

We were in France only three weeks that summer. Everyday we had seven hours of lessons and several more hours of French through audiotapes and earphones. The rest of our waking moments we spent speaking French with our fellow classmates. Every night I went to bed with a headache. But the results were amazing. In just three short weeks, we had the confidence to converse in basic French, albeit with a limited vocabulary. The University campus reflected the international flavor of the College of 'Propaganda Fide' in Rome.

The only difference was that this summer campus had male and female students from all over the world with secular, not religious, vocations.

My French improved and so did my interest in a Greek girl, who initially told me that she was interested in my Indian culture and background. I was drawn to her because at that time I was studying Greek philosophy in Rome; so we had common philosophical interests besides trying to work on our language skills. From Shabnam, the Muslim high school girl in Bombay, to Chryssanthie, my current Greek friend, there was a lot more stirring within me than just the desire to become a priest.

My studies of Philosophy were also causing a spiritual upheaval within me. Being very docile and obedient as a child, I had never questioned my beliefs and values. With rational, philosophical ways of thinking and searching for the truth, I began to question and doubt everything I had believed and blindly accepted as a child in India. Since I was barely sixteen years old when I joined the seminary in Bombay, I did not have the opportunities there to be distracted or attracted by the opposite sex. It was different in France and in Italy. I was now entering my twenties and I did not have the protection of family or religious institutions as I did during my teens in India. In many ways I was alone and on my own.

Philosophy and rational thinking were not the only obstacles to belief. It was one thing for professors and philosophers to challenge your precious childhood beliefs, but another to have an attractive young Greek woman ask you why you want to become a priest or what would happen to the world if good people like me refused to populate this world with more good human beings like myself! How do you reason with that line of thinking?

I had never ever gone out on a date in my life. When I was growing up in India, you dated the person you would one day marry. Teenagers hung out in groups. You went to the movies or to the beach with your friends. You played with your peers and were never seen alone with a person of the opposite sex. It simply wasn't a part of the culture or of my upbringing.

The 1960s and the 1970s were very difficult for clergy and for Catholics everywhere. Right after the Second Vatican Council ended in the year 1965, there was so much openness and so many radical changes taking place in the church that many priests and people did not seem to know anymore what to believe and generally how to behave and act as members of the Catholic Church. The familiar traditions and practices were gone. Some priests abandoned ministry and many laypeople left the Church. They were not leaving their faith or their discipleship of Jesus Christ. They were simply not able to adapt to the changes that were taking place after more than four hundred years of uniformity and unquestioned certainty.

Changes were introduced into the liturgy of the Church. Seminary formation seemed to have lost its constancy and consistency. Before the sixties and the seventies, Latin was the language of worship and seminary studies. All seminarians that came to study in Rome from many parts of the world and of the Church felt like equals. But once the local languages were used both in Worship as well as for instruction in the seminary classrooms, the professors were at a loss because they had no updated textbooks from which to teach. The old texts were outdated. Even as they taught each day, these post Vatican II professors were either in the process of writing new theology books or mimeographing their notes daily like bulletins, hot off the press, for all the new international students.

Many Italian seminarians, in this new Second Vatican Council environment, criticized and challenged everything. Nothing was taken for granted or considered 'sacred' simply because it was taught consistently in the past for many centuries. New ideas were flooding the seminaries. Since the Propagation of Faith college seminary was considered the training ground for future bishops in mission lands, professors with modern ideas were constantly scrutinized and investigated by the Holy Office and the Congregation for the Propagation of Faith. A popular professor of dogmatic theology was fired when he wrote a book about theology and belief as process and development and not as unquestionable fixed absolutes.

Our Moral Theology professor was appointed by the Vatican to evaluate and correct errors in the popular Dutch Catechism. Some of our Italian seminarians ridiculed this choice of the hierarchy, because they claimed that a professor who recognizes the 'missionary position' to be the only moral position allowed in the bedroom was too narrow minded to deal with the Dutch

Catechism, which was written with the broad minded openness of the Second Vatican Council.

It would be false to claim that everything and everyone in the Church were falling apart. Many professors and seminarians remained faithful and calm despite the storms of change raging all around them. Many of them are exemplary parish priests, seminary professors and bishops in every part of the world today.

I questioned my motives and myself: What made me stay in the seminary when everything seemed to be crumbling and falling apart around me? To whom could I go or to what certainties could I grasp as I was being tested at every turn?

Painfully, I realized that I was becoming an adult in the faith. It was an agonizing process, but I was learning to think and believe for myself.

I also learned to pray spontaneously from the heart and to pray about the issues that troubled me. I realized very early on that I could either make or break my life.

Change can be very painful, but without change there is no growth in spiritual life. As Blessed John Henry Newman once said, "Growth is the only evidence of life."

*****

After I finished my study of French that summer, I was invited by a friend named Frank from the Seychelles to hitchhike with him throughout Europe. I knew this friend from my seminary days in Bombay because he was my classmate then. But he had left the seminary and decided to settle in France. I had never hitchhiked before. Not knowing how to explain this new adventure to my parents in India, I simply wrote them a letter saying that I would be vacationing in Europe by car with friends. The truth was that I did not really know which car would be our means of travel. The Holy Spirit came to my rescue so that my explanation to my parents turned out finally to be true. A young Frenchman named Michel wanted to share our adventures. He owned a car, a sturdy '*Deux Cheveux*'! We decided to share the expenses for gas and food, and travel as a trio through most of Western Europe.

My universe was expanding and I was becoming adventuresome and a risk taker.

It turned out that each one of us had friends scattered in different countries of Europe. We covered almost six thousand kilometers in three weeks, starting first in Paris, France where we met; then, we drove through Belgium, Luxembourg, Germany, Switzerland, Northern Italy, Austria and the northern part of the former Republic of Yugoslavia, which is now an independent country known as Slovenia.

Sometimes we slept out in the open countryside in a makeshift tent. When we arrived at the homes of friends, we had a chance to have warm showers, clean clothes and comfortable beds.

This traveling adventure was filled with excitement. When I feel like traveling to new places today, I think back to that time when I decided to 'hitchhike' across Europe.

Two countries for two different reasons were going to affect my life and my future. The first was Germany. Our French companion introduced us to his German friends, Franz and Maria Opwis, a wonderful, caring elderly couple. Franz was well known in the area and in surrounding countries like France, Holland and Belgium because of his hospitality and generosity towards young people and families and his knowledge of European languages. He and his wife were very devout Catholics, regular churchgoers and very supportive of the clergy. Everyone called him the Mayor of this little German village of just seventeen households. Once, a letter arrived at his door, which had as address his last name, below that, the word, 'Lascheider Hof' (the name of the little village where the Opwis couple resided) and, finally, Germany, in bold letters. The letter was promptly delivered!

Being a mailman in this region of Germany must have been a very spirit-filled profession because whenever you delivered mail to a household especially in the winter, the people would invite you into their homes for a quick shot of 'schnapps.'

When we the three 'musketeers' arrived at his simple home, his eyes began glowing when he recognized the fact that we represented three different continents: Michel from France, Europe, and Frank from the Seychelles islands, off to the south-east of Africa, and, finally, me, from India, Asia. He was so excited to welcome us to his home and to Germany that he wanted everybody to know who we were right away.

The evening of our arrival he and Maria took us to the quaint resort town of Reinsfeld, which in God's mysterious providence was going to play an important part in my life later on as a deacon and a priest.

Reinsfeld had about two thousand inhabitants. In the town's center was the parish church of St. Remigius. The town was nestled in the hills close to the wine growing area of the Mosel River. The historical city of Trier was about thirty miles from Reinsfeld. The Diocese of Trier was also going to play a prominent role in my future. But, back then, as a tourist, I was more interested in the fact that Trier was considered to be oldest Roman city in Germany. The 'Porta Nigra', built two thousand years ago by the Romans still stands tall, strong and defiant as the main entrance to the city.

Maria Opwis was the only one who drove the family Audi. Franz gave private lessons in Mathematics, Electrical Engineering, Languages and Mechanics, but he was too nervous to drive a car. So, Maria got her driver's license at the age of forty-seven to chauffeur her brilliant and popular husband and their many international friends.

In the summer and in the winter, the tourists added to the local population of Reinsfeld. Many of them came from Holland, Belgium, France and other parts of Germany. The social gathering places in many of these small European towns were the local bars. In these locales, you could get food as well as beer, wine and schnapps. In the evenings, after a hard day's work, the locals and tourists would hang out in the bars to relax and to meet friends and neighbors. Besides the outdoors activities, like hiking in the summer and skiing in the winter, there was not much else to do around these parts for entertainment.

After a few drinks, the townspeople loved to sing and dance. Franz found out that I played the guitar and that I also loved to sing international songs. In Germany the second most popular spoken language is English, and I soon found out that Germans of all ages loved well-known and classic English melodies.

Growing up in India without television, I had learned and memorized many popular English and American songs.

Music appeals to people of all ages because we come into this world with a sense of music and harmony right from birth. And this sense is also the last to go. So, even the elderly who might lose their sense of speech or forget details of events from their past, will come alive when they hear familiar tunes and melodies from their childhood and from their cultural and religious backgrounds.

Thus, music is definitely a universal language. I grew up loving and enjoying music. And I loved to perform!

That evening, after we were introduced as 'stars' from three continents, friends, strangers, locals and tourists welcomed us warmly and began to sing and dance in the Reinsfeld bar. In between our singing and dancing, we were given plenty of sandwiches and snacks to eat and beer and wine to drink. Germans love their alcohol and they also love their food.

A few hours into the lively and laughter filled atmosphere, a young German soldier walked into the bar. In a few minutes he taught us how to drink Schnapps, which I had never tasted before in my life. Even without knowing the language, he showed us how to hold our hands behind our backs and merrily drain several small bottles of fiery Schnapps with our eyes closed. It was a fun evening till I began to feel the effects of the singing, the dancing, the food and the beer and wine mixed with Schnapps.

There was no mandatory drinking age in India when I was a child. Occasionally beer was brought into our homes, but most of us found it to be so bitter that we would mix it with lemonade. Living and studying in Rome was different. At every table of six students, there were two bottles of table wine for every meal. But the cheap wine tasted so sour that we would end up simply drinking water, and once in a while having pizza with beer in restaurants.

That night in a stranger's home and in a strange land I threw up for the first time in my life from partying and drinking too much. I had no idea where I was or what was happening to me. For the first and only time in my life, I was truly drunk.

In the morning as we prepared to leave Germany, I was too embarrassed to look at the faces of our genial, smiling hosts. They told me that they were not upset with me but they had a good laugh at my expense when they noticed that even my brown skin had turned pale from throwing up all night. I realized later on that with the Germans' fondness for beer and Schnapps, it was not uncommon for some of the locals to get drunk frequently in that country.

In subsequent years, when I would attend a *'Kirmes'* or a village festival, I would see young Germans lining up all the empty beer bottles they had consumed on the dining table, as a mark of pride.

My practicing Catholic German new friends knew that I was a seminarian, and yet they were not judgmental towards my hangover experience and me. We said our morning prayers together, and then, with just a cup of black coffee (good remedy for hangovers), we said goodbye to each other. In my embarrassment I was wondering if this was going to be my first and last visit to the home of this delightful couple.

Everything happens for a reason. Even though I was embarrassed with my first experience of getting drunk, I endeared myself to my new German friends and family. After my return to Rome, we stayed in touch and became and have remained very close friends. Divine providence can bring people together not only through joyful events, but also through embarrassing moments and even tragedies.

God works in mysterious ways.

*****

From Germany, my friends and I traveled through the beautiful and picturesque European countryside. The artwork and the awesome churches we visited fascinated me. I realized that true education is not limited to staying within the walls of schools, colleges and universities. If you have an adventuresome spirit, the whole world can become one huge fascinating classroom.

Among all the countries we toured on that trip, I loved wandering through Austria, especially gazing at the hills and the flower-decked homes along the winding country roads. One of my cousins, a nun, worked in a nursing and old folk's home in Vienna. She spoke German fluently and thus became our guide through the streets of the Austrian capital. A walk in Vienna can turn into a waltz as you listen to beautiful, classical music at every turn.

I had mentioned earlier that two out of the many European countries we visited were going to strongly impact my life and my future. The first was Germany. And now we were about to enter the other country, linked to communism and to Eastern Europe.

This second country was Yugoslavia, and it would be my first visit to a Communist country. I love history. I remembered that when I was growing up in India, there were three world leaders, who were held up as models of moderate centrist politics, as opposed to the extreme ideologies of Capitalism, with the United States being its strongest advocate, and Communism, spearheaded by the Union of Soviet Socialist Republics. The three moderate leaders were Nehru from India, Nasser from Egypt and Tito from Yugoslavia. I was born and raised in India, of course, where Nehru was elected as the first Prime Minister. When I flew to Rome, my flight had a brief stopover in Cairo, Egypt, I can still recall the beauty of flying into the rising sun over the skies of Cairo.

And now I was experiencing a historical moment as we crossed the Austrian border into Tito's Yugoslavia.

Yugoslavia as a nation was a blending of several diverse republics and that was the genius and strength of President Tito. But after his demise, the republics began to break away from each other. The Republic to the north of Yugoslavia was Slovenia. Today, Slovenia, like Croatia, Serbia, Bosnia, and Macedonia, is an independent nation.

In Slovenia, Michel, our French companion, knew a young Slav, by the name of Milan, whose family we decided to visit. He welcomed us warmly into his home and asked us to stay for a few days. His peasant family collected hops that made for a very strong local beer. We were having a wonderful, relaxing time enjoying the simple hospitality of these peasants, even volunteering to collect hops with the rest of the family, when one evening during dinner, I accidently found out who our hosts really were.

I understood why they say that it is a small world after all.

Our Rector in Rome was born and raised in this region of Yugoslavia. I was surprised and shocked to find out that this was the house of his sister. The young friendly Slav, our host Milan, was none other than the Rector's nephew.

In spiritual life there are no co-incidences, they say. There are only God-moments. At that time I did not possess or internalize this sense and idea of spirituality. I was simply perplexed at this strange co-incidence. How did I end up even with so many other communist countries and thousands of families all around me at precisely the home and farm of my Rector from Rome?

Today I understand that everything happens for a reason. At that dinner in Northern Yugoslavia I felt totally perplexed and confused.

It could have remained a pleasant surprise to meet our Rector's sister and to enjoy her hospitality. But the surprise changed into a personal shock for me, because I was due back in Rome at the college by a certain date and our time in Slovenia had already delayed my return by a whole week.

How does one keep to a tight schedule on an unplanned, open ended trip? There was no way I could return to Rome on my own. How was I going to explain my tardy return to the Rector? Or was he even going to offer me a chance to give an explanation?

I couldn't make up a story even if I wanted to because he was definitely going to hear about my visit to Slovenia from his sister or his nephew. In fact, that's exactly what happened. Upon my return to Rome, the Rector in an icy and sarcastic tone informed me that his sister had called to notify him about an Indian seminarian studying in Rome who was kind enough to grace their home in Yugoslavia!

While my experience in Germany gave me a sense of belonging and connection with humanity, the extra late week in Yugoslavia began causing ruptures in my spirit and in my understanding of the priesthood.

Rules and regulations are there for a purpose. Especially in formation years, seminarians should take them seriously to prepare someday to take the vow of obedience that the priesthood calls for. The Rector was keenly aware of this and in his position was simply doing his duty.

He was a very good communicator and participated fully in the life of the Seminary College. He would eat meals with us and play volleyball, basketball and soccer with the seminarians.

As he often reminded us in his spiritual reflections, Europe and her secular ways would turn out to be great sources of temptation and seduction for us young men who had come from simple and traditional societies of the Third World.

The rules of the Seminary were established to protect and not jeopardize our vocation to the priesthood.

As far as I could recall, it was my first serious conflict with authority. I did not know what to say, except to look down and be filled with fear and trepidation. I had always been a good kid at home and in school. At St. Pius X College Seminary, I was considered to be the best seminary candidate in my class, which was also the reason why I was selected to study in Rome.

Conflict with authority figures is a strange experience. On the one hand there is a power differential for which you feel victimized; on the other hand, there is nothing you can do when you are definitely in the wrong except to admit your wrongdoing.

The authority problem becomes complicated when there is a power difference between you and the person in authority, and you feel strongly in your heart that what you have done or failed to do was subjectively right with no intention of malice on your part. Your conscience feels no sense of guilt and your innate sense of justice makes you think and feel that the person in authority is now victimizing you in this particular situation. You have no choice in the matter. You have no other recourse. You feel alone and abandoned.

In my seminary days, authority figures behaved as if their authority came directly from above. So even if you were victimized you had no way to argue your case. There was no way to prove your innocence because there was no room for dialog. You were at the mercy of the superior, who arguably was carrying out the Will of God. Even to call someone 'Superior' denotes a power differential that may be knowingly or unknowingly abused in certain situations.

We constantly run into people who affect our lives and our destiny. The 'coincidences' are simply mind-boggling. Why does God choose a certain individual, couple or family to cross your life's path? My German friends, despite my hangover, became my extended family; and my Yugoslav friends, despite my best behavior, unknowingly embarrassed me and shocked me into a corner with no escape.

All of them, the good and the bad and the ugly, changed the course of my life.

Only later after accumulating a lot of wisdom and experience, I began to realize that the people who came mysteriously into my life were only catalysts or instruments in God's hands, to bring about personal growth and radical changes in the direction of my vocation and the priesthood.

Most of the seminarians in Rome disliked the 'Monsignor' (which was the Rector's title) and saw another side of him. He was a smooth talker, very diplomatic in speech, and too much of a disciplinarian for them to confide in him. Being athletic he would join us in many of our outdoor games and sports in order to prove that he was one of us.

And now he and I were in a conflict situation due to my 'disobedience' and late return from vacation.

More than anyone, a future priest (and possibly, a future bishop) from Rome was expected to be totally faithful to all prescribed rules and regulations, including the ones governing vacations.

I happened to be selected that same year to be one of the twelve 'apostles' whose feet would be washed by the 'Monsignor' during the Mass of Holy Thursday. It was a confusing moment for me, when he bent down on his knees and kissed my feet after washing them.

A new Rector took the place of the 'Monsignor.' By contrast, he was a humble, cigarette-smoking Franciscan, who had worked for many years in mission lands and did not come from the ranks of the Vatican diplomatic corps. The seminarians liked him instantaneously. He personally delivered some of our mail just to have a look at our smiling faces. He knew how much we longed for mail from our loved ones in distant lands. If you needed to talk to him, he would stay awake with you till late into the night.

He restored trust in us, a quality we had lost with the previous administration.

In this atmosphere of trust and openness, he confided in me one day that there was a negative and unsavory comment from the previous Rector in my personnel file. Instead of being excited about my visit to his sister's home in Yugoslavia, he had made a note in my file that because I had returned late from my vacation by one week, I was unsure about my vocation to the priesthood.

It was one of the darkest days of my life. I wept bitterly. I was mad and scared at the same time. "How could he do such a thing?" I asked myself. My tardiness, after all, was an innocent mistake. Was I going to be expelled for that? I had never felt so alone and so afraid.

The new Rector was at first surprised to see my reaction. He comforted me and told me not to be afraid. There were not going to be any repercussions, he reassured me.

But something happened at the core of my spirit that day. The 'Monsignor' planted seeds of distrust in authority within me. The innocence of my childhood was being shattered by the suspicions and doubts that come from being misunderstood and falsely accused. When you take away the lens of innocence and trust, the world begins to appear as a frightful and oppressive place.

*****

Many great holy men and women have shared in their spiritual writings how a journey radically altered the direction of their lives. Blessed Mother Teresa of Calcutta is one such example. During a train journey in India, she decided symbolically to jump over the walls of her comfortable Loreto Convent that she had first joined and start a new vocation of service in the slums of Calcutta among the poorest of the poor.

My car ride to Yugoslavia would radically affect my thinking and my vocation several years later. At first, it diminished my trust in authority. I came to realize that most authority figures were not there for my benefit. They weren't thinking about me all the time. They seemed to be more concerned about the rules and laws that their subordinates were expected to obey. If they had reached the top of the ladder of authority and privilege, they would continue to maintain their superior position, even if it meant stomping on the progress and dreams of those below them.

Jesus criticized the Scribes and the Pharisees for placing burdens upon the poor and the weak and not lifting a finger to help them.

Fortunately, our new Rector restored my trust in authority. He showed us a new way of leadership and service. The new Rector's behavior was modeled after the example of Jesus who washed the feet of his disciples so that they would do likewise for one another. He healed us when he personally delivered to us our mail and asked us about our families. He comforted us whenever he took the time to listen to our problems.

A priest is often referred to as 'another Christ' or a 'man for others.' Our new Rector, who is today a bishop in Rome, was, like Christ, the perfect model of priesthood and humility. His first name Pellegrino in Italian was identical to the English word: Pilgrim. That's what he was for us: a fellow pilgrim, who lived up to his name and his calling.

With him and with his support I began a new chapter in my life and journey of priesthood.

Does God send conflicting opposite personalities into our lives so that we can learn from them and see both sides of the picture? Do these contrasting individuals reflect the 'Dr. Jekyll and Mr. Hyde' aspects of our own hearts and behaviors?

When several years later, Fr. Pellegrino came to pay me a visit in Bombay, I asked him what he had come to do and what other visits he needed to make in India. He surprised me by saying that he had traveled all the way to Bombay simply to see me and to find out how things were going in my life.

In this tale of two Rectors, I realized that each of us could be a blessing or a curse in the lives of others, especially our subordinates when we are in positions of authority over them. The choice is ours.

I recall a prayer of St. Teresa of Avila that speaks to me in my journey and in the conflicting personalities I meet along the way:

> "Within you may there be peace today.
>
> May you trust God that you are exactly where you are meant to be.
>
> Let this presence settle into your bones,
>
> And allow your soul the freedom to sing, dance, praise and love.
>
> It is there for each and every one of us."

*****

After two years, the required study of Philosophy ended. I received my Bachelor's degree in Philosophy *summa cum laude*. I enjoyed the two years of questioning, doubting, learning, growing and soul searching from the giants of philosophical thought, starting with the Greeks and the Romans, that it seemed at that time that there was no other field of study I would ever enjoy more.

But that was not the case because I now moved into the profound and fascinating study of Theology. From the philosophical questions concerning human existence, we shifted gears to the theological questions concerning the divine and the interaction of the divine with the human. From sensing that I had become a more mature human being with the explorations of human and metaphysical thinking, I began now with the study of theology to feel that I was truly in training to become a priest and fulfilling God's purpose for me in coming to Rome.

It became apparent to me as the months went by that I was being challenged to integrate my humanity with my call to priesthood. I still remember what a kid said when he noticed a pair of pants underneath a priest's long white cassock: "Look, mom, there is a man under the priest!"

A priest continues to be a sign of contradiction. While he is immersed in the world, he is expected not to be of it.

In Rome, although we were seminarians, we had no external symbolic sign of religious commitment because we wore neither a white cassock as we did in India or a clerical black shirt with Roman collar in public as priests did in Europe. Soon after our arrival in Rome, we had been given two sets of black robes or cassocks with red stripes and red buttons, which served as our seminary uniform. But we never wore these robes to the University or into the city. We usually wore them for daily Mass and for services at St. Peter's Basilica in the Vatican. Because of the red buttons and the red stripes, occasionally the Swiss guards would salute us as we entered the walls of the Vatican.

After the Second Vatican Council, most of the minor orders were eliminated. We were considered to be clerics only after ordination to the transitional diaconate. That was still three years away. So, gradually both because of our lay state and the cooler Mediterranean climate, I built up a wardrobe of suits, ties, sweaters and overcoats. Clothes make the man! I felt like I was a regular university student on the outside, and a seminarian preparing for the priesthood within the seminary walls on the inside.

This secular way of dressing, studying and living allowed me to meet and be friends with several Italian families. This contact also enabled me to understand cultural differences. Once I was invited to have my birthday party at the home of an Italian family, and there I was given several presents. The way I was raised in India, it was not proper to open presents in front of the people who had given them to you. I thought I would quietly take them home and then open them. Instead, the whole family insisted that I open my presents. Needless to say, I was somewhat embarrassed. However, I learnt quickly and adapted to my new cultural surroundings. There is definitely a value in seeing the look of surprise and joy when presents are open. Both the giver and the receiver are linked by the gift.

In Bombay when we were interviewed by the Spanish Jesuits to discern our vocations, one clear statement to us was that we should not be joining the seminary if we do not care about the opposite sex. From childhood, I had constantly felt comfortable around girls and women. I could always count on my mother's strong maternal and feminine presence. I was also surrounded by the care and wisdom of five sisters. From grade one to eleven I attended a co-ed school. It was there while growing up that I began to slowly get exposed to some of the intricacies and intrigues of relationships with the opposite sex.

I began to see that women seemed to be more grounded and more open to life. Women complemented and completed my manliness and my humanity. I knew that one day in the future, as a priest, I would have to work closely with women in the Church. God prepared me for ministry in a Church supported today largely by women, as the women disciples of the early Church that were always there to accompany and assist Jesus, the Apostles and their successors.

After that initial interview to discern our vocations there was no more talk of sex, celibacy or women in the seminary formation years. On the other hand, in seminaries today, there is much more openness in talking about sex and sexuality. Even though Roman Catholic priests take the vow of celibacy, today's seminarians are asked to think about priests as being married to the Church. If the Church is their spouse how does that make them feel? If young men have issues regarding sexuality, it is better to find out about them before they are ordained priests. Such open conversations and teachings help greatly in the maturing process of future priests.

Towards the end of my second year in Rome I felt homesick and wanted very badly to visit my family in India. I stayed in touch with my parents and siblings through postcards and letters. But the mail system was very slow and replies from India did not always reach us.

There was a joke told among my international peers that if mail had not arrived it had probably been dumped into the Tiber.

When I mentioned my homesickness to my superiors in Bombay, I was informed that because of a famine in India, it would not seem proper that a seminarian should travel all the way from Rome on vacation. Families who were having a hard time because of the famine would be very upset. Sometimes I wonder if this refusal from my superiors also served to alienate me from my own roots in India. After all, the saying goes, "out of sight, out of mind." Although I missed my family terribly, I felt more and more distant from my homeland.

The opposite also seemed to be true for me. The world was becoming my home. I felt at ease wherever I went. I grabbed every opportunity to travel in Italy and beyond. The world was now my school and every aspect of life and travel fascinated me.

The college of 'Propaganda Fide' would organize tours within Rome and outside the city. I loved visiting museums, churches and quaint little historical towns all over Italy.

*****

One thing I never had since I joined the seminary right after High School was paid work experience. It wasn't common in India to do summer jobs or part time work during the school year. With the help of your family you first finished all your studies. After that you would start looking for a full time job. Thus, I never had the satisfaction of earning my own money.

So, one summer, like most seminarians, I applied for a part time job in Germany. The German Mark seemed very attractive to us students. Some of the seminarians received yearly allowances from their Bishops or dioceses. I did not receive any from India. Considering my young innocent looks I was offered a summer job in a bank in northern Germany.

Because I was so far away from my own parents and family and because I had no other relatives close by to help me in my needs, Franz and Maria Opwis who lived in the western region of Germany decided to 'adopt' me and become my European parents.

When they heard about my desire to do a summer job in their country, they suggested that I come to their home and work instead in a nearby factory that made parts for Mercedes-Benz cars. This was a golden opportunity for me to earn some pocket money and to learn the German language from none other than the very talented polyglot, Mr. Franz Opwis. Since he lived close to France and had many French-speaking visitors, he was also known by the endearing term '*Tonton* Francois' (Uncle Francis) and his wife was everyone's '*Tante* Mia' (Aunty Mary).

I agreed to take the offer of my foster parents. It would have been foolish to refuse. Each weekday morning, Mrs. Opwis would wake me at five o'clock, give me breakfast and then drop me at the local bus stop to catch the bus to work. While most of the early morning German workers napped peacefully in the bus, I would use the time of the bus ride to learn conversational German.

At the factory, the work we did to manufacture shock absorbers for Mercedes cars was called 'Akkord Arbeit,' or piecework. It was basically an assembly line. We were expected to mechanically thread four hundred pieces every day. In the beginning, being enthusiastic and inexperienced, some of us doing part time summer jobs tried to make more pieces than expected of us each hour to earn extra money. But the regular workers warned us against increasing our hourly numbers; for fear that they would have to do the same increased number for the rest of the year but without the extra pay.

Thus, at my first paying job I learned the importance of teamwork and survival.

When I received my first ever paycheck, I was very happy and deeply moved. I had never personally held so much money in my bare hands. I called my family in Bombay and told them that I was planning to send them all of my first earnings out of gratitude for all that my family had done for me since childhood. They simply laughed and said that even though it was a nice gesture on my part, they had not expected me to pay them back for all the love they had shown me growing up in the city of Bombay. They asked me to spend the money on myself, which was difficult to do since I had such generous foster parents in Mr. and Mrs. Opwis. They took care of all my needs.

So I learned another important lesson regarding money, namely, how to save it for the future.

My foster parents would remind me that Germany was a very cold country and I needed more fat on my body to stay healthy. The Indian 'Bony Wrestler' would not have been able to survive in the low freezing temperatures of Germany. A whole cooked chicken would be placed on my plate, and I was expected to finish it all in one sitting. They also taught me how to apply butter properly on bread. They pointed out that all the holes on the surface of a slice of bread had to be filled with a thick coating of butter. That was the best way to eat heartily and to keep warm in Germany.

Every Sunday we attended Mass at Reinsfeld, the town where I had my first hangover. The church of St. Remigius was almost a thousand years old. While I was working at my summer job at 'Bilstein' during the week, I noticed that a lot of the young boys and girls who were getting a practical technical education there happened to be parishioners of the town of Reinsfeld. We became good buddies both at work and in church.

This close relationship I had with the youth of Reinsfeld and of the larger town of Hermeskeil led me to headlining a concert and social evening in a youth hall that shared the premises with a local bar. We enjoyed singing American and German songs together. The German youth and families joined me wholeheartedly, when I sang songs like: 'This Land is Your Land,' 'Michael Row the Boat Ashore,' 'When the Saints Go Marching In,' 'If I Had a Hammer,' and 'Jailhouse Rock.' I still cherish to this day the special African drum they gave me as I entertained them with my guitar into the night. Our evening of music ended at three in the morning, when we were gently forced out of the public bar and hall by the stout and burly bartender.

Although I had a decent and dignified experience of working during my summer vacation for a living, some of my African classmates did not have it so easy. I remember especially the case of Daniel, a tall, handsome Sudanese. His skin was blacker than black, almost purple. He also got a summer job in Germany but he ran out of money after working for a few days, and payday was still a long ways off. He wasn't as fortunate as I was to be living with friends who took care of all my needs. He did not know anybody in that German town where he worked and was too embarrassed to ask for money to buy food. He told me later that he had starved for three whole days, while working full time; and finally, when he received his paycheck, all he could do was look at the money in his hands and weep bitterly.

I have been very fortunate in my life. God was constantly blessing me and watching over me. I ran into the right people and generally found myself in the right places and circumstances. Life was never an unmanageable and burdensome struggle for me. So many people struggle each day to make ends meet. I have always been richly blessed. It's not that I have too much of

111

anything at any time in my life. I have always found whatever I needed to live a decent human life wherever God led me and placed me. I have never felt abandoned or orphaned. I have never gone to bed hungry, unless I chose not to eat.

Thus my heart is constantly filled with gratitude.

I owe a big debt of gratitude to my parents. They did not have much by way of money and possessions. Yet, they were never found dissatisfied or complaining. They trusted in God and they worked hard to feed and educate all their children. They taught me to trust and to have faith.

Since my family allowed me to hold on to my first paycheck that summer, I began to understand the value of saving and the value of money. Money was never going to be my master, just a very useful servant. Fortunately, I did not have any major expenses at any time during my sojourn in Rome.

When I left for Rome in the year 1970, I was allowed to take only twenty-one British Pounds with me because I was traveling as a student. Indian Rupees had no international value and were not considered hard currency. I held on to the twenty-one British Pounds as long as I could. In the summers when we traveled to other parts of Europe, as Indian citizens, we had to apply for transit and regular visas, which cost money. Then there was the cost of local transportation and food. My European friends were very understanding of our financial situation and thus were very generous toward us 'poor, starving, third-world students.'

My early experience had influenced me so much that even today, I do not spend money carelessly. I prefer to save rather than spend on unnecessary things. In some ways, I have become like my parents, trusting in God and being satisfied with the little I have.

The Beatitudes remind us: Blessed are the poor in spirit; blessed are those who are detached from the things of this world; blessed are those who fully trust in the Lord, for the kingdom of heaven is theirs.

It is surprising that Jesus who was born poor and lived poorly talked so frequently in the gospels about money and wealth. For Jesus, the love of money, not money in itself, was the root of evil. Jesus was aware that one needed money to survive. If the disciples learned to remain detached and to be poor in spirit, money could be a good and useful servant. For, as Jesus said, one cannot serve both God and Mammon.

What my first paying job in Germany helped me realize is the sense of accountability and to have the healthy perspective of the relative value of money and material things in one's life. When it's not your own money or you don't have to pay for it yourself, you don't treat things the same way and with the same respect. Before I earned my own money, if I was invited by friends for dinner and did not have to pay the bill, I would insensitively order the most expensive items on the menu.

Blessed are the poor, not because they have no money but because even if they did, they would remain detached from the things of this world. I have met many who are ordained and do not have a proper perspective on the temporary value of money. They end up being greedy for material things or lack a sense of accountability and stewardship.

There were two instances when I was embarrassed not to have my own spending money. The first time was in Great Britain when I visited my sister and her family. In order to use the public lavatories, I had to ask my brother-in-law for a few pennies. Sometimes it costs money to relieve yourself in public places. The second time happened in France, when an acquaintance invited several of us to join him for a dinner in a restaurant. When we finished eating, he began collecting money from each one of us as our share of the expenses for the dinner. Fortunately, I did carry some money with me that day.

In Asian cultures, when you invite someone you don't expect them to pay for anything. Hospitality is sacred. There is no obligation for you to invite anybody and you should never make your guests pay. If you cannot afford to pay for everyone, it is important to say so at the very beginning, so that all the guests can be prepared to pay for their own meals.

Since we were dealing in those days in Europe with several foreign currencies, I had opened a small savings account at the Vatican Bank. I had asked myself the question why the Church would need a bank for its spiritual mission. At our young age, the seminarians were such idealists that we believed the Church could be managed on love and prayers alone.

While I was working at the Mercedes factory in Germany, there were many youngsters who belonged to the parish of St. Remigius in Reinsfeld. They informed their Pastor about me. After I met him one Sunday, Reinsfeld's Pastor was keen that my presence should be an inspiration to the youth of his parish. Perhaps, he thought, we might also inspire some of the youth to think about a vocation to the priesthood and the religious life. After our initial encounter, we met often to discuss youth and religious issues. When he realized that one day I would return to Rome to finish my theological studies and then go home to India to serve my people, he personally requested the Bishop of Trier to consider ordaining me a deacon in his parish.

An ordination ceremony in a country parish had never happened before, to my knowledge, in this ancient city and Diocese of Trier.

When the auxiliary Bishop of Trier decided to come to Reinsfeld to ordain me a deacon, the news spread like wildfire in all the neighboring towns and villages. These simple, devout Catholics had never witnessed an ordination before, because ordinations only took place at the Cathedral and were attended mainly by family members and friends of the 'Ordinandi.'

For the first time I realized that my own life and story could become a model for future vocations to the Catholic priesthood.

It was the end of August in the year 1975 that hundreds of people from several towns and villages gathered at the parish church of Reinsfeld to witness my 'Yes' to ordination and to the transitional diaconate.

I was the only candidate for ordination and visibility was an issue in this old, historical stone church. Hence, during the litany of the saints, when the ordination candidate is supposed to lie flat on his face seeking the help and prayers of all the saints and holy men and women of the Church, I was asked to lie on the three marble steps that led to the altar rather than lie face down on the floor of the church. Needless to say, I was very uncomfortable on the hard and uneven marble surface.

During the relatively long litany of saints, I needed to blow my nose but simply could not get to my pocket to pull out my handkerchief (those were the days before Kleenex). So, there I was sniffing from time to time as various saints were being invoked. I learned later on that when people, especially the elderly, saw me sniffing, they thought I was crying, and that led to many tears in the congregation.

The Bishop reminded everybody about the seriousness of this ordination ceremony. He invited and challenged the youth of Germany to consider service in the Church by becoming priests and nuns. He was happy about the opportunity to come to a village parish to ordain me, a foreigner for a mission diocese. But his hope and dream would have been to come more often in the future to ordain more young German youth to the priesthood and the religious life.

This ordination event was so significant that it was reported in the local newspapers of at least six neighboring towns and villages. Many families till today have pictures of these ceremonies. When the town of Reinsfeld published the chronicles of its thousand-year history, my diaconate ordination featured prominently in the book.

The whole assembly gathered outside the church after the ordination ceremonies. The Mayor of Reinsfeld greeted the Bishop, the Pastor, the many visitors and me, as the guest of honor, showering praises on us for bringing such fame and recognition to a small resort town of about two thousand inhabitants. It was a beautiful, sunny day and a perfect setting for a joyful community celebration. I replied in German, thanking everybody for the great privilege of being ordained a deacon in this beautiful and unforgettable Mosel River vineyard covered region of Germany.

Some of my seminarian friends came to the ordination from Rome. My two 'hitchhiking' buddies from France also made it to the celebration. The very first friends I had made in 'Ponte di Legno,' Italy, namely, Mirella and Giovanna, came with their parish priest to share my joy. A special priest friend from Rome was present that day by the name of Fernand Franck. Later, he became the Archbishop of Luxembourg.

The following Sunday, as a deacon, I baptized a set of twin boys, Karl and Johan, and Sonja, a beautiful girl whose family I would meet on subsequent visits to Germany. I also had opportunities to improve my knowledge of the German language because, from time to time, I was given the task of preaching at Sunday liturgies. I enjoyed doing ministry. From the start I felt I was fulfilling the mission entrusted to me by God and by the Church.

When the moment came for me to leave Germany for the last time as a newly ordained deacon, we all gathered at the tiny airport of Luxembourg. After tearful goodbyes, I left for Rome expecting to never see my friends again.

My five years in Rome and Europe gave me a great appreciation not only for my own country and for what I had left behind, but also for the whole world in all its diversity, complexity, mystery and beauty.

What would I face upon my return to India?

CHAPTER 5

GOING HOME

I N ROME I began preparations to return to Bombay after being away for five years. In September of 1975 I said '*Arrivederci Roma'* (goodbye Rome) and flew back to the country of my birth.

A few days before my departure, I had made friends with an important official from Air India. He told me that I could take as much luggage as I wished on the return flight. Was he aware how much 'baggage' I had accumulated over the years in Europe? If he did, he may not have made me such a generous offer. When you grow up in poverty, you tend to save everything. And when you return to a poor country, literally everything seems to be useful enough to be packed and eventually given away as gifts to people who anxiously await your return.

One important piece I was carrying back with great care was a black-and-white, thirteen inch television set. When I left for Rome in the year 1970 there was no television in India. The first programs I had ever watched on television were in Italy. I was now bringing home a symbol of my window to the world that I had discovered and explored, as I matured from my teenage years to adulthood.

By 1971, *Doordarshan* (the Hindi name for State-run television) arrived on the Indian sub-continent and spread rapidly. In the beginning it was a government monopoly because it was seen as a very powerful medium of communications and control that could politically influence the thinking and the habits of the Indian people. My thirteen inch television set was going to be too small to have any effect on the sub-continent I had left behind five years earlier. But it was still an important symbolic treasure for me.

When I landed at the Bombay International Santa Cruz Airport, I realized that I would finally have a chance to embrace my beloved family in person. When I had left them I was almost twenty years of age; now I was returning as a young, hopefully mature, man, almost twenty-five years old.

From inside the airport terminal, I could see my entire family waving excitedly, and I could feel the tears of joy streaming down my face. It was a wonderful family reunion with many hugs and kisses. I held each member of my family in a tight embrace as long as I could, especially my mom and dad. It's a strange feeling that when you come home even after you've been gone several years, the magical moment you experience when you reconnect with family members, makes you feel as if you never left.

I remembered the greeting I received in a farewell card: "Goodbye for now. When we meet again we will carry on as if we never parted." On the flight home I was wondering how everything would turn out. There was no need to worry or be anxious. After all, blood is thicker than water and there's no place like home.

When I landed it felt safe. I felt loved. I knew in my heart that I belonged here.

I was so absorbed in my family that I barely noticed a stranger picking up my bag with the precious thirteen inch black and white television set. One of my family members asked me to look over my shoulder. I nabbed the stranger-thief just in time, and he, with a straight innocent face, told me that he owned a similar piece of luggage.

The harsh realities of returning to and living in India were just beginning to stare me in the face. If my thirteen inch black-and-white television set was to be stolen, it would still not have been the end of the world for me; yet, I could have lost an important symbol of my window to the rest of the world, which had fascinated and excited me for the last five years.

As we grow older symbols are all we have to jog our memories and to help us pass on our stories and wisdom to others.

*****

It wasn't long before I was assigned as a deacon to a parish called Sacred Heart in Santa Cruz, Bombay. There were five priests who ministered to this faith community. At the church, I would preach on Sundays and help with the distribution of Holy Communion. There were no lay Eucharistic Ministers in those days, so very soon people seeing me give out communion, began to address me as 'Father.' After all, I wore the same white cassock as the other priests of the parish, and I was publicly doing almost everything else priests do in church. The only exceptions were that as a transitional deacon I could not celebrate Mass, anoint the sick or hear confessions.

Almost every parish in Bombay had a school attached to the church. Although the Pastor (called simply, the parish priest in India) doubled up as the school principal, the other clergy in the house were also assigned to help with school administration by taking on the role of grade level principals. As the deacon, the new kid on the block, I was asked to be responsible for the elementary school children.

One of my responsibilities was to hand out the examination report cards to the best performers and the worst students. The best received an applause initiated by me, while the worst were expected to get a public flogging in the classroom also administered by me. Returning from Europe where I did not see any signs of physical punishment meted out to kids, this requirement of me from the school principal to publicly embarrass the poorly performing kids was a rude awakening.

It brought back childhood memories of being in a crowded classroom of fifty-five children in the second grade, where the teacher and disciplinarian was a priest. He had given us some homework that several of us had failed to do. We were barely eight years old. This sadistic priest went to each child who had forgotten the homework and went about cruelly bending one of their fingers till it touched the back of their palms and the child yelled in pain. I wasn't sure which was more painful: to be tortured physically in this way or to know that you were going to be next in line for punishment. As he moved from one row to another and came close to my seat, I almost fainted. When I opened my eyes, I realized that a miracle had taken place. This scary person in a priest's robe had accidentally missed my companion and me. There's definitely some advantage to having many kids in a class.

After five years in Europe I knew that I was a changed person. I could not accept the *status quo*, much to the annoyance of the stern school principal and parish priest. "I know you have been away in Rome," he said to me one day, "but this is the way it's done over here." "Whether you like it or not," he reminded me, "you have to punish these kids, otherwise they will never improve."

I simply refused to hurt any of the children. Instead, I invited the ones who had fared miserably in class to come to my office for a chat. Many of these kids were so tiny and emaciated that their feet barely touched the ground when they sat opposite me in my office.

In my conversation with them, I observed that all these kids with failing grades came from a particular slum area of the parish called *Golibar* I also found out that these kids being raised in poor families came to school without any breakfast. I was shocked. An army marches on its stomach. In the seminary we were reminded that one couldn't even philosophize on an empty stomach. How could one pay any attention to a teacher in class or do well in their tests without having eaten any breakfast in the morning?

Rather than flogging the kids for having failed in the examinations, I went over to visit this huge slum area and their families. Although I was born and raised in Bombay, as a kid I had closed my eyes to the harsh reality of slum life that existed in pockets all over the city. Many international cities in the world have slums. But often, the wealthy and the poor do not have to cross paths, because their dwellings are separated. Bombay does not have separate sections for expensive high-rise apartments and miserable slum dwellings. They co-exist.

Forty-two percent of the city's population lives in slum pockets and the largest of them called *Dharavi* may have upwards of several hundred thousand inhabitants. Some of the brand name products sold in high-end stores in Europe and in the United States are made in these slums.

Sacred Heart Parish in Santa Cruz, Bombay, was considered to be a wealthy community. Yet, the slums of *Golibar* were spread out right behind the church and school property.

Most of these single-family slum dwellings were made up of corrugated metal sheets, which got to be very hot and unbearable in the heat of the day. They were built next to open sewers, breeding grounds for rats and mosquitoes. Water had to be brought in from a distant public tap and the whole family cooked, ate and slept in the one single room, which they called 'home.' Some could be fortunate to have public toilets that were usually dirty and unsanitary. Many of the poverty issues of the Bombay slums were recently highlighted by the movie 'Slum Dog Millionaire,' a movie that for obvious reasons was not well received in India by Indians.

As I visited *Golibar*, the slum dwellings and neighborhood of many of our school children, I heard constant noises and loud blaring music from the many and varied religious festivals of Hindus and Muslims, who form the majority of slum-dwellers. There was no quiet area for study and for doing homework. How could one sleep, study or do any homework in such miserable, noisy surroundings?

My solution was to help start a breakfast program for these poor kids to help them improve in their performance in school. I approached some wealthy parishioners for donations. Then, I talked with the Social Justice Committee of the parish to gather volunteers and provide some simple nourishment for the poor children of the slums before the beginning of class each day.

The breakfast program gradually created some happy smiling kids, who also showed improvement in their test scores. This simple program made me realize that the solutions to the problems in the Third World countries are very often to be found in the community itself.

Mahatma Gandhi, known as the Father of the Nation, once said: "For the poor, bread is God." Even though the stern school principal thought that corporal punishment was the best way to help the under-performing kids to do better, it was a known fact that it was the same kids who would be repeatedly and publicly flogged and humiliated every year.

On a full stomach, all the kids looked happier and did much better in their studies and exams. The dreaded punishment cane could be put away because there was no one left to be flogged and publicly embarrassed.

I was beginning to look at India's reality with new eyes. I remember standing on the balcony of our eighth floor family apartment in Bombay with my brother who is several years younger than me. I was looking down at the pockets of slums and poverty around our apartment building and being very disturbed by what I saw.

This stark reality filled with misery and inhuman conditions was not new. It existed even before I left for Rome. My new awareness was sharpened by all the traveling I had done in the past five years. I kept saying again and again: "How can such conditions exist in these modern times? How can anyone live this way?" When my youngest brother saw my troubled face and heard my depressing ranting and questions, he said to me: "You will get used to it."

At that moment I wanted to scream: "No, I do not want to get used to it because I cannot accept it." I was too discouraged and frustrated even to protest or scream.

There are poor people all over the world. What I was seeing with new eyes was not poverty, but misery. When you are poor, you may not have all the luxuries you want, but at least you have the basic things you need. The misery I saw was not even fit for animals. It was the kind of misery the prodigal son experienced in the parable of Jesus. In the story the younger son, after irresponsibly spending his inheritance, ends up so hungry and miserable that all he can find is what the pigs refuse to eat.

How could human beings live this way? Where was God in all this?

I could not get any satisfactory answers from either Indian politics or Indian religions.

India is still today the largest democracy in the world with over a billion inhabitants. The system of government is bicameral: the 'Rajya Sabha' and the 'Lok Sabha', similar to the House of Lords and the House of Commons in Britain. The Prime Minister is usually the head of the Majority political party, while the President is the symbolic head of the country, much like the Queen of England.

What I read and observed was that the politicians of the country had exploited the poor by using them for votes and making impossible promises to them. Sometimes hundreds of thousands of illiterate villagers would be taken in open trucks or lorries, as they are known in India, to polling booths where their votes would be coerced and manipulated. The poor and illiterate were promised clean, running water, decent housing and health care, lower food prices, free education, minority rights, *et cetera* prior to the elections but very few promises were kept after the elected politicians came to power.

R. K. Laxman was a very famous cartoonist, whose work and political humor appeared daily in the newspapers. It was always the first thing I would look for when reading the daily news. His cartoons were entitled "You said It by Laxman". In them he always had a central character that was the ordinary guy in the streets commenting on the political reality of the country. In one such cartoon, we see a helicopter circling over the slums of the city, and the common man says to himself: "It must be election time. These politicians show up only once every five years."

The religions of the country from my limited perspective appeared to encourage the poor to accept their miserable conditions rather than to improve and change them for the better.

India is the cradle of many important religions. The majority of Indians, about eighty-four percent, are Hindus. Islam also spread in India during the Persian invasions and represents about eleven percent of the population. Buddhism originated in India but spread more quickly in Far Eastern countries: in Cambodia (95 percent), Thailand (94 percent), Burma (89 percent), Bhutan (75 percent), Sri Lanka (69 percent), Tibet (65 percent), and in large parts of China, Laos and Vietnam. India is also home to other religions like Jainism, Sikhism, and very ancient forms of Judaism and Christianity.

From time to time religious extremists have tried to take hold of power by violent means. There have been a number of Hindu-Muslim clashes and there has also been a strong movement to establish a Hindu State. Some political parties have nourished and stoked the fires of religious extremism.

Catholicism spread with the coming of the Portuguese, especially Vasco da Gama, who found his way around the Cape of Good Hope at the end of the fifteenth century. Today, almost three percent of India's population is Christian. Some evangelical Protestant churches are making converts in sensitive border areas. These fundamentalist Christians tend to portray Hindus and Hinduism very poorly. Hence, recently there have been sporadic clashes between Hindus and Christians, churches have been destroyed, and poor tribal Christians forced to return to Hinduism, something unheard of for many centuries. Those who seek to do harm do not distinguish between Protestant and Catholic communities. Since Catholic churches have many more openly displayed religious symbols, like statues and crucifixes, they are more often the targets of religious fanaticism.

The tolerant nature of India is being corroded and destroyed by extremists of all religions. In the movie, 'Gandhi,' the Father of the Nation reminds the people that if they follow the practice: 'an eye for an eye and a tooth for a tooth' then, everyone will be toothless and blind. When the Hindu-Muslim hatred and fighting was getting out of control, he reminded them that they were like the two eyes that we need in order to see, and the pair of lungs that we need to breathe and survive. They needed each other. So, therefore, they should learn to be tolerant and to co-exist as brothers and sisters.

In my childhood Hindus, Muslims and Christians had always lived together in harmony. Next to our home lived two Muslim families and on the other side of our home facing the main street was a restaurant run by Hindus. Everyone got along wonderfully well. I was raised in a neighborhood where we played together, attended one another's festivals and tolerated all our differences. When religions become intolerant, and fundamentalist religious groups tend to be that way, then violence ensues and innocent people suffer the consequences. It is temples, mosques and churches that are destroyed, and people lose homes, livelihoods and the lives of loved ones as a result.

Catholicism has made a huge positive impact in India through her schools, colleges, hospitals and care for the aged and the needy. Even Indian politicians who hate the British and the colonial past of Europe want to send their children to Catholic schools and colleges. They know that they and their children will receive the best of discipline and the best of education at these institutions. Even though Christians comprise only about two and a half percent of the entire country's population, one might say that about fifty percent of the best schools, colleges and hospitals found in India are efficiently run and maintained by Catholic parishes, dioceses and religious orders.

It is amusing to read matrimonial advertisements offered by Hindus, Muslims, Sikhs, Jains and Buddhists, who will claim that they are highly suitable as marriage partners because they are convent-educated!

Muslims who were poor generally seemed to remain poor because they lived as a closed community that accepted help only from their own religious and social institutions. Most of the facilities they built were places of prayer, not of social action. Girls and women were generally discouraged from attending elementary and higher educational institutions. There seemed to be very few visible professional women. Their role was limited to family life.

Hindus were very peace-loving neighbors. I believe that the poor among them continued to be poor probably, from my biased Christian perspective, because of the Hindu belief in reincarnation. This doctrine appears to be very logical and reasonable, namely that one cannot accomplish and complete everything and arrive at total fulfillment with the benefit of only one life cycle. We have so many loose threads in the short span of our earthly existence. So, the belief in reincarnation asserts that there must be many cycles of life that we need to go through before we reach fulfillment and Nirvana.

Of course, a simplistic logical reasoning that is tied to the belief in reincarnation would go like this: "I will try to live a good, moral life, if my next life is dependent on the present one. But knowing that I do not want to mess up my next life or regress to a lower life form, like that of an animal or that of a lower caste, what could there be to motivate me to be more involved and passionately committed in this present life, here and now?"

I wonder if a lack of social involvement and risk-taking emerging from a simplistic interpretation of reincarnation can create apathy, which then perpetuates poverty and human misery.

According to the Buddhist version of reincarnation, misdeeds in past lives affect today's life situations. Do something bad in this life and you will probably come back as a sentient being of some kind in your next one, but not necessarily as a human being. Buddhism emphasizes moderation, which is a good thing and makes the followers of Buddha very calm and compassionate human beings. But where is the passion needed to create social change, to improve human lives?

A famous young Buddhist monk, who tries to make the practice of Buddhism relevant to the West, also speaks out against the value of Hope. According to him, Hope creates desire and increased desire leads to more pain and suffering. From a Christian perspective, I find that hard to understand. Christians do not run away from the reality of the cross or of suffering in their lives. Jesus said: "If you wish to be my disciples, take up your cross daily and follow me." Jesus himself has shown us by example the way to face suffering. In Luke's gospel we are reminded: "Was it not necessary for the Christ to suffer?" We arrive at life and Resurrection through suffering and the cross. Hope strengthens our resolve not to give up. Without Hope we are practically lost and spiritually dead.

Christians do not actively seek out suffering. But if suffering comes into our lives, we are called to believe that light will come from darkness and that life and Resurrection will come from death. Again Jesus says: "Unless a grain of wheat falls to the ground and dies, it remains just a grain of wheat; but if it dies, it bears much fruit."

In keeping with Buddhist principles, during Burma's bloody crackdown, some soldiers tried to 'defrock' monks prior to detaining them, in a bid to soften their own karmic crimes.

126

Hinduism and Buddhism have given rise to New Age religions and New Age ways of thinking in the West. It's all about me and my self. Everything around me is illusion. Even suffering is in the mind and therefore can be set aside with meditation, right thinking and consciousness.

New Age thinking has crept into churches, retreat houses, convents and Christian colleges. The Paschal Mystery – the life, suffering, death and Resurrection of Jesus – are unfortunately watered down and weakened as a result. If it's all about me and my self, then Christ is only a figment of my imagination or consciousness, and not the Word of God who historically became flesh, who suffered and died on the Cross and who rose from the dead for our salvation.

I don't have the answers to India's political and religious dilemmas. I don't claim with any certainty that it is religion that makes us poor or rich. I do believe in the power of religious beliefs that inspire us and motivate us to do the right thing for ourselves and for our fellow human beings. I believe that we can make the world a better place. The proper religious beliefs will help our fellow pilgrims and us to get there. It is easy to blame God for what we fail to do for ourselves. If we see ourselves as stewards of God's creation, then accountability and responsibility will follow.

A young Hindu told me recently that God allowed religion and religious practices in order to overcome fear. But extremists in every religion seem to create fear among people through violence in the name of the same God who wants us to overcome fear.

As in the different Christian denominations in the world so also among the religions of India there is a lot more that unites than divides us. All religions speak of peace and try to urge their followers to keep the golden rule. We need to understand each other's beliefs, live together in peace and harmony and strive together to make this world a better place for all.

Victoria Schmidt, the Director of Theresian World Ministry, an international Catholic women's organization, shares a story that came from traveling in Thailand. She visited a Fatima Self-Help Center run by the Good Shepherd Sisters. The Center invites women from the slums to learn a variety of trades, like hairstyling, sewing, embroidery and weaving, which give them an opportunity to support their families. She noticed one day that the Buddhist children before leaving the grounds that afternoon to go home stopped in front of a prominent statue of Mary and sang a lovely hymn to her. Singing a hymn to Mary is a traditional Catholic practice. When she inquired why Buddhist children were following this practice, she was told that Buddhists honor the spirit in every house. Victoria asked herself that day what would happen if everyone in the world were to honor the spirit in every heart, in every house, in every religion? What if each of us honored the faith of every tradition and welcomed all their followers as brothers and sisters? What she saw in those children praying and singing in front of Mary's statue was for her the journey we all need to make toward living with reverence.

This is the peace and unity that I believe God aches for us to understand, accept and live.

I was now beginning to look at my homeland and my roots with new eyes. The eyes are the windows of the soul. Like looking through a peephole, my spirit was observing and evaluating what was all around me in India.

I was glad, however, that no one could look in reverse through the peephole into my heart and into my spirit. I was already beginning to feel very small and insecure in relation to the immensity of India and her many serious problems.

I had returned to India from Rome filled with confidence. This self-assurance was slowly being eroded as I grappled with the reality, the contradictions and the complexity of India.

The three months of transitional diaconate at Sacred Heart Parish in Santa Cruz passed quickly, almost like a honeymoon. The wedding was soon to take place and the marriage journey in all seriousness was about to begin. The Ordination ceremonies to the priesthood were set for December that year.

*****

Physically, I was sick almost every day since I returned from Rome because I wasn't used to Indian spices in my meals anymore. I loved the taste of Indian food and its flavorful spices, which brought back childhood memories, but my poor stomach could not withstand this hot and flaming gastronomical assault at every meal. After consuming what Indians consider bland Italian food for five years, largely from the Lombardy region where our Italian nuns came from, my stomach linings were rendered delicate and weak.

I went for an Executive Health Checkup to a well-known hospital in Bombay, where they did a full physical examination. At the end of the day, three specialist doctors met with each patient to go over the results of all the tests. You even received a half hour of yoga and breathing exercises. During the day, I noticed among the patients a Buddhist monk with saffron robes drinking only bottled water. Since the hospital had a good reputation, I did not worry where my drinking water came from or how the salad and vegetables were washed and prepared for all of us attending the health sessions of the day. In Bombay they commonly use filtered water for drinking purposes but the water is not necessarily boiled before being filtered for use in drinking containers. After eating the salad and vegetables provided for lunch and drinking filtered water, I began to feel somewhat queasy and bloated as the afternoon session progressed. By the time we got to the yoga exercises, I was feeling sick all over.

I picked up my test results and hurried home. All my reports were great, but when my siblings saw me, they said: "The reports are excellent, but the patient is dead."

I was constantly reminded that everything gets better with time. The excitement of being at the threshold of priestly ordination and all the ensuing preparations made the peripheral issues of readapting to home life go away, at least for a while.

Before ordination to the priesthood there is one final retreat that a transitional deacon needs to make. Because of my studies in Rome, I was on a different academic track than my Indian classmates from the seminary in Bombay. They had an extra year of pastoral work between their studies of Philosophy and Theology. I missed the experience of a pastoral year, living in a foreign country. I was thus going to be ordained a priest a year and four months before my companions who started seminary life at the same time with me. I ended up having to do a personal directed retreat with the help of one of the Jesuit spiritual directors by the name of Fr. Feliu from Spain.

He was a very dynamic priest, well loved by all, including my family. What was even more significant was the fact that Fr. Feliu was one of the three Jesuits who had interviewed me several years earlier and welcomed me into seminary life. With this conclusion of seminary life retreat, I experienced with and through him one of the many circles of life in my faith journey.

The journey of faith is not a straight, logical line. It is more of a spiral that either takes you deeper into spiritual realms or higher into heavenly insights.

Each morning of my ten-day retreat I met with my spiritual director for about an hour, when I would receive from him guidance and spiritual direction. He asked me to meditate seriously on the story of the rich young man in the tenth chapter of Mark's gospel, verses 17 to 31.

The encounter that Jesus has with the young man in this story reveals to us what discipleship is all about. The young man asks Jesus what he should do to inherit eternal life. Jesus points out to him the ten Mosaic commandments, which can be summarized in the love of God and neighbor. In one of very few instances in the gospels we are told that Jesus loved this young man who faithfully observed the commandments from his youth. He had never strayed from the path. Yet Jesus in his insightful wisdom knew that the young man still had one major attachment and that was to his possessions. Jesus challenges the young man to be a full and true disciple by selling what he has, giving it to the poor and then following him with an unencumbered heart. We are reminded at the end of this encounter, how the response to discipleship can be very difficult because the young man's face fell and he went away sad because he had many possessions.

My meditation task was very simple and direct. On the threshold of ordination to the priesthood, I, as a young man of twenty five, was asked to look deep into my soul and find out if there was anything I was attached to, like the rich young man of the gospel, that would make me turn away from serving and following Jesus faithfully for the rest of my life.

In the gospel story we are reminded that Jesus looked into the soul of this young man and saw possibilities for the Kingdom. God works through human beings and Jesus needed faithful stewards to announce through their simple, committed lifestyles the advent of the Kingdom of God. Yet, any major earthly attachment could come in the way of total commitment, which discipleship (and the priesthood) calls for.

A humorous way of understanding what I was getting into comes from the story of a chicken and a pig that are having an argument as to who gives the most. The chicken says that by laying and giving eggs she is making a major contribution. The pig, on the other hand, counteracts with: "In my case it is a total commitment."

In Italy during some of our wild seminary days, we would jokingly comment on the three promises of priestly ordination in this way: Obedience, yes, but with Dialog; Poverty, yes, but with a 'Cinquecento' (the 500, the smallest Italian car of those days) and Chastity, yes, but with a Secretary!

Like the rich young man, to what was I still attached in my life? Since his riches possessed the young man of the gospels, I decided to prayerfully make a list of what I could be attached to.

As I looked at the items on my list I became more aware of my weaknesses and I was troubled since I was so close to ordination. So I went to my spiritual advisor and sought his counsel. He said that there was a difference between being attracted to something and being attached to something. One can have possessions, for instance, and be also detached from them, but one may end up, as in the case of the rich young man, being possessed by one's possessions.

He spoke to my questioning, troubled spirit. He described for me the first disciples that Jesus himself had chosen. Jesus did not choose them because they were perfect human beings. Peter may have appeared to be a passionate leader, yet when Jesus was arrested, Peter denied him three times. James and John were youthful when they were called but they seemed to have cravings for position and power. Matthew was already a tax collector, belonging to a hated profession among the Jews, yet Jesus called him. Judas may have started out as a team player but in the end he sold Jesus for thirty pieces of silver.

Somebody who starts out with a lot of promise may end up shockingly in the opposite camp. Conversely, somebody who starts out weak may surprise the world with their passion and commitment.

Although my spiritual director could not read into the future as Jesus did with the rich young man, he told me that I needed to firmly say to myself: "Today, at this time in my life, and hopefully in the future with the help of the Holy Spirit, I am willing to be detached from all the things and people on my list. I am willing to enter into ordination without any serious attachments, mental reservations or heavy burdens that will prevent me from following Jesus faithfully as a priest."

I willingly, fully, consciously and strongly said: "Yes" to the above.

Further in my retreat meditations, I remembered the promise that Jesus makes to those disciples who are ready to live a detached life. On one occasion Peter says to Jesus: "We have given up everything and followed you." And Jesus responds: "Amen, I say to you, there is no one who has given up house, or brothers or sisters, or mother or father, or children or lands for my sake and for the sake of the gospel, who will not receive a hundred times more in this present age; houses and brothers and sisters and mothers and children and lands with persecutions, and eternal life in the age to come."

*****

It turned out to be a joy-filled retreat as I came away with a greater awareness that I was going to be ordained a priest not for myself but rather to live a life of service in the Church for others. I came away with the assurance that I was not alone in my decision. I knew that I was being called to share in the priesthood of Jesus himself, who was calling me to follow him to be a fisher of people just as he had called those first fishermen two thousand years ago by the Sea of Galilee.

I could feel Jesus looking into my eyes, calling me by name and loving me. As one popular refrain in Church puts it: "I have loved you with an everlasting love; I have called you and you are mine."

My family in Bombay lived in a parish run by the Salesians of Don Bosco, an Italian religious order well known for its catechetical and youth work. In fact, St. John Bosco of Turin, Italy, was the first living saint to be part of a live press conference. My classmates at St. Pius X College Seminary still had a year of studies to complete but there were three Salesians who were ready to be ordained the same time I was. Although I was becoming a diocesan priest, the Bishop ordained the four of us at the Shrine of Don Bosco in December of the Holy Year, 1975.

For those who are not familiar with ecclesiastical terminology and distinctions, I like to think of diocesan priests and religious order priests as being part of a great heavenly soccer team. In the goal area, we find those orders that are contemplative and spend more of their time in prayer and meditation like the Cistercians, cloistered nuns and other contemplative monastic orders. In the middle or the center we have those religious orders that are partly contemplative and partly action and mission oriented. They spend a certain number of hours in community prayer and an equal amount of time in service, outreach work and evangelization. Finally, there are the forwards like diocesan parish priests who do not live in community and are totally out in the world, among the people, ministering directly to their spiritual needs.

My energy comes from people; therefore I could see myself only as a parish or diocesan priest. Sometimes people ask me what kind of priest I am. I usually respond that I am a 'regular' guy (as opposed to a member of a religious or monastic order).

Because of the crowds, the four of us were ordained in an outdoors ceremony on the school grounds of the Shrine of Don Bosco. Besides my parents and all my siblings and their families, there were many neighbors, friends and parishioners who were present. Most especially, there was Sister Crispina, who foretold when I was three years of age that I would become a priest. Mr. and Mrs. Franz Opwis, my German foster parents, were also there to link me to my years in Europe and my ordination to the diaconate in Reinsfeld, Germany. All my classmates from Bombay were there and many other priests from the Archdiocese and beyond. The Salesian community was large, so there were many priests and brothers who came to support their fellow Salesians who were being ordained with me.

There are powerful moments in every ordination celebration. I recall three such moments.

The first is lying down flat on your face, humble and contrite, during the litany of the saints. It is quite a spiritual experience. It expresses an act of surrender and a profound understanding that you cannot do God's work only by yourself. Thanks to the Communion of Saints, you are made aware that you are not alone; that the entire Church stands with you and prays with you. It is a humbling experience.

The second is being empowered by the Holy Spirit. As you kneel and as you humbly bow your head, first, the ordaining bishop approaches you; and then, one by one, all the priests silently lay their hands on your head. They all invoke the Holy Spirit upon you; and as you feel the touch and warmth of their hands, you also realize that these will be your co-workers in the vineyard of the Lord. Because you have your head bowed down, you do not know which priest it is who is praying for you. There is a sense during this ritual that there will be many hands to join yours in spreading the gospel. The fraternity and the unity of the presbyterate are felt strongly at this sacred moment. It is a unifying experience.

Finally I was moved to tears when my parents dressed me up in priestly vestments for the celebration of my first Mass. It reminded me of all those years when my parents had dressed me for bed, for play, for school and for church. It was a strong reminder that my family and friends would always be there to support me in the ministry of priesthood. Yes, I had given up family to follow Jesus, yet my family would always be there in spirit wherever my ministry would take me. It is an experience of intimacy.

At the end of the Ordination service the bishop had a great smile because he was the first one to kiss your consecrated hands. After the final blessing of the Mass, which we did together, the four of us newly ordained priests went to the people. Several hundred family members and friends came forward to plant a kiss on our consecrated hands. Only later I understood how truly important are the hands of a priest.

A priest's hands will be called upon to bless marriages, to baptize babies, to absolve sinners, to consecrate the bread and wine into the body and blood of Jesus Christ and to give communion, to anoint the sick, and to comfort the poor, the disabled, the homebound and the dying.

A wonderful, surprise party followed the ordination ceremonies. The Salesians of Don Bosco realized that I was the only non-Salesian in the group of four newly ordained, so they invited me and my entire family and all my guests to this memorable reception and party.

My German foster parents were very comfortable in this international gathering. Since the Salesians were founded in Italy, there were many Italian priests and brothers who joined us in the festivities. Beer flowed like water and there were all kinds of finger-licking delicacies: spicy chicken wings, vegetable and meat samosas, a variety of papadams, egg rolls and burrito-style Frankies. My siblings could not sit still when the party was warming up and very soon they were on the dance floor, entertaining the clergy with a variety of classic and modern dances. One of the Salesian brothers played the guitar while a small choir of seminarians regaled us with English and American songs into the night. It was a fun evening and everyone, without exception, enjoyed it.

The seminary formation journey of priesthood is a very long process that can last from six to fourteen years. Some of the religious order priests, like the Jesuits, take a few extra years to specialize in a particular field of education and study. They may take several more years to arrive at ordination.

On the day of my ordination, I had a sense of fulfillment. I felt strong and secure in my identity and vocation.

*****

Although your ordination Mass is your very first Mass, yet the principal celebrant during the ordination ceremonies is the Bishop. The following day, I had the opportunity to be the main celebrant or presider of my first 'solo' Mass. St. Joseph Church in the west of Wadala, Bombay, was our parish church. The Salesians of Don Bosco were in charge of this parish.

Normally the pastor and the associates of a parish help a newly ordained priest celebrate his first Mass in his home church. But all the priests of St. Joseph Church were Salesian priests and I was ordained, instead, a Diocesan priest. Salesians like other religious orders have community life while diocesan priests do not. Since the other three newly ordained with me were of the Salesian religious Order, all the priests of St. Joseph Church decided to join their fellow religious community members for the festivities that took place in another Salesian parish.

I was alone. Yes, I had participated very often in the celebration of Eucharist all my life, but this was my first opportunity to be the leader of worship. In those days there were no liturgy coordinators to help in the planning and implementation of Mass. The priest practically did everything. I marked the Sacramentary (the book of prayers with rubrics and instructions for Eucharist) with as many ribbons and Post-it notes that I could find. I would be embarrassed if I was to miss my place in the flow of the Mass and I also wanted to be sure at all times to know what I had to do next. I am not a perfectionist but I like to be well prepared. Always!

Liturgy is prayer and also theater. One is called not only to be a leader of prayer, but also to be a sacred performer, who maintains the flow of worship and keeps it engaging for all. I had four altar servers: my youngest brother and three nephews, all of more or less the same age. A classmate seminarian helped with the readings and a small parish choir did the best they could to sing hymns everybody knew and could easily join in.

The homily was my responsibility. Since no other priest was around to preach on my behalf, I had to do a solo performance. They say first impressions are lasting impressions. I still remember the homily I gave at my first Mass. I talked to the assembly about a movie I had seen, entitled 'My Name is Nobody.' The main actors were Henry Fonda and Terence Hill. In the movie Henry is the fastest gun in town but he doesn't know that someone who is following him everywhere is trying to be better than him. And Terence follows Henry like a disciple wanting to be a faster gunman than the Master. Finally, in a shootout, the disciple guns down his idol.

I shared in my reflection that even though Jesus is my hero, he notices me and calls me by name. In Jesus' eyes, I am not anonymous. As a matter of fact, I am 'Somebody,' unique and important. Since God gives me a sense of my own worth, I do not have to destroy my model and hero to be a better person or to be the best. As a disciple, I will always learn from my Master and grow each day to be more like Him. My Lord will always be in my life, as I am in His life. In fact, a day will come when, as St. Paul says, "It will be no longer I who live but Christ who lives in me."

Mentioning the movie at the beginning of my homily was like throwing a hook to grab the attention of my audience. This was an important aspect of my preaching style that was observed and reflected back to me by a school principal. Whenever I am called to speak or preach, I like to begin with a story, a joke, a question or a description of a real life event, in order to capture the attention of my listeners, before I go into the subject matter itself.

St. Paul, at the Areopagus, first spoke to the Athenians about their shrine to the unknown God, before broaching the difficult subject of the resurrection of the dead.

In the beginning I did not completely understand the value of preaching the Word of God. Only gradually from talking with people in informal settings, I began to realize that people are hungry for God and as a result are very grateful for a good homily that can sustain them through a busy week. Just as people come to be fed at the table of the Eucharist, so also they gather to be fed at the table of the Word of God.

Just like preaching, only gradually, I began to understand the power of priestly ministry in the lives of ordinary believers. I realized how powerful symbols and sacraments really were. Pastoral ministry of visiting the sick or just spending some quality time with families and listening to their concerns can do a world of good. There is a great deal of brokenness and alienation in the world. I slowly discovered how as a priest I am given the power to bring comfort and healing to people of all ages.

Major parish assignments for priests were given out in May or June in India each year. Since my ordination took place in

December, I was first given a temporary assignment. I was sent to Bandra, to a rather affluent community in the suburbs of Bombay. Besides helping the other priests in the parish with daily Masses and ministry, I was asked to be the Principal of the parochial school temporarily in the absence of the regular Principal.

Right from the beginning of my assignment I began to sense the special place a priest has in the community. Besides being addressed as 'Father,' I was consulted by many on almost every subject as the 'expert in residence.' Somehow they felt that I had knowledge and insights directly from above. A few, who knew that I was recently ordained, tried to manipulate my decisions. Even though I did not have much pastoral and worldly experience, common sense came to my rescue.

I remember when it came time to finalize the admissions for the kindergarten class in our Catholic school a woman insisted that a child she represented had to be included in my final list. She was acting as an agent for the family. She reminded me, first of all, that, if admitted, the child's non-Christian family was going to make a sizable donation to the needs of the school. It was a well-known fact that every parochial school was overcrowded, and the buildings and classrooms were badly in need of repair. When I insisted that a Catholic school cannot be bribed and should follow strict rules of moral behavior, she added that, second of all, I may be lacking the understanding of what should be the right thing to do in this case probably because I was just a newly ordained priest.

She was telling me in no uncertain terms that I lacked experience. A seasoned Principal, according to her, would never make such a mistake.

What my common sense told me and what I realized quite clearly was that a deserving poor Catholic child would be denied a good education simply because we would allow ourselves to be bribed by a wealthy non-participating, non-Catholic family. I could not tolerate this injustice. And I'm glad I did not cave in to the demands of this sweet-talking, manipulating individual.

This was the first of many similar incidents I experienced living in India, where bribing and corruption are a way of life. Reminded about the remarks of my youngest brother, as we looked some months earlier at the slums and the miserable life of so many disadvantaged children and families, I was simply not ready to get used to this way of life.

I felt very proud that day when I said 'Yes' to the future of a poor child, and 'No' to the lure of bribery.

To help them in the process of discernment in the spiritual life, some Christians will ask themselves: "What would Jesus do?" In this school situation, I think I did what Jesus would do to help in the education of a poor, needy child. The poor do not have a voice, so a priest, especially, has a mission to care for the downtrodden and to be the spokesperson for the voiceless among us.

What I was being awakened to was the reality of social problems in India. I was totally unprepared. After all, I had joined the seminary right after high school and the five years in Rome did not help my readjustment to life in India.

*****

During the six months I was in my first temporary parish assignment, I had an opportunity to attend a three-day counseling workshop at the Pastoral Center of Bombay, facilitated by an American Jesuit. Having no counseling and psychology background in my seminary studies I enjoyed the workshop and learned a lot. The basic skill of effective counseling we learned and we practiced through role playing was to be good listeners. The workshop affirmed my natural skills of being an effective counselor.

Sometimes when you attend a good workshop, you feel you've become an expert in that field. From that very moment your main desire is to convert everyone to your new ideas and to your new way of thinking.

But there were some other thoughts going on in my mind. While I was at the workshop I decided that I should educate myself in a lengthy program of study on Indian soil, so that I would get to know the people of India better and I thought I would be able to serve them more effectively with the proper tools and skills. Before leaving for Rome all I had in India was a high school education. My five continuous years in Rome seemed to have alienated me from my Indian roots and from the reality of Indian life.

My life in Rome had, for better or for worse, made me an 'independent thinker.' I felt I had to figure things out for myself first and foremost and then, with proper research, reasons and facts make my presentation to someone in authority for their approval.

Is it possible in the Church to become an independent thinker and to act on your own thoughts and ideas? I was soon going to find out.

I wrote to the Bishop about my well-researched plans. I told him that I had decided to pursue a Master's degree in Social Work in Bombay and my reasons for doing so.

As soon as I returned from the counseling workshop, I found a letter waiting for me from the Bishop. His response was succinct and direct: "I have decided that you will **not** pursue a Master's degree in Social Work."

I was shattered. I ran back to the Pastoral Center to meet the American Jesuit and I was fortunate that he was still around. Instead of feeling like a reasonable Counselor after a good workshop, I felt I was in dire need of counseling and therapy for myself.

In Rome for five years, I had to make my own decisions. I was aware that I could either make or break my life. When I wrote to the Bishop that I had made my decision, I thought he would be glad to know that I was a self-starter and confident in myself and in my abilities. His response shocked me. He was not open to dialog and he was not happy that a subordinate would dare to make a decision by and for himself.

Since the American Jesuit was a visitor and a guest of the Archdiocese, he preferred not to give any advice. He listened to the best of his ability; putting into action some of the principles he had taught us during the workshop. I continued to share with him my realization from this confrontation with the Bishop that I was like a fish out of water. I told him that when I was studying in Rome, I had to make my own decisions and very few cared then in the turmoil of the seventies whether I made it or not to the priesthood. Many seminarians had quit but I had remained faithful and persevered because I believed in my vocation and my call.

For five years my sense of 'Time' and 'Space' had radically changed. I was used to processing everything before I made an informed decision. Now I was feeling like I was going backwards to a Church structure programmed for blind obedience. What had happened to dialog and the spirit of the Second Vatican Council? Even though I gave clear reasons to the Bishop about my education plans for the future, instead of inviting me to friendly dialog on the issue and seeking the Will of God together he simply replied with a blunt, confrontational, unidirectional and authoritarian denial of my request.

On his behalf, I must say that the Bishop was generally a kind man of God who cared for his priests. He modeled for us a simple life of prayer and commitment. When the first Cardinal of India was grievously sick, this Bishop who was temporarily put in charge did not want the Archdiocese to end up in a chaotic state. He felt that his responsibility was to avoid any signs of unrest so that the transition and the road to his eventual leadership of the Archdiocese would be smooth and without problems.

We were still in the first decade after the Second Vatican Council and the winds of change were affecting every stratum of religious and parish life. The upheaval in the Church was widespread in Europe and in North America; and the Bishop definitely wanted to avoid any chaos in the Church in India.

When a ship is tossed about in stormy seas, the Captain must take control. The Bishop realized that the reins of leadership were now entrusted in his hands and he had to manage the Archdiocese responsibly.

The Bishop was short in stature but strong in his ways. A leader is sometimes born to lead but usually a leader emerges in difficult and challenging circumstances, as in the case of the Bishop. The first Cardinal appeared to be a born leader maintaining the strength and wisdom of the pre-Vatican II Church he inherited; his successor emerged to respond to the call to leadership in the challenging post-Vatican II Church.

In Chapter Six of the gospel according to Mark, Jesus summons the twelve Apostles and then begins to send them out two by two to spread the Good News of God's kingdom. He tells them how to prepare for this arduous journey. If people welcome them they are to stay. But if people reject them and do not listen to their message, he asks them to "leave there and shake the dust off your feet in testimony against them."

On the roads of India or the Middle East, dust can stick to your feet for the entire journey. The feet need to be washed before entering a home. Shaking the dust from their feet was a symbolic act performed by Jews returning home from travel or exile in a foreign land.

What I understood from this particular passage in Mark's gospel was that in priestly ministry, as in all other forms of ministry in the Church, one may not be warmly welcomed and sometimes one may experience total rejection. The important thing, according to Jesus, was to leave the past behind by shaking the dust of rejection and then move ahead with clean feet and fresh faith to the mission of announcing the reign of God. The ultimate priority for a Christian and for a priest should always be the Kingdom of Heaven.

Life, they say, is about correcting mistakes and learning from them. When you fall don't focus on the place where you fell, instead see the place from where you slipped so you can pick yourself up and move on with your life. Rather than fret over a failure or disappointment, Jesus was asking me to pick myself up, dust myself off and start all over again.

Shaking the dust caused by the rejection I experienced at the hands of my Bishop meant that I needed to revisit the meaning and the identity of the Catholic priesthood. When married couples begin to have problems, they need to go back to their wedding day, their marriage vows and most importantly, to the reasons that brought them together in the first place. I had to return to what was essential in becoming a priest.

Of course as the documents of the Second Vatican Council remind us, the Bishops, in as much as they are the successors of the Apostles, have a share in the fullness of the priesthood, and the clergy are helpers of the Bishops in the mission of the Church. But I also gathered from the 1971 document of the

Synod of Bishops, called 'De Sacerdotio Ministeriali' that priests find their identity to the extent that they fully live the mission of the Church and exercise it in different ways in communion not only with their Bishops but also with the People of God.

The purpose of priestly ministry is to serve the entire pilgrim Church, which is the family of God. I realized that I should stay on course with the mission of Jesus himself in and through his Church by helping the pilgrim people of God to arrive at their heavenly destination by sharing fully and living totally in the mystery of God.

I vigorously shook the dust from my feet when I understood that the priest's first task is to proclaim the Word of God. I decided not to take the Bishop's rejection of my plans personally but to keep my eyes on what is essential to the mission and identity of priesthood.

*****

The only reason why I looked back was to ask myself how this priesthood vocation journey began for me in the first place. Why did I choose to become a priest? Did I choose this vocation or did God choose me? Perhaps if you know where you've come from, this realization may help direct your path towards the future and also help to confront the obstacles on your onward journey.

I recalled that I had decided to become a diocesan priest, as opposed to joining a religious order, because of the strong, early influence of my childhood parish priests and priests at my parochial school. At the tender age of sixteen, I was not aware of other choices.

The only fleeting idea I once had was to check out the Jesuits. At Andheri, Bombay, there was a Jesuit novitiate or Jesuit formation house up on a hill. At that time the famous Fr. Anthony De Mello, S.J., was the Rector of the novitiate. Fr. De Mello became quite popular as a speaker and retreat preacher in the United States and some other English-speaking countries. Like Thomas Merton, he, too, wrote books that blended Catholic and Buddhist teachings. He was famous for his Zen meditation stories. He died rather young on his way to conducting a retreat in the

United States. After his death he came to the attention of the doctrinal watchdog Holy Office of the Vatican because of his controversial writings.

I had a very honest and straightforward conversation with Fr. De Mello regarding my vocation to the priesthood. I told him that I had doubts whether God wanted me to become a Jesuit instead of a diocesan priest. His response was blunt: "If you have any doubts, then God does not want you to be a Jesuit." In one sense I am thankful to Fr. De Mello because he enabled me to enter the diocesan seminary without any doubts or hesitations.

Somehow, in those early years, I was under the impression that belonging to a religious order meant having a rigid and rigorous community life with the added burden of total, blind obedience. In a parallel sense, the diocesan priesthood, where the priest has to deal only with his Bishop, appeared to be a way of life more open to dialog and growth.

Already a few months after ordination, I was shocked into reality. It seemed like dialog in the diocesan priesthood was not an option.

Fr. Edward Hays, a poet, artist and author of many books on prayer and spirituality, opened my eyes to the beauty and power of the life of a diocesan priest. Being a diocesan priest himself, he remembered the time when priests who were not members of religious orders, like, for instance, the Jesuits, Franciscans and Dominicans, were called 'secular,' or worldly. To some the term secular seemed diminishing, so they came to be called diocesan priests.

Fr. Hays hails the notion of being a secular, or worldly, priest. He views the world as the domain of the Spirit, and says that Catholic Christians, believers in the Incarnation, should be especially worldly people. There was a time in the early Church, when hermits and 'religious' people fled the world and escaped into the deserts and forests. But if God chose to enter our world as a human being, in Jesus Christ, God has made our world into a place of encounter between the human and the divine.

The main task of a diocesan, secular priest is to help people sense and connect with the divine mystery that is within us and around us in this world.

As a young, secular priest from America Fr. Hays found something lacking in his interior prayer life. With the support and permission of his Archbishop he went to India to learn how to pray again. With an interpreter, he visited Hindu holy men living in caves at the base of the Himalayas.

On one occasion he met a Hindu holy man sitting silently in a cave. He had taken a vow of silence for over forty years. Fr. Hays wrote this question on a slate: "Have you ever seen God?" The holy man wrote his reply: "Yes, several times." Then Fr. Hays asked: "What is necessary to see God?" The Hindu monk grabbed the slate again and wrote: "You must have a pure heart."

For Fr. Hays that was an epiphany. He remembered that those were the same words that Jesus said proclaiming the beatitudes during his sermon on the mount: "Blessed are the pure of heart, for they shall see God."

Fr. Hays returned from his spiritual search in the Himalayas with a strong conviction about priestly ministry, which has inspired my own life as a priest. He has enabled me to look at priestly ministry as a dream worth giving your life for, even though you don't know how it is going to end.

That explains why you can continue to be happy and to love being a priest, even when disappointments and disillusionments come your way.

The pain of rejection was my fall in imitation of Jesus carrying his Cross on the road to Calvary. I needed to do what Jesus did: pick up the broken pieces of your life and move on. Never give up. Jesus himself fell three or more times on the Way of the Cross, and I'm sure that to rise each time was more difficult than the time before.

The correspondence with my Bishop regarding continuing education appeared to be my first fall on the journey of priesthood. In the rest of my life, there would be other weak moments that would make me fall and collapse on my priestly journey of faith. But the wisdom that you acquire from an earlier experience prepares you for similar and related challenges in the future.

As one reads in the concentration camp of Dachau, Germany: "One who does not learn from the past is condemned to repeat it." The ultimate goal as it is expressed in several languages in Dachau regarding the holocaust is: "Never Again."

The important thing was for me to get up and to move on and more importantly never to give up.

*****

So with renewed courage I accepted my first regular parish assignment as Parochial Vicar of St. Ignatius Church. I was very happy.

This parish was located in the heart of the crowded city of Bombay. There was a roundabout close to the church with seven exits. So this area came to be known as 'Sath Raasta' or 'Seven Roads.'

The parishioners were simple and devout. It was a poor community, and it was the intention of the Archdiocese that a young priest, especially one who had studied abroad, should get his feet wet from the very beginning of his ministry in poor, needy surroundings.

As Mother Superior, Blessed Mother Teresa of Calcutta would follow the same process with the nuns she would send abroad for ongoing education and formation. She did not want their higher education and degrees to go to their heads.

Assignments were given to clergy without any fanfare or discussions. You were summoned to Archbishop's House, where in a large room with several other anxious and nervous priests, you waited for your name to be called. Then you entered a cavernous room with a very high ceiling and sparse décor where the Archbishop would be seated behind a large desk in his impeccable white cassock. He would say 'hello' to you, and then give you your assignment while you were still standing at a distance. Then you approached him and kissed his ring like you would a mafia boss and then left to pack your meager belongings in order to report for duty and service at your new assignment the following day. Clergy assignments in those days were quick, cold, impersonal and undemocratic.

Today's assignment process has come a long way from those dark ages. Every year you are asked to do a self-evaluation, which is then passed on to members of the personnel board. This is an advisory board to the bishop that is comprised of pastors, associates and other chancery personnel. Before a pastor's assignment is made there is a parish consultation to find out the challenges and strengths of a parish community that is in need of a new pastor. Then it is the task of the personnel board to match the best skilled priest that is available to the needs of the parish community.

During the consultation process it appears that every parish dreams of getting Jesus himself as their new incoming Pastor!

Even after this current lengthy process, a priest is asked whether he is willing to take on the new assignment. Only after he agrees, a recommendation is made by the personnel board to the bishop, who gives his approval and his blessing. The priest is informed that the bishop has agreed to his assignment, and then he has still a couple of months to work through the transition before he shows up at the new rectory for duty as a parish priest. The assignment of Parochial Vicars is less complicated. A pastor is asked whether he will accept a certain priest as his associate, and the associate is also asked whether he would be willing to go to a certain parish. When both agree, the Bishop is informed and the assignment letter is sent to both the associate and to his new pastor.

The process is still simpler today because not every priest has the calling to take on the responsibilities of pastor, and there are not too many associates to choose from when a parish expresses a need for one or when a parish is financially able to accept a second or third priest.

Sometimes, through pastoral experience and previous assignments, a priest understands that he is not the only one who is making a transition. His community, too, is going through a process of deeply felt emotions and an experience of death and dying. Such a priest will be sensitive to the transition process affecting him and his parish community. Not only will he deal with his own process but will also help his parish community grow spiritually from the experience of transition of pastors and associates.

*****

Now back to the 'Seven Roads' parish. Surrounded by poverty, I focused my ministry like the good sisters of Blessed Mother Teresa of Calcutta on the poorest of the poor. There was a playground a good distance from the church called Vallabhbhai Patel Stadium. Behind these grounds could be found several pockets of slums. The city sewage flowed through these open spaces along the stadium; and right next to all the unbearable and unhealthy stinking sewage, many families, including my own parishioners, had their miserable shanty dwellings.

This makeshift, temporary housing was created out of corrugated metal sheets that made it a living hell in the hot sun of the tropics. But it provided some shelter at night for these poor families, and especially from the monsoon rains.

My first trip to these slum dwellings was a pastoral visit to the families to get to know my parishioners. I already had one great experience under my belt when I visited the slums of '*Golibar*' as a deacon in the parish of Sacred Heart in Santa Cruz.

Once again I was reminded that no life experience is isolated or useless. Every human experience prepares us for similar or more complex and challenging events later in life.

Every moment lived in the here and now is a learning experience for life.

The families were happy to see me and welcomed me warmly into their sparse living quarters. Often, I would be asked to sit on the only available chair in the house and offered, as a sign of hospitality and goodwill, any drink available at that moment. Sometimes I would get a glass of milk, at other times a cup of tea or coffee. Usually, I would be given a plain glass of water to drink. Even though it wasn't the safest drinking water, not accepting it would be an insult to the family.

I realized that these poor people needed a lot of help to have any experience or semblance of human dignity. I remembered the scene in the gospels where Jesus looks at the crowds following him for days and his heart is moved with pity and compassion for them because they were like sheep without a shepherd. The help these families needed was both spiritual and material.

In one of my trips to Germany as a seminarian, I had met two gentlemen, one a businessman and the other an eye doctor. Both had offered to help me if I ever got involved in a project of helping the poor in India. I contacted my German friends and described the situation of these slums to them. I asked them whether they would be willing to help. They offered me their full and unconditional support.

In the beginning, our poor parishioners in these slums simply wanted to clean and improve the front common gathering area where there was a huge wooden Cross. This was their own public prayer space, just as the Hindus had their own small temple for worship and prayer, and the Muslims their own little mosque. It was a reasonable project, and we fixed the area very quickly with everyone's help and soon celebrated the first Mass at the foot of the Cross. There was an immediate sense of pride and joy in the entire community. After the Mass, the whole neighborhood was invited. There was music and spicy snacks for everyone to enjoy.

My German friends were not interested in the religious life of these slum dwellers. The work of cleaning around the Cross was done by the people themselves. Any changes or modifications were paid for by the slum inhabitants. Even though these people were so poor and urgently needed a lot of help, what really mattered to them was their faith and how to celebrate it. They were truly detached from the things of this world.

In Matthew's gospel, the first beatitude says: "Blessed are the poor in spirit, the Kingdom of heaven is theirs." The word 'blessed' in the beatitudes can also be translated as 'happy.' No wonder the children and the families here always appeared to be happy and smiling. The poor do not have the anxiety the rich have to protect their wealth and manage their finances. If you have very little or nothing, all you can do is trust more fully in God.

My German benefactors had bigger plans for this slum area. With my help, they wanted to improve the housing and the living conditions of these poor people. They were willing to provide the necessary funding for construction of family dwellings. I called a meeting of all the adult slum dwellers. For the first time they were able to meet and welcome these blond

Germans. There was a great deal of excitement at shaking hands and touching these generous foreigners and at the prospect of improved housing and living conditions. The 'town hall' meeting appropriately took place at the foot of the Cross.

These poor people wanted the Cross area for worship, decent living quarters for eating and sleeping but definitely no bathrooms or toilets in the house. They were surrounded night and day by raw sewage, so they preferred to have cleaner separate public toilets rather than have facilities so close to their kitchens and their beds. At first my German friends could not understand why these families did not want self-contained homes, complete with kitchen, bedroom and bathrooms. Only when they saw for themselves the miserable and filthy surroundings in which these poor families lived each day, they were able to separate need from want.

At this stage, an aspect of Indian life reappeared and exposed its ugly head. I was once again troubled and concerned: it was the widespread use of bribes to get construction permits and other approvals from the city municipality officials. In Indian society, almost in every public domain, there is a hierarchy of workers. To get to the top in order to procure needed permits, one is required to bribe every level of peons, secretaries and minor officials along the way. This was frustrating to me, especially because of the nature of our work: to help the poorest of the poor. But people in India were so used to this corrupt way of life that no one seemed to bat an eyelid when it came to bribes. I finally realized, grudgingly, that I had to work within the system or simply abandon any hope of doing some good among and for the poor.

Several months after we began the construction project, we had the grand opening celebration of twenty five decent dwellings. We sang and danced for joy. Everyone loves a good party and the poor don't need a whole lot to show their appreciation and express their joy. I was treated like a hero.

More than anything, I realized that a priest is a shepherd who is called to tend to the needs of his flock. He needs to energize their souls by restoring their hope and their human dignity. Christ, who became human and poor, was present that day not only in that symbolic Cross, but also in the hearts of the poor who took ownership of their new dwellings with a sense of pride. They were not palaces, but they were definitely a huge step up from the mangers of Bethlehem and the shanty slums of Bombay.

Sometimes, in one's entire life, just one important task, joyfully completed, can become a metaphor and paradigm of fulfillment. Such was the contentment that came to me from the completion of this slum rehabilitation project. I was ready to appear at the judgment seat of God and hear the words from the twenty-fifth Chapter of Matthew's gospel: "Whatsoever you did to the least of my brothers and sisters, you did it for me."

Jesus reminded his disciples that "the poor you will always have with you." That does not mean that we can neglect the poor because we cannot eradicate poverty. It simply means that we ought to do everything we can, with persistent perseverance, to restore the dignity of all needy human beings. Each one of us needs to do our part, however small and insignificant it might appear to be.

Our task as Christians is to show up and to show that we care.

Persistent perseverance means that we acknowledge that hunger, for instance, may never disappear from the world in our lifetime, yet we still need to do all we can and consistently, to eradicate hunger, homelessness, abuse, discrimination, prejudice, slavery and other anti-human and immoral issues of our world one situation at a time however small and insignificant.

The story is told of a little kid who was bothering his father for attention while at work. So to keep him occupied, the father gave his son hundreds of pieces of a puzzle of all the countries of the world to put together. The man thought that he would be left alone to work in peace for a very long time. But the son surprised his father by finishing the puzzle in a very short time. When asked how he had done it, the son said that on the other side of the puzzle were pieces with the image of a man. By putting together one human being, the whole world was put in place.

Any personal or communitarian rehabilitation endeavor calls for a well structured follow up. The problem with India and many Third World nations is not the lack of goodwill and creative endeavors, but the dire need for follow up and funds for future maintenance. New high-rise, impressive buildings, for instance, are built quickly with shoddy materials that get totally damaged with the monsoon rains that follow. Earthquakes may cause more damage and take more lives in poorer Third World countries than elsewhere in the world, where fortunately long term safety and maintenance plans are put into place.

While we were in the construction phase, I noticed that the Sisters from the religious community of Blessed Mother Teresa of Calcutta often visited our slum families. When the project was complete and the festivities ended, I asked the Sisters to provide ongoing health care and religious instruction to these families and their children. Whatever money was left over from the generosity of our German benefactors, I handed it over to the leaders for ongoing maintenance of the Cross and the new houses.

The word 'Eucharist' means Thanksgiving. We had much to be grateful for. From time to time I had celebrated the Eucharist with the entire slum community and truly gave thanks for all the wonderful things God had done in our midst. Our final celebration of Eucharist at the foot of the Cross was truly a climax celebration of the Paschal Mystery, our community rehabilitation work immersed in the Passion, Death and Resurrection of Jesus, Emmanuel, God-with-us.

I remembered Jesus going back to Nazareth, as the Scriptures remind us, where he had been brought up and as usual he went to the Synagogue on the Sabbath. When he stood up to read, he was given the book of the prophet Isaiah. He opened it and read: "The Spirit of the Lord is upon me, because he has chosen me to give the good news to the poor."

If a priest by Ordination is another Christ, an 'Alter Christus,' then his first and most important task is to work among the poor and to bring them hope by sharing the Good News with them. In Mark's gospel, Chapter 10:45, we are reminded that "the Son of Man did not come to be served but to serve and to give his life as a ransom for many."

I'm glad God gave me this opportunity to make the presence of Jesus known and felt in an obscure slum of Bombay.

*****

My first assignment lasted only a year. The following year I was sent to a wealthy suburban parish of Bombay called St. Andrew where I spent the next five years of my priesthood.

Every assignment has its share of challenges and blessings. If what I took away from my first short assignment were my shepherding of the poor in the slums and celebrating the sacraments and the mysteries of our faith, this second assignment would give me the unique experience of priestly collaboration, fraternity and team work.

We were five priests living in the rectory: the pastor, the school principal and three associates. From the very beginning we were like the five fingers of one well fitting glove. We worked so well together that we became the model of priestly ministry for the whole Archdiocese.

What this team work established for me was the effective combination of the social and the spiritual in a priest's life and in the life of a Catholic parish. Parish life is the religious commitment of a community of disciples and the family of baptized Christians. The life of a parish is wholesome when people not only pray together but they also enjoy one another, work together and love each other.

A priest is both a spiritual guide and a community leader. Whenever we had social gatherings in the parish like the one called "Parents Day," all the five of us clergy joined in and helped with the fun theatrical productions. We sang and danced with the parish families and for the entertainment of all. We were always ready and willing to make fools of ourselves for the greater good.

There was a very popular Bollywood movie called, *"Amar, Akbar, Anthony."* These were three common and popular names representing the three major religions in India: Hinduism, Islam and Christianity. When the three associates, including myself, came on stage mimicking these movie stars and the three religions, the people simply could not control their laughter.

Because of the friendly, welcoming atmosphere of this parish, many youth would spend their evenings on the church grounds. They would inform their parents that they were going to church and that's where they would hang out with their friends and with their priests.

One huge successful community building venture in this parish was known as the "Zonal Talent Show." The parish was divided into four zones, and each zone had to come up with local parishioner talent in singing, dancing and dramatic plays. The four zones of the parish would compete with each other for bragging rights to see which was more talented. The final day of performances and competition was always the highlight of the parish's calendar of events. The competitive spirit of this annual Talent Show simply heightened the quality of the performances. What was truly amazing was the outpouring of talent from ordinary parishioners of all ages, who gave of their very best, and the sense of community and unity the show created in the parish.

Truly, as St. Paul reminds us in his Letter to the Corinthians, together we are the one body of Christ. There are many parts in the body, each one important to the others and each one needing the others. When one part suffers, all suffer. When one part rejoices, all share in the happiness. We are all blessed with many unique gifts. The purpose of these gifts is to build up the community of the body of Christ.

What a joy for me to see the Word of God come alive in the community and among the priests of this dynamic parish.

Every parish is like a live cell in the worldwide body of Christ. Just as cells need blood and oxygen to survive and to thrive, so also do parish communities in the universal Catholic Church. The sustenance and nourishment of parish life are spiritual and social activities. If the preaching, the music and the sacramental celebrations are of high quality, and the parishioners find opportunities to socialize and have fellowship with other worshippers, the entire parish becomes vibrant and filled with spirit and life. Other people begin to hear about such a lively community and they flock to every advertised event.

Tertullian, a church father of the third century reported how pagans described the Christians among them: "See how they love one another."

Within a year of being planted in this wealthy, vibrant, suburban parish community, I began to blossom as a priest and as a human being. I thrive on other people's energy. While celebrating Mass, for instance, I may start out feeling a bit down at the beginning, but soon the presence and the participation of the assembly before me lift up my spirits and I come alive.

In this second assignment there were many resources available for the social and spiritual growth of the many families in the parish. Their enthusiasm positively affected my priestly ministry and my social skills.

I was soon involved in a major multi-media youth production called 'Shadow of the Son.' It was a religious, multi-media, theatrical show complete with singing, slides, acting and audience participation. I played the role of Jesus Christ, with my friend Tony as my understudy. Together we put on almost fifty shows to full houses.

Since it was theater in the round, the actors had to walk among the audience, who sat on the floor everywhere in this compact parish hall. Many in the audience were moved to tears feeling the pain of Jesus in the Garden of Gethsemane. But with the grand finale of the Risen Savior entering the hall with white, sequined and glistening robes came the delightful 'oohs' and 'aahs', especially from the children. They would joyfully touch my robes as I passed by, truly sensing the difference between the earlier suffering Christ on the Cross and now the glorious Savior of the Resurrection.

I did my best to stay in character till the end of every show. The show impressed the audience and deeply affected my faith life. I truly had to understand who Jesus was for me in order to effectively be the presence and the power of Jesus for others.

This was the one and only time I grew a natural beard for about six months. Since my understudy was slim with a bony structure, and I had a full figure with enough flesh to cover my bones, he was referred to as the suffering Jesus of the Cross, while I was known as the well-fed Jesus of the wedding at Cana in Galilee.

Besides acting, singing and playing the guitar I also began to get involved in the Charismatic movement. This form of prayer and worship was first made popular by the Pentecostals and then adopted into mainline Christian denominations, including the Catholic Church.

As a young novice priest I began to see how the life of the Church is enriched by a variety of spiritualities. I believe that the Holy Spirit works in many ways to enable and help human beings to pray and deepen their spiritual life.

In the history of the Church, there have been inspiring saints who have developed special gifts and spiritualities that have enriched the whole Church.

The Franciscan spirituality involves people with simplicity of lifestyle and service to the poor, while the Dominicans use their talents to preach effectively the Word of God. The Jesuits have immersed themselves in the field of education, while the Sisters of Blessed Teresa of Calcutta reach out to the poorest of the poor.

As a parish or diocesan priest my vocation and gift have been to work in the front line, where people live daily their call to holiness. In the busyness of everyday living, I am called to enable people to hear the voice of God and the promptings of the Holy Spirit. I try to help people see the Paschal Mystery in their own daily experiences of dying and rising.

What I have stated in the paragraph above in summary form is my spirituality as a diocesan parish priest. It directs and inspires what I do and how I live.

One size does not fit all, so I stayed open to the many ways in which the Holy Spirit could open the hearts of modern men and women to their spiritual purpose and goal. Through the Charismatic movement, I found I could help people express joyfully, with the help of music and gestures, the life of the Spirit within them. This was a dynamic form of prayer more suited to my own personality. People who gathered for Charismatic prayer lifted their hands more, sang joyfully, shared deeply in the Scriptures and prayed often in tongues. New words were coming into church vocabulary, like 'Healing Masses,' 'Gifts of the Holy Spirit,' 'Praying in Tongues' and the notion of being 'Slain in the Spirit.'

This style of prayer affected my priestly ministry. In the beginning of my pastoral work in parishes, I would just mumble the prayers and sacramental words under my breath, as if I did not strongly believe in their power to heal and to communicate the grace of God. But now, thanks to the Charismatic Prayer Movement, I was not afraid or embarrassed. I would proclaim aloud the prayers at every celebration. I was a new man, a courageous, faith-filled priest.

There can be sometimes a lighter side to every sacred ritual and celebration. In one parish where I was celebrating a Mass of healing in Charismatic style of prayer, several people approached the altar for hands-on healing and then lay on the floor as they were 'slain in the Spirit.' Some migrant, Hindu and Muslim poor workers from a nearby construction site walked into our open church and curiously looked around as parishioners were falling down and lying on the floor on all sides of the altar. These workers decided to join the 'party' and walked up to the altar area and lay down quietly next to the ones 'slain in the Spirit.'

I was part of a team of four young people, who were invited to conduct Charismatic retreats and 'Life in the Spirit' seminars all over India. When I was studying in Rome, I was made to believe that I was an ambassador for my country, but, in reality, I knew very little about India. People in Europe asked me a lot of questions about my country and my culture. In my youth my family regularly visited and vacationed exclusively at the farm of my maternal grandparents, so I was ignorant about the rest of India. That changed radically for me when our Charismatic team traveled to preach and facilitate retreats in many parts of India. We would spend a few extra days either before or after the retreat-seminar and, with the guidance of our hosts and other local people we would visit as much as we could places of interest in that area of the country.

I realized how big, complex, and mysterious the Indian sub-continent really was!

*****

In the Charismatic movement, my gifts were in celebrating the sacraments, in teaching and in singing. One year a team of Catholic American Charismatic healers came to Bombay to lead a healing convention. Francis MacNutt, who was then a Dominican priest, was the leader of the team, which included the famous Jesuit Linn brothers, and several well known Charismatic healers from the United States. My ability to sing and play the guitar had made me a popular priest in Bombay and thus I was chosen to spearhead the Music Ministry at this national Catholic healing convention.

About 20,000 people came to the convention from all parts of the country. It was a powerful experience of prayer, healing and grace. During the four-day convention, I had my own personal experience of healing. Even though I loved to sing, my throat was perhaps the weakest part of my anatomy. In the singing itself of healing songs, I experienced the healing touch of God, which enabled me to sing for hours without being tired or hoarse.

My personal healing made me realize that there is direct power in prayers and sacraments. In Baptism we are cleansed from original sin; in Reconciliation we are truly forgiven; in the Anointing of the sick we are healed in the way God wants us to be made whole; in Confirmation we are filled with the gifts and fruits of the Holy Spirit; and in the Eucharist, we are truly fed and strengthened by the Body and the Blood of Christ. In the sacraments of service, namely, Priesthood and Matrimony, the priest and the married couple become the sign and sacrament of Christ's presence in the world, called to serve and to proclaim the kingdom of God.

For those who believe and can see with the eyes of faith, God's Spirit is always at work. During the convention, I felt God's Spirit was opening a door for me and preparing the way for a major transition in my life.

Among the American healing team members there was a visiting Dominican Provincial who came from Rome. We became good friends. Although I had lived and studied in Europe for five years, I never had the opportunity to visit the United States of America. One day I asked this Provincial whether he could help me find a summer ministry position in a parish in the United States. He told me that he was raised in the Boston area and that the Pastor of his family parish would definitely be looking for priestly help in the summer months. He made the necessary contacts for me to help out six weeks in a parish in the Boston Archdiocese.

The very first Catholic community I was going to visit in the United States was Sacred Heart Parish. As a deacon returning from Rome, coincidentally, the very first parish of ministry for me in India was also Sacred Heart. Later on when I would make a permanent decision to live and work in the United States, the first parish I would be sent to would be none other than, you've guessed it, Sacred Heart!

The Sacred Heart of Jesus is the symbol of God's real, incarnational love for us. God is love and we believe that we are made in the image and likeness of God. Therefore the purpose of our lives is to love and to be loved. The Sacred Heart reminds us of this reality. And as a priest I am called to preach and live this reality in season and out of season. My ministry and priesthood have been nurtured and nourished in the loving Sacred Heart of Jesus.

That summer I flew directly from Bombay for the first time to the United States. It cannot be compared to my very first flight several years earlier to Rome as an inexperienced teenager and seminarian. But the leap into the unknown and the desire for discovery and adventure were still the same. It was a very long, tiring flight. Even though I was gaining several hours flying west yet I was in the air for almost twenty-four hours. I had ten more years of priestly experience and maturity since the first flight to Italy, but the same sense of adventure and excitement at rediscovering 'the new world' of Christopher Columbus.

I arrived in Boston where I was met by the enthusiastic parish secretary. She had never met anyone from India before and was so excited to welcome me to the United States that she decided to show me almost all the highlights of historical Boston that very first day. Since I had flown for almost twenty-four hours through different time zones, as we breezed through the beautiful, historical and cultural city of Boston, I did not know whether I was coming or going. The good thing about flying to the United States was the English language we shared in common. We could understand each other (well, almost, because Americans from Boston and Indians from Bombay have unique accents) even though I hadn't the foggiest idea where I was. I had arrived in Boston on a Friday afternoon, so my first weekend of church services followed immediately. I celebrated the Masses and preached with great enthusiasm and, in my heart, felt right away that I belonged here.

For some strange inexplicable reason it felt like I had come home.

On Sunday night when I went to bed, I was out like a light when my head touched the pillow. I thought I was still dreaming when I heard in the distance some loud knocks on my bedroom door, with a desperate voice asking, "Are you okay? Are you alive?" Jet lag had caught up to me, and I had slept soundly for a whole twelve hours. The Rectory housekeeper was afraid something drastic had happened to their foreign visitor.

This parish in the suburbs of the city of Boston had two priests, both of them in their late fifties or early sixties. The Pastor was jovial and kindhearted. He tried to impress me with a delicious prime rib dinner, which, unfortunately, ended up being too well done, almost black and burnt. We laughed about it. The Associate Pastor had a short temper and seemed to get upset very easily. During his Mass on my first weekend at the parish, I wanted to observe how things were done or celebrated liturgically in America. So I stood in the back of the church behind the glass doors sometimes pacing back and forth, which distracted and upset him.

There is much we can learn from dealing with difficult people. They do have valuable lessons to teach you, only if you are willing to go beyond your personal hurt and humiliation. I learnt from this Associate that during prayer and liturgy it is very important to be still. Unless there is an emergency, no liturgical minister, much less a priest, should be moving about and distracting the prayer of the community.

In the end, they were both helpful guides for me, in their own unique ways, to my understanding of the Church in the United States.

One of my earliest cultural shocks was to learn that the Associate Pastor had a sibling who was divorced. In my ignorance of life in America I could not imagine how family members of a Catholic priest could even entertain the thought of divorce. Divorce for me happened on television or to Hollywood celebrities, not in real life, and especially not to family members of clergy.

This experience took me back to how I felt when I heard of the first seminarian in Bombay who had left the seminary and the first priest in Rome who had left the priesthood. Such things were never meant to happen in my Catholic Church.

When you are young you tend to live in a perfect, ideal world. These bubbles of perfection and idealism were quickly being burst as I traveled and lived around the globe.

Travel opens you up to the height, the breadth and the profound depths of human reality, both its weaknesses as well as its strengths. Travel helps you understand that there is a bigger reality than just your own personal world. Travel can help you mature as a human being by confronting you with opposites, with differences, with contradictions and with a sense of mystery. You begin to see others as either similar to you, or to understand why others are different from you. The world is a much bigger place and houses all kinds of characters and situations. In such a world, diversity and complexity are commonplace.

Until I traveled to the United States, I did not realize that there were so many Christian denominations in the world. In India I was only familiar with Catholicism and perhaps a touch of Anglicanism because of the limited religious influence of the British. If there were so many ways of being Christian, would there not also be room in the Catholic Church for diversity and differences? When one has never traveled or read a variety of books, pluralism in society can seem to be very threatening and scary.

In the college seminary of Rome I discovered that all the cultures surrounding me were really a part of my own humanity waiting to be discovered and opened like a treasure chest. Now my exposure to life and religion in America made me more tolerant of others and accepting of diversity.

The parishioners of my first American parish community of Sacred Heart were wonderful. For Catholics, the Sacred Heart of Jesus is a symbol of Christ's bleeding and sacrificial love for all humanity. The people, young and old, of the Sacred Heart parish took me into their hearts and into their homes. They knew that it was my first visit to the United States and they wanted to make it memorable for me.

Some of them introduced me to a youth program called "TEC – To Encounter Christ." It was a powerful, weekend experience to share faith with young adults and to hear their faith stories.

At different times in her history, the Catholic Church seems to have neglected the needs of certain populations. In the beginning of the 20th century, it was workers who did not get the attention they deserved. In the latter part of the 20th century, young adults from the ages of eighteen to thirty-five felt a lack of belonging to the Church. The To Encounter Christ weekend truly responded to the faith and the world of young adults. I had such a good experience on my weekend, especially because I was a young adult like all the other participants that I ended up being on team as the Spiritual Director and, eventually, introducing upon my return this weekend program to young adults in Bombay, India.

Another prayerful and beautiful experience on the east coast for me was to visit the Western Priory Benedictine Monks. They had some of the most moving and inspirational music I had ever heard. Since 'Work' and 'Prayer' are the two oars of the boat of monastic life, these monks would return from working in the fields, and then, still in their work clothes, would sing and chant the Vespers or Evening Prayer. Visitors like me were allowed to join them for prayer. I began to understand how work can be a part of prayer and how prayer can make work meaningful. Thus the whole day is sanctified and God is glorified in everything. This beautiful setting of the Western Priory and the singing of the monks touched the contemplative side of my soul. I felt a deep sense of peace and inner joy. I was very fortunate, after Vespers, to be introduced to the two monks who had composed most of their beautiful music.

It was my interest in music ministry that had led me to the shores of America. I learned that when one is awakened to certain interests in life, echoes of that harmony continue like ripples to be felt and found all through the journey of life.

Six weeks of summer come to an end very quickly when you are 'having fun' and enjoying, as in my case, ministry and people. On my last day, at the end of my final Mass in Boston,

I was astonished when I got a standing ovation from the entire congregation. Someone even said later that I could easily have stood for Mayor of Boston and won the election hands down with so much popular support!

I left Boston thinking I would never again have a chance to return. But a door had opened in my life, and the Holy Spirit was going to take over if I was willing to listen and obey. I asked myself if and when the time came would I be able to say like Samuel in the Hebrew Testament: "Speak, Lord, your servant is listening"?

*****

My traveling days were definitely not over. Since my youngest sister had become a flight attendant, she decided to treat my parents to a trip across Europe. While I was still in Boston, my parents and my youngest sister first flew to Scotland to spend a few days with the family of my eldest sister. Then, after traveling to London, they flew to Frankfurt, where I was expected to meet them after I left Boston. In Germany I introduced my family to all the wonderful people I had got to know in Reinsfeld and Hermeskeil.

It is not often that others, including family members, have a chance to experience what you have lived and have only communicated in the past to them through postcards and photographs. I felt the joy of my parents as I took them to all the familiar sights, people and places of my past. In some ways I was reliving my time and experiences in Europe through the eyes of my parents.

I was ordained a deacon in Germany in 1975, and now as a priest, a few years later, accompanied by a part of my family I was able to celebrate the Eucharist on German soil in the German language. At St. Remigius church in Reinsfeld, standing at the altar with my parents, it was the completion of one of those circles of life that I have come to recognize so frequently on my spiritual journey.

From Germany we took the train to France and then to Switzerland. After spending the weekend there with friends we traveled to Italy, ending in Rome. When traveling we find interesting and unusual associations with places and people. In Germany, while visiting some friends who owned a bar, my dad was asked whether he wanted some whiskey to drink. In India my dad often enjoyed a stiff cocktail before dinner, so he happily welcomed the thought of a Scotch and soda. When he saw my friend who was a bartender pouring just one measured shot of whiskey, my dad turned to me and said in Konkani: "Why is the man dirtying the glass?" Needless to say, I did not translate that query to our hosts. Traveling through France, my parents were reminded of the open, green countryside of Mangalore, where they were both raised. In Switzerland, my parents felt privileged to visit the country where Charlie Chaplin spent the last years of his life. We never know what we are going to be reminded of or what memories are going to be evoked in our travels.

For three full days in Rome my parents experienced in a concise and limited way a summary of my five-year Italian sojourn. They loved St. Peter's Basilica, and I took them to Castel Gandolfo, the summer residence of the Pope, where we were part of a crowded papal audience.

Another fascinating aspect of travel is the surprising possibility of running into people you have known and don't ever expect to see again in your life. At Castel Gandolfo, I met a Monsignor, who was an Irish priest studying in Rome when I was a seminarian student myself, and now here he was functioning as the personal assistant of the Pope. Later on, I found out that being appointed as the personal assistant to the next Pope as well he got ordained as bishop of a diocese in Ireland. When Pope John Paul I, also known as 'The Smiling September Pope,' (since his papacy lasted less than a month), died mysteriously, a fiction novel was written allegedly implicating six characters who worked in the Vatican at the time of the Pope's death. One of them was the Irish Monsignor!

My parents were not interested in any of this intriguing history or politics. What concerned them the most in Italy was that the Italians were eating food without the benefit of Indian spices. "How could anyone live this way?" they asked. I had my parents stay at a *'pensione'* run by nuns. After tasting the cooking of the Italian nuns, my parents simply could not imagine how I had survived on bland Italian seminary food for five years!

164

When my dad made his one and only trip to Europe, he was almost eighty years old. I was so happy to see him share my past and the places that he had indirectly said "Yes" to, without having ever experienced them in this personal way. If my dad had not asked me to pursue the call that God had given me, when I had doubts about it after the passing away of my eldest brother Charles, God alone knows what would have happened to my life and to my future.

Moreover, my dad had asked me not to worry and that God would provide. That's exactly what happened. God rewarded my dad's trust and took care of my family's needs.

That is what made my dad and my mom awesome in my sight. They were raised in small, unknown villages of Mangalore, India, and yet they always encouraged me to dream big and to see as much of the world as possible. My parents were not worldly, so I believe that this adventurous spirit they always had came from their lives of being faith-filled individuals, and their constant trust in God's providence and protection over their children.

Their impact on my life was simply exceptional and awe-inspiring.

In Rome I put my parents on a flight back to Bombay with wonderful memories of their first ever trip to Europe. My Dad returned with long sideburns and everybody thought he looked so good for his age. My youngest brother, who was only sixteen, then, went to pick them up at the airport. He was driving a car for the very first time.

Every event leaves a mark and has an effect in our lives. In a few years, my youngest brother would be the next sibling to leave Bombay and join me in the United States of America.

*****

After waving goodbye to my parents in Rome, I returned to Northern Italy to visit the friends I made when I was studying in Italy. I first went to Cremona to see Mirella and Giovanna, the very first Italian girls I had come to be friends with when I was on vacation in Northern Italy at 'Ponte di Legno' (The Wooden Bridge) with other seminarians. Through our correspondence they knew that I was a seminarian and they had even made the journey to Reinsfeld, Germany, when I was ordained a deacon there.

I am glad we stayed in touch because wholesome and healthy friendships are so important and precious in one's life and journey especially in the life and calling of the priesthood. A Catholic priest is called to celibacy but not to a life of isolation and loneliness.

I stayed with Mirella and her mother. At their home I experienced Italian warmth and hospitality at their finest. When we were seminarians in Rome, we got some opportunities to meet Italian families, but we never stayed with them. Even the food we ate in those days was prepared by simple nuns from Bergamo, Italy, who were familiar with only two major spices: salt and pepper. No wonder my parents thought that all Italian food was bland and lacked flavor. But that was not the case with Mirella's mom's cooking. Italian food is delicious as long as you don't have to eat it in a Catholic seminary!

Mirella's home was on a street that ended in a square or 'piazza' called *'Fine Mondo'* (the end of the world). I laughed to myself realizing that for a lot of people who don't have the opportunity to travel, where they live day in and day out must appear to be the end of the world as they know it.

Later on I thought about a small town in California called 'Freedom.' The townspeople had once put up a sign at the end of the town which said: "Freedom Ends Here." The neighboring town was not amused, so the sign disappeared.

From the end of the world which was Mirella's home, I went to visit my friend Mario in Bergamo, which is also a beautiful historic city in Northern Italy. Mario was my classmate in Rome and sat next to me during our boring philosophy lectures. He kept me awake and entertained, with his smiling, impish eyes and Italian sense of humor. He also taught me to drive on the crowded, impossible streets of Rome. He was too emotional to live the disciplined life of a religious. So, he left the religious order he had joined and went back to his hometown of Bergamo to artistically paint houses (his occupation) and to marry his childhood sweetheart, Margherita (his passion).

Mario also happened to be the nephew of the brother of good, Blessed Pope John XXIII, the elderly 'transitional' Pope who succumbed to the promptings of the Holy Spirit, and introduced the Second Vatican Council to the Church and to the whole world. He was the Pope who realized in the early sixties that it was not the Church that needed to change. It just happened that the world had changed so much and so fast that the Catholic Church had to move with the times and be ready to dialog with the modern world. 'Aggiornamento' became the rallying cry and task of the Second Vatican Council.

Good Pope John XXIII, like many other Popes who were not beatified or canonized, was in a sarcophagus below the Vatican in the tombs of the Popes when I was a seminarian in Rome. Later on when I visited Rome in the Jubilee Year, 2000, I was moved to tears to see the remains of the Pope in the main basilica of St. Peter's, under one of the side altars, after he was proclaimed 'Blessed' by the Catholic Church.

While visiting my friend Mario in Bergamo, he took me that first evening to meet the brother of Blessed Pope John XXIII. Mario's uncle was ninety-six years old and had a delightful sense of humor. He was happy to meet me and told me that he was only forty-eight years old – per leg! He went down to the basement cellar and brought us some good wine. He also imbibed a good deal with us that evening. The next day, I was told, this ninety-six year old Italian farmer was unable to attend a family wedding where he was expected because he had one too many with some young visitors the night before. I'm sure that Blessed Pope John XXIII, like his brother whom I met, must have also enjoyed a good glass of Italian wine in his days as a Vatican diplomat and the Patriarch of Venice. That's what makes saints so much like the rest of us.

As the saying goes, "There is no saint without a past and no sinner without a future."

When Pope John XXIII was asked how many people worked at the Vatican, he is reported to have said: "Half of them." When he went to bed at night, he would conclude his night prayers saying: "O God, I have worked all day. This is your Church. I am going to bed. Good night!"

How I wish all of us, especially priests, could pray like that every night!

*****

From Italy I returned to Bombay and I went back to parish life immediately. Travel affects people like no other experience in life. I came back with many new stories and memories to share of my six weeks in the United States and of my return journey to Europe as a priest.

But it wasn't very long before the inner turmoil surfaced again. Once more I began to feel like a fish out of water. The trip to Europe and the United States served only as a temporary distraction. The inner turmoil I experienced did not reveal any doubts about priesthood or about the effectiveness of priestly ministry. It was just the location where I was serving the people and exercising priesthood that bothered me and filled me with sadness. India still did not feel like home to me. I tried, unsuccessfully, to suppress this inner agitation and turmoil.

From my experience in Boston, I launched the young adult weekend called: "TEC – To Encounter Christ." In the Archdiocese of Bombay I received a lot of support from enthusiastic young adults and families. In starting this much needed young adult program I discovered that God had blessed me with strong skills of organizing and motivating people. Such a weekend as "TEC" was meant to be, would train and nurture potential leaders in the Church, who would be passionate about their Catholic faith. Even the Bishop was happy to support me in this venture.

Our weekends were packed with young adults who came to celebrate their faith. The structure of "TEC" called for several adults to witness to their faith in different areas of Church life and spirituality. Some of the topics dealt with the practice of religion, the sharing of faith, and the challenges of growing up in the Catholic Church. I had the gift of recognizing the talents of people and of inviting them to do something they were not used to or had never done in the past. This was to speak in public about faith issues and struggles in their own journey of faith. Such witness talks can be very powerful and are beneficial both to the ones who share their story as well as to those who come to search what God wants of them.

As a young priest I began to understand what kind of leader I really was becoming. I had a firm desire to empower others. Lao-Tzu once said that a true leader is one who can step aside at the right time and the people can then say we did these things ourselves. True leadership is not about who is appointed to a position of power, but who has the capability of motivating and empowering others to lead and to take over the reins of leadership when called upon by the community. After the Second Vatican Council Church ministry was being handled and run more and more by the laity, but due to the lack of empowerment, the Church still seemed to have a dearth of motivated, educated and self-starting leaders.

On any given "TEC" weekend, as many as eighteen lay people would be called upon to give talks and personal testimonies. Fifty to seventy-five young adults would register for each weekend experience. The more weekends we organized the more leaders emerged and the popularity of the program spread.

Basically, these weekends were making young people adults in their faith. When we are children, we are told what to believe. There is a sense of obligation about what we should believe and very little understanding of why we believe. As we become teenagers, we begin to question and challenge these beliefs. Mentors are very important at this stage to help teenagers with their questions, so that they are not misled by the allurements and distractions of this world. Finally, one hopes that after the questioning phase, young adults will be able to stand up for what they believe. Unfortunately, this is not always the case, because many children and teenagers do not carry their faith education into adulthood. Many adults remain puerile in their spiritual life and journey. That is why a "TEC" weekend was so crucial to young adults who had fortunately not wandered away and who were still interested in searching for the right faith foundation and direction in their lives.

On one "TEC" weekend I was talking with a young woman professor who was fascinated by how much I gave of myself for the success of these weekends and the energy and time that was needed to make them successful. After I shared my motivation, purpose and vision for organizing these weekends, she simply asked me, "You give so much of yourself to others. Who gives to you?"

The thought of thinking about me and my needs had never crossed my mind. In the minor seminary of Bombay, during the first intense six months of spirituality, we were constantly reminded that we were like soldiers of Christ on duty twenty-four hours a day; that we should jump out of bed each day at dawn as if our beds were on fire; and that a priest is never on vacation from priestly ministry and always on duty, twenty four hours a day, seven days a week.

As newly minted priests the concept of a day off never appeared in our job descriptions. Even the words, 'Job Descriptions' were not introduced in seminaries and parishes. Since clergy retirement was not known then, the only time a priest could rest was on his deathbed. The benefits of priesthood were truly out of this world. You were urged to see your life as a candle burning at both ends.

Anything less than full-time total commitment was seen as a weakness in your response to the call to priesthood.

The question from the young professor, "Who gives to you?" haunted me for a long time. I did not know how to integrate my personal needs with my sense of total commitment to the priesthood, without appearing to be selfish or self-centered. If and when I took some vacation I would feel guilty and anxious that I was not busy constantly doing God's work.

It did not cross my mind that the Scriptures say that even God rested on the seventh day after creating the world. The Sabbath was sacred. Rest and Work were polarized in my psyche because of the intense formation that was offered in the first six months of seminary life in Bombay. We were first and foremost soldiers of God, members of Christ's army. When a soldier finds himself in the trenches in the front line of battle, even during a lull in the fighting, the soldier needs to stay alert at all times. It can be a matter of life and death. But can one emotionally and mentally survive in this constant, eyes wide open alert mode?

It is tough to maintain a sense of commitment when one is polarized in this way. One often experiences restlessness. St.

Augustine reminds us that our hearts are restless because they are meant to find their rest in God. But the restlessness I experienced came from the lack of balance in my life between the personal and the professional, between my human needs and my priestly commitments.

I remember one day wanting to talk about this feeling of constant restlessness with a mature fellow priest, who lived in the same house with me. I thought I could benefit from his wisdom and from his many years of priestly experience. When I approached him, he told me he was busy because he had to finish his breviary readings and prayers first. He had to fulfill his obligations as a priest to meet God at an appointed time in the prayer book of the Church, rather than to spend time counseling and offering spiritual direction to a fellow priest in need. I was disappointed and hurt.

When I sadly returned alone to my room that morning, my thoughts went to the parable in Luke's Gospel of the Good Samaritan. Here on the road was a needy human being, who was robbed and bleeding from his wounds. And the first person to come that way happened to be a priest who decided to leave the wounded soul and hurry on the other side of the road to his place of worship and duty. I felt abandoned by a man of the cloth, who forgot that God requires mercy, not sacrifice.

Jesus and his disciples were overwhelmed by the crowds that followed them everywhere hungry for God and for healing. So much so that Jesus had to remind his disciples that they would always find poor people in need. Thus from time to time Jesus would ask his disciples to come away with him to a secluded place or to the top of a mountain, so that they could be alone and spent some time in rest and prayer.

In my mind I understood why my fellow priest did not have the time to listen to my woes and help me immediately; in my heart, on the other hand, I felt alone, sad, hurt and abandoned.

There are only twenty-four hours in a day. A priest has to constantly make choices about what ministries to exercise and who to serve. Besides all that a priest has to pray the liturgy of the hours several times daily. Parish life is so centered on the leadership of a priest that a young priest always seems to be inundated with needs and demands on his precious time.

One of the first things sometimes that may drop out of a priest's life is the breviary, the prayer of the Church that he is obligated to pray. In the beginning when he is extremely busy a priest might say all the prayers of the morning, afternoon and evening at one time before midnight simply to fulfill the obligation. Such moments might be compared to a person eating breakfast, lunch and dinner all at the same time. That would make for some heavy indigestion! Gradually, even this stuffing method of formal prayer seems impossible to maintain and the breviary may disappear from the radar of a priest's life.

Diocesan priests, unlike religious and monastic orders of women and men, do not have community life in parish rectories and therefore lack the perfect setting for the liturgy of the hours.

Priests jokingly say that if a priest were to die suddenly, a fellow priest would rush to his bedside and arrange the ribbons of the breviary to the updated and correct prayer times.

It is ironic that in many parishes lay people are discovering the liturgy of the hours even as some priests seem to be abandoning its regular practice.

The liturgy of the hours is a priest's privilege to connect and pray with and for the whole Church. I am glad that I have personally never given up on praying the breviary. Like faithful lost friends, we return to each other, and enjoy each other's company even more intensely than before. The challenge for a diocesan priest like me continues to be the regularity of saying the breviary without the benefit of community life.

From the very beginning after ordination I realized that a priest is called to be a man of prayer. People are constantly asking a priest for prayer for themselves and for their loved ones. Prayer is also my soul's life breath and helps to deepen my relationship with God. I love to pray and I lift up my heart to God in many different wonderful ways.

It is said that "Peace is seeing a sunset and knowing who to thank." Prayer for me is becoming more and more an act of gratitude and mindfulness. Blending Eastern and Western spiritualities, my prayer often begins with 'The Morning Offering' and then, an awareness of my breath and the Spirit within me. The psalmist reminds us: "Be still and know that

I am God." I breathe out what is not of God (all my anxieties and concerns) and breathe in the life giving gift of the Holy Spirit. While I still continue to pray in a formal way my morning and evening liturgy of the hours and my prayers before and after meals, I enjoy my union with God through spiritual reading, nature walks and even the music that is streamed through my I-Pod. Every Advent, Christmas, Lent and Easter seasons I spend six minutes daily with the 'Little Book' series of meditations. Celebrating daily and Sunday Eucharist, baptisms, weddings and funerals and other liturgical events with the community completes my time of prayer and union with God.

Prayer is essential because priestly life can be very busy. Blessed Mother Teresa of Calcutta reminded her missionary sisters that having so much to do the whole day serving the needs of the poorest of the poor; they definitely needed to spend daily at least an hour before the Blessed Sacrament. Above the Crucifix in their chapels of prayer, the Missionaries of Charity were always reminded of the words of Jesus on the Cross: "I thirst." Martin Luther once said: "I am so busy now that if I did not spend two or three hours each day in prayer, I would not get through the day." St. Francis of Sales put it another way: "Every Christian needs a half hour of prayer each day, except when he is busy, then he needs an hour."

I understand that life is fragile even for a priest and needs to be handled with prayer.

CHAPTER 6

A VOCATION WITHIN A VOCATION

B ACK IN India, after my vacation in Europe with my parents and my summer parish experience in the United States, my restlessness continued. The ordination to the priesthood had completed and fulfilled an important stage and goal in my life. Now I began to seek a vocation within my vocation.

Was God calling me to do something specific as a priest? While religious order priests like Jesuits, for instance, specialize in specific areas of education, a diocesan priest is by and large a generalist. In imitation of St. Paul, he is called to be all things to all people. Is this how God wanted me to continue my priestly ministry or was there a specific contribution God wanted me to make for the good of the Church?

In preparation for my ordination to the priesthood, I had splurged on postal stamps by sending invitations to almost all my traceable Roman classmates who were scattered throughout seventy five countries. When we left Rome in 1975, the understanding was that we would return some day to continue our religious studies at one of the many Pontifical Universities of Rome. At the Urban University where we studied Philosophy and Theology, there were only non-ordained seminarians. Rome, however, houses other Pontifical Universities where priests go for specialized research and studies, like the *Gregorianum*, the *Angelicum* or the *Theresianum*. Moreover, there are many other religious colleges and universities in Rome and elsewhere in Italy and the rest of Europe and North America where you can obtain advanced degrees. Several of my classmates did return to Rome to finish what they had started as seminarians.

The new Archbishop did not have any specific plans for me since he had his hands full running the most important Archdiocese in the country. He also had huge shoes to fill taking over the reins from the Cardinal, well known as a spiritual leader in India and also in many parts of the Catholic world.

The Cardinal was the one who had decided to send me to Rome for seminary studies, rather than to a Pontifical seminary just outside of Bombay. He had a vision for the future of the Archdiocese, and somehow my vocation, and I believed also my future, was tied to that vision.

The Cardinal was a well known orator. He had shared with us that one method that contributed to his effective speaking skills was two blank notebooks: one, he kept by his bedside and the other, in his pocket at all times. At night, if he had an inspiration, he would wake up and make a note of it right away. Thus his talks and speeches were always interesting, relevant and inspiring.

I have learned a lot from him to make my homilies and presentations relevant, effective and passionate.

His blank notebooks remind me of the man who was inspired in a dream at night, woke up instantly and went down on his knees to thank God for the inspiration. When he stood up to write down his wonderful idea, he could not remember it any more. The moral of the story is to first write down what inspires you and then go down on your knees to thank the Almighty.

While the Cardinal was tall, well-known and well-liked, the new Archbishop was small in stature and generally unknown. Moreover succession did not imply continuity. The vision for the Archdiocese that led me to Rome was soon abandoned and forgotten. I found myself hanging in thin air. What was going to happen next in my life? Did anybody want to know? Did anybody care?

Every diocesan priest is accountable to only one Bishop, even if the Bishop has auxiliaries to help him. Before and after ordination you develop a strong, fraternal relationship with your Bishop. If you are fortunate you will have that same Bishop for the rest of your life as a priest. But sometimes due to sickness, death or transfers to other assignments and dioceses, you lose the ties you have developed with each other. A new Bishop comes in and a brand new relationship needs to be established. Permanent relationships are hard to develop and to maintain. That is why in life we have many chance acquaintances but very few permanent friends.

Every bishop comes with his own agenda and style of leadership. Even though he may acknowledge his predecessor in talks and in public prayer, he basically feels called to run the diocese entrusted to his care in his own way and with his own unique style.

This creates a special dilemma for the international immigrant priest, who no longer has ties with his country, former bishop or fellow priests. Relationships in new foreign cultural settings have to be set up from scratch and are not easy to develop and nurture.

I was fascinated by the modern media of communications. When I was a seminarian in Rome I attended a Media workshop offered by the Jesuits on Communications and Radio Technology. I was easily drawn by the media because there was so much excitement attached to them and I had a personality that I thought was a perfect fit for the world of media and communications.

When I found out that there was a program of catechetical study in France called AVEX (Audiovisual Expression of the Faith), I approached the Archbishop to allow me to attend this program funded by a world-wide Catholic missionary organization in Germany, appropriately named Missio. This time was different. The Archbishop and I entered into dialog on the value and need for continuing education.

Life is full of surprises. When you least expect it, people change. After doing his research by consulting a well-known Spanish Jesuit, Fr. Balaguer, from whom he gathered that this was a good program, I received the necessary permission to take a year off for study in France.

*****

In 1980 I left for Ecully, near Lyons, France, to study the use of audio-visuals for faith and evangelization purposes under a well-known dynamic catechetical French priest, Fr. Pierre Babin.

Before arriving in France, since Israel was on my way, I flew to Tel Aviv and the Holy Land, for the first time in my life. I was invited by an Indian parishioner who had settled in Israel by marrying a Jewish man. I stayed with them for four days. On my own I traveled to Bethlehem, Nazareth and the holy sites of Jerusalem. I was deeply moved by my visit to Calvary, to the Empty Tomb of Jesus and the Church of the Resurrection. It was such a powerful experience of faith to see the real places with the familiar sounding names that I had heard all my life in church and in my Scripture studies in the seminaries of Bombay and Rome.

Both while entering as well as exiting the place and church of Jesus' birth in Bethlehem, a name which means the 'House of Bread,' one has to bend down and be humble. To be humble is to be literally close to the earth, in the spirit of the Incarnation, of the Word of God becoming human. In this environment of simplicity and humility, one is also reminded about the reality of war even in the birthplace of the Prince of Peace. At the door of the Church of Jesus' birth at Bethlehem, there were two Israeli soldiers with machine guns monitoring closely and scrutinizing the movements of all the pilgrims.

Later on I experienced the agony of Jesus in the Garden of Gethsemane, and I knew in my heart that I would continue to experience this agony in my own life in the future whenever the time would come to make difficult decisions.

In Nazareth, I tried unsuccessfully to locate fellow Palestinian seminarians by asking around for them by name. Just as many of our Vietnamese seminarians could not return to Vietnam in 1975, when the communists took over the entire country by overcoming the might of the United States and the forces of South Vietnam, so also the Palestinian seminarians must have had a very difficult time returning to the Israeli occupation of their Palestinian homeland.

And I thought I was the only one having huge reentry problems!

The situation in the Holy Land where I tried unsuccessfully to find companions from the past taught me the painful lesson that one cannot easily recreate and relive the past. Memories are wonderful and necessary, but we all need to move on with our lives.

Next I stopped in Athens, Greece, just for a day. I had continued to correspond from India with Chryssanthie, the Greek girl, who was my summer French conversation partner when we were at the University of Caen in Normandy, France. Chryssanthie had given me the impression that she was fascinated by Indian culture but secretly she was interested in me. I have to confess that I expressed to her as well how much I was fascinated by Greek culture (especially due to my philosophy studies in Rome); yet as a young man of twenty-one then, was I also interested in her? I don't think so. I never toyed with her emotions or made any promises to her. She was just a friend I happened to meet on the campus of a French university. Our mutual cultural interests motivated us and helped us to improve our knowledge of conversational French. That's all that mattered to me, then.

While I went ahead with my studies and was ordained a priest, Chryssanthie had since got married to a teacher twice her age. In our correspondence over the years, Chryssanthie made it clear to me that she simply could not understand the notion of celibacy. In fact she had said to me once that our world needs to be populated by good people; therefore good individuals like me, according to her theory, should procreate and fill the earth with goodness.

Another reason why celibacy did not make sense to her was because she was raised in the Greek Orthodox tradition. The Orthodox Church split from Rome in the year 1054. While the Western Church carried on its tradition of requiring the clergy to be celibate, the Orthodox churches of Greece and Eastern Europe allowed their priests to have the option to marry before and even after ordination. The only restriction applies to their Bishops who are to remain celibate. Even though like most cradle and cultural Orthodox Christians Chryssanthie did not practice her faith, she definitely had a strong opinion about the issue of marriage and celibacy for Catholic priests.

At the age of twenty-one, when we first met, I was not sure I could easily explain to her the nature of celibacy. I was also not sure whether we would ever see each other again after I returned to India. But there she was waiting for me at the airport of Athens, with the same familiar smile and her head tilted to one side, with her husband beside her.

Just as I had visited the Holy Land for the first time, this was also my first visit to Greece. I was the proverbial modern tourist trying to see a lot in a short period of time. While four days cannot do justice to the Holy Land, one day is just a drop in the bucket for visiting the ancient civilization of Greece. But my gracious hosts gave me a taste of the flavor of life in Greece, from eating delicious Greek food to touring the ruins of the Parthenon. They reminded me that if I had had a few more days at my disposal, we could have done a tour of the islands, the true heart of romantic and cultural Greece.

When one has had a sampling of something unforgettable, one is filled with the desire to return for more. Eventually, I would return both to Greece and the Holy Land for memorable, lengthy visits and tours.

Just as the liturgy of the hours (the breviary) calls for companions to pray with, so also celibacy as a discipline makes total sense for priests, monks and religious who live in a community. In the life of a religious community everything is shared in common. The community becomes your family. You do things together and you share responsibilities as in any normal family.

This is not the reality of diocesan and parish priests. We do not live in a community and we are allowed to hold on to our personal possessions. Some of us work and worship with hundreds of people on the weekends and then find ourselves alone in rectories with no one to talk to.

Many centuries ago, some historians tell us, the Church could not control how married clergy would dispose of church property, because their spouses and children would inherit all that they owned including the material assets of the church. Mandated celibacy that was put in place about a thousand years ago in the universal Church removed this inheritance obstacle and church property was held secure by the institution of the Church, rather than by individual clerical families.

Since then the Church has proposed a spiritual reason for celibacy, pointing out to Jesus' choice to be unmarried and the long tradition of celibacy in the Catholic Church, while acknowledging all along that celibacy is strictly a Church discipline. It is not a mandate from Christ to be celibate because the Apostles, like Peter for example, were married and so were several Popes, Bishops and Presbyters in the early Church. Still it is a personal choice at ordination that every man who wishes to become and remain a Catholic priest be sworn and committed to celibacy, like Christ himself.

Since celibacy is required of Catholic priests, a priest is now seen as being married not to a single woman but to the Church herself.

After all those years Chryssanthie still regretted my choice of celibacy and for the last time in Greece, on her territory, asked me what I thought about it. When I clearly expressed to her that it was my choice to be and continue to remain a celibate Catholic priest, she waved good-bye and never again communicated or corresponded with me.

*****

From Greece I arrived finally in France to begin my program of study. As in Rome, I was once again part of an international group of students. This group was not limited to clergy, so we had religious sisters and brothers as well as many lay people, both single and married, that came from many parts of the Catholic world to study the modern means of communicating faith.

This program in France was held in two segments simply called Avex 1 and Avex 2, about three months each in duration. We learned to use slides, photos, magazines, radio, various sound and light technologies, and even television. We developed our own pictures in dark rooms and used large images to tell stories and to reflect on difficult issues of faith. We were challenged to collaborate and build on one another's meager resources. At the end of each segment we also produced our own short television shows.

The emphasis throughout the program was not only to communicate but to communicate effectively. We had to constantly keep the attention of our listeners and viewers and to bring relevance to our message and ideas.

Many of the participants came from Third World countries. We knew that we did not have the money to buy expensive technologies for our parishes and catechetical centers. In 1980, for instance, a portable, heavy and bulky color video camera cost around $12,000. Today, generally speaking, the only thing that comes down in price and also gives you more for your money is electronics and digital technology.

So, many of us from poorer countries had to think in terms of the simplest and cheapest methods and technologies to share the good news of the Gospel. And even if we had thousands of dollars to buy the equipment, we were also aware that very often in the villages, where most people lived, there would be no electricity.

In one of our sessions we were fascinated when a missionary told a story in the dark with just a few pictures and a flashlight. We were glued to his every word as well as to every movement of light. Communication does not have to be expensive to be good and effective.

The patron saint of television is St. Clare of Assisi but in my spiritual perspective, the model for media communicators should be none other than St. Mary Magdalene. When Mary Magdalene went to the tomb to see where they had laid her beloved Lord and Master, she found that the stone had already been rolled away. She was heartbroken because she thought that the body of Jesus had been stolen. When she saw the gardener, who really was Jesus, she asked him in her state of sadness if he knew where they had taken the body of Jesus. When she heard her name, "Mary," from the lips of the gardener, she immediately and joyfully recognized the Risen Savior. Then Jesus asked her to go to the disciples and tell them what she had *seen* and *heard*. This is the basis for the audio-visual communication of faith and Mary Magdalene is known as the Apostle of the Apostles.

Recently, I was deeply moved by praying at and touching the relic of St. Mary Magdalene, brought over from France to some of the parishes of our diocese by the Dominicans of Saint Baume. Mary Magdalene reminds me that we are all called by name and loved with an everlasting love. When we know we are loved so intensely, we are passionate about spreading the Good News.

During my six months in France I visited a few inspiring places. One of them was right there in Lyons, the second largest city of France. When I had joined the seminary in Bombay, as part of our spirituality program we were asked to read the lives of holy men and women. The first book I chose was the life of Peter Damien, a priest from Belgium, who ended up as a missionary in Molokai, Hawaii, an island where lepers were banished to die. Leprosy was considered a very contagious disease in those days. Finally, Fr. Peter Damien became a leper himself, sharing fully, in complete solidarity, with his family of exiled lepers. Peter Damien was recently canonized a saint in Rome and I was happy to visit the church in Lyons where he had celebrated his first Mass.

Pope Benedict XVI declared 2009-2010 as 'The Year of the Priest'. It was the 150th anniversary of St. Jean Marie Vianney, the patron saint of diocesan parish priests. Ars is a small town just outside of Lyons. That's where Jean Marie Vianney was sent and that is where he came to be known as the Curé d'Ars.

The story goes that Jean Marie Vianney did not know where Ars, the place of his first assignment as a priest, was located. He met a child on the way and said to him: "Show me the way to Ars and I will show you the way to Heaven." I was deeply moved by my visit to Ars, where Jean Marie Vianney lived an ascetical life, heard confessions sometimes for as long as fifteen hours a day, and through pastoral concern and visits brought people back to the Church. He was truly a shepherd of his flock and I felt inspired to live my vocation in the footsteps of this patron saint of parish priests like me everywhere.

The final inspiring healing shrine I visited after many hours of train travel was Lourdes, in the Pyrenees between France and Spain. It was touching to see the simple faith of Catholics in the nightly candlelight procession praying the Rosary. It was an amazing sight to see so many sick people on wheelchairs and stretchers out in the open praying for miracles.

The climax for me was to participate in the Stations of the Cross, and witness through the life-size statues, the conversion of the centurion. In the beginning he looks away from Jesus simply carrying out his duty as a Roman soldier. Gradually he seems interested in this bleeding, suffering man. There's something different about him and he even turns in his direction. Finally, it is the same soldier who looks up at the crucified Jesus after he gives up his Spirit, and makes a confession of faith: "Truly, this man was the Son of God."

It is ironic that a gentile achieves the insight no Jew achieves in the passion story of Mark. Even Jesus' disciples are portrayed in Mark as rather thick-headed, slow to catch on to Jesus' true identity. That Roman centurion always reminds me how fortunate I am to know and to believe in Jesus' true identity as the Son of God, as my Lord and Savior.

In the year 2009 Peter Damien, the leper of Molokai, was canonized a saint in Rome by Pope Benedict XVI. From St. Peter Damien I learned to show solidarity as a priest with the people I work with and for. From Jean Marie Vianney, the patron saint of parish priests, I learned to have passion and pastoral concern for the flock entrusted to me as a shepherd. And finally in Lourdes, from Mary, the Mother of Priests, and the converted Roman centurion from the Stations of the Cross, I learned to draw others to Christ and to salvation.

At the end of Avex I and II, I got to spend some relaxing time in the French Alps. I spent Christmas in Abondance, a beautiful snow-covered Alpine village. How did this trip come about? A parish priest from Abondance, with a group of seven French parishioners, had stayed at the Taj Mahal Hotel in Bombay, and my sister, Rita, who worked for the hotel, had befriended them. These French visitors had come over to our house in Bombay for dinner and Indian hospitality and had given us an open invitation to visit them in France. So, here I was in their town on my first "White Christmas" and asked to give the Christmas sermon in French. I shared some of my childhood Christmas stories in my homily. The snow-covered picturesque village of Abondance was the perfect setting for my first Alpine Christmas.

While some parishes offer a blessing to those children and adults who don't or cannot receive Holy Communion, here in Abondance I was introduced to the concept of Friendship Bread. Since these Alpine villages draw a lot of tourists and families with little children, a piece of unconsecrated bread is offered to those who will not be receiving Communion, so that everyone feels included in the parish family celebration of Eucharist.

When I left for France from India I was given a year's study leave from parish ministry. Since the program in France lasted only six months, after the Christmas break in the French Alps, I flew to Montreal and then to Ottawa, Canada, for Avex III. This segment was the theoretical component of Communications Media taught at St. Paul's University, which was affiliated with the University of Ottawa, the capital city of Canada.

This was my first trip to Canada and became the clearest proof for me why one should not think of settling in such a cold place (especially, for an immigrant from the Tropics). It was forty degrees below zero when I arrived. Rooms and buildings in Canada are well heated. So, I was pleasantly surprised when I saw an ice-cream machine in the foyer of our residence. In India, in the Tropics, people drink hot tea on sunny afternoons, so that when they sweat, the pores of their skins open up and consequently with the gentle breeze their bodies begin to cool down. The huge contrast in the temperatures between the cold outside and the heat inside the building made the ice-cream treat the perfect welcome to cold Canada.

For students the best advantage of a severe winter is to stay indoors and study. This is exactly what I did. I knew that my time in Canada was going to be very short and every hour of the day mattered.

But I did not travel to Canada simply to study. Ever since I stepped onto Italian soil many years earlier on my very first flight to anywhere in the world, travel has meant so much more to me. Traveling can be such a great education tool. It can open your eyes and heighten all your senses to absorb the beauty and the progress of humanity in all its diversity and complexity.

Therefore the theory of Communications Media was not the only reason why I chose to come to Canada. I also wanted to experience Canadian life. In North America, Canada is not very different from the United States. In fact, some make the claim that when the United States has a cold, Canada sneezes.

Despite the similarities, each country has its unique flavor and culture. The best way for me to experience Canadian religious life was to help out at a parish. Every parish can use some extra help. I found myself accepted for the summer into a local progressive parish in Ottawa, called Holy Cross. There was a young dynamic pastor who was happy to welcome me and introduce me to life in Canada.

Through him I got introduced to the game of ice hockey. In India, field hockey is a national sport. This pastor played ice hockey and had some major bruises to prove to me how much of a contact sport it is and how much Canadians love it.

In Holy Cross parish I discovered the power of good sound and music in liturgy. In Indian churches, because of the oppressive tropical heat and the lack of air-conditioning, the doors and windows often stay open to the noise of traffic, barking stray dogs and crowds of people. In Canada, at least in the winter, everything is shut tight as in a huge sealed box, but this makes it much easier to focus on the prayers and the celebration of the liturgy.

I remember one Indian church not having any doors or windows, literally opening up to the outside world and at the same time welcoming the environment and the surroundings to the sacred space of the church. Western churches prefer to have huge glass windows to have the same effect and avoid wind, dust and noise from the outside.

Since the canal circling Ottawa for six miles is usually frozen in the winter, it ends up being the longest public skating rink in the city. Some adults skate to work while children skate to school. A great attraction in the winter is the frozen sculptures, beautifully carved in ice. Human beings, wherever they find themselves, adapt even to such cold, freezing conditions. Instead of being miserable and homebound in the winter, they create a festival of ice sculptures, drawing tourists and visitors from everywhere. Humans are simply amazing!

I envied the skaters as they glided smoothly on the canal to school, to work or for pleasure. But skating was not for me.

There wasn't enough time for me to learn at my age and as a sport it just didn't seem to be a lot of fun to completely lose control and fall on your behind again and again. Moreover, one of our mature students, a nun from Papua New Guinea, had a life altering experience on the ice. As she walked on the frozen black ice to school the very first day, she was thrown up into the air and landed on her face. She was so still the onlookers thought she had a heart attack and had died. She was alive and breathing, just not able to move. She was rushed to the local hospital and did not get out for almost three weeks having broken her pelvic bone and fractured her hip. She wasn't able to return to the 'Avex III' program. From the hospital she returned to Papua New Guinea to rest and recover from her surgeries. If I had any desire to skate or take up a sport like ice hockey, it was gone after seeing the falling nun.

There's a reason why the best time to learn new games and sports is when you are a child or teenager. You have less to fear at that age and that helps in the learning process. It's amazing to see at the summer Olympics how fearless young gymnasts somersault and land on balance beams that are barely four inches wide. I have realized also that one should learn as many languages as possible when one is young. At a more mature age it's more difficult and challenging. Moreover, it gets harder to remember as one grows older.

Many Canadians are bi-lingual, speaking English and French. Even though Canada was a British colony, Canadian English sounds more American than British. Signs of American culture are everywhere, from television to billboards, from fast food restaurants to all kinds of businesses. Coming directly from France to Canada, I found the Canadian French from the province of Quebec to be very melodious. It took me a while to adjust to it, but I was not there long enough to enjoy it.

With the theoretical component of Avex III and the practical applications we learned in France during Avex I and II, I felt my program in audio-visual communications was complete. I was happy to have this opportunity to study in such unique surroundings and to have a vocation within my priestly vocation.

*****

Since I had two more months left of free time before my expected return to Bombay, I decided to re-visit the Boston area, which I had loved so much the first time I was there. When I left Boston, I never thought I would have a chance to return so soon. I was invited by the same Pastor who no longer had an associate to help him at his parish in Revere near the city of Boston.

Another circle of life!

Revere Beach is one of the more popular beaches of the New England States and of the East Coast. Prior to this visit of mine, the Pastor and his associate, another dynamic priest, had decided to work as a team rather than have titles of Pastor and Parochial Vicar. They saw themselves as co-pastors, co-shepherds, and as equals in their responsibilities. This teamwork was so successful that people from all over the greater Boston area came to attend services at their vibrant parish.

In this community I quickly made a lot of new friends, including a permanent Deacon, his wife, and their children. Even the deacon's family did not live in the town of Revere. People are drawn by charisma. It is true that the Eucharist should be the principal center of Catholic worship and the main reason why people go to their parish church, yet people are constantly looking for more: for a sense of community, for good music, for hospitality and welcome and finally, for good homilies on the Word of God.

Not every ordained deacon, priest or bishop can preach a good homily. As an aside, in homiletics training in the seminary, we were told, with a touch of humor, that you have a good homily if you have a good beginning, a good ending and you keep them not far from each other. You also have a good homily if you reach your destination and then simply land the plane instead of circling around again and again *ad nauseam*. Very often, the problem with preachers is that they have good material but they don't prepare the ending. So, they don't end; they simply stop when they run out of gas. Finally, a good homily, someone said, is like a miniskirt: short enough to draw attention and long enough to cover the essentials!

The community of this Revere church and its co-pastors provided the best of all of the above and more.

The Pastor worked the harder of the two but the associate was more popular with the people. The latter was the first to suffer burnout. Popularity has its price. He told me later, with some exaggeration but nevertheless to make his point, that he never had a personal moment to himself. Even when he returned from his day off (which he would spend with his fellow priests), there were several messages for him at the rectory on the steps leading up to his bedroom. The pastoral need was so great and the parishioners were so hungry spiritually, he felt he had to step down and go away for awhile. He quit the team. The Pastor was now alone in this large parish and he was very glad when I arrived to help him and to give him a break for the summer.

After hearing about what happened to the associate I began to understand a little bit more the validity of that young Indian professor's haunting question to me: "You give of yourself to everyone. Who gives to you?" No one can take good care of you better than yourself. When you are in a leadership position, like a pastor, for instance, people may be under the impression that you are always mentally and spiritually strong, and never in need. When a priest takes a leave of absence due to stress and burnout, everyone is surprised.

Carl Jung, the psychoanalyst, once commenting on the words of Jesus at the last judgment, namely: "Whatsoever you do to the least of my brothers and sisters, you do it for me", asked, "What if you found out that the least among your brothers and sisters is really **you**? Wouldn't and shouldn't you take better care of yourself?"

I now understood the value of having a day off to relax and to recharge my batteries. It is so easy in ministry to burn the candle at both ends. How can you give yourself to others, when you have nothing left to give?

This is what the associate sadly discovered about himself. Burnout and stress can destroy one's core and sometimes, even one's vocation and faith. The associate took a long leave of absence from active ministry and even asked himself if God was now calling him to marriage and to give up his life as a single, celibate Catholic priest. As he painfully found out, if you don't get away from your work for at least a day every week, then you find yourself constantly checking e-mails, answering the phone and the doorbell, and responding to sick calls and emergencies. You feel like you are constantly putting out fires and the worse thing is that you feel guilty if you neglect to answer all needs immediately.

The story of the stressed out associate has a happy ending. Several years later when I revisited the Boston area, I met him once again, now functioning as the pastor of his own parish, much more relaxed, talking freely about days off and retirement and as passionate as ever about ministry and priesthood.

Every crisis can become an opportunity. In Mandarin, apparently, the same symbol of letters is used to indicate both the words 'Crisis' and 'Opportunity.' Instead of being discouraged by what happened to the associate, I resolved that I would do everything in my power to take better care of myself. Often priests are placed on pedestals and treated as superheroes, always on call to help the needy around them. Giving to yourself is an acknowledgement that you are human and that you, too, have needs like the rest of humanity.

One good memory I have of that summer is that of practicing driving on the streets of Boston. The Pastor gave me the use of his car. I had received my driver's license when I was studying in Rome, Italy. They say that if you can drive in Rome, you can drive in any part of the world. The problem was I did not own a car then, so all the driving lessons were apparently wasted. When I returned to India from Rome, I had to get a new driver's license because, as in Great Britain and many Commonwealth nations, you drive in India on the other side of the road. Once again, failing to own a car in India made the new driving lessons somewhat useless. For eight years I drove a Vespa scooter on the streets of Bombay.

I can also add from lived experience that if you can drive in Bombay, you can definitely drive in any part of the world.

The first thing Indian drivers do is to toot their horn even before the car moves. I guess they do that to make sure it works if and when needed, or they simply blow their horns to announce to everyone who can hear to watch out because they are now preparing to drive on the crazy city roads. The advantage of driving a scooter on the congested roads of Bombay was twofold: it was easy on the pocket book because gas is so expensive in India, and secondly, if the traffic was horrendous, which was usually the case, you could either weave in and out of traffic or take the scooter onto the pavements of Bombay in either direction. As you constantly tooted your horn you kept pedestrians on their toes.

The pedestrians of Bombay are well trained. They know how to step away quickly from the onslaught of crazy drivers. "He who hesitates is lost" is a proverb that must have come from the streets, the traffic and the pedestrians of Bombay and Rome.

After all the years of maniacal driving in Bombay, it was fun to drive a spacious American automatic car on the streets of Boston.

I had an interesting experience of Church politics in this parish of the Archdiocese of Boston. Even though the associate had moved on after experiencing burnout, the parishioners were still eager to continue to have the team structure of parish leadership. It had been a good experience of parish life for them and so they requested their regional bishop to continue the same model.

The regional bishop came with his consulters for what was announced as an open parish-wide listening meeting. Many parishioners took the time from their busy schedules and filled the parish hall. People were then invited to come to the microphone and say aloud what they liked about this team leadership model. Since I had come from an audio-visual program in Canada, I used my micro tape-recorder to record the comments and reactions from the floor.

I had never before heard such powerful testimonies of how parish life had enriched the lives of so many people. They said they were happy to come to church. Their children and youth had good sacramental and catechetical programs. They felt a sense of ownership because of their many involvements in parish life. People had tears of joy as they narrated how their spirits were fed and nourished in this community.

The bishop and his consulters seemed to listen patiently to all these positive comments. But they did not say anything to reveal their own personal thoughts, reactions and impressions.

A little after I left Boston to return to India, I heard that my friend, the Pastor, was transferred from this popular parish and an elderly 'lone ranger' pastor was appointed in his place, who quickly removed all traces of the Team Leadership Model. The "Co-pastors Team Model" was considered to be unhealthy by the Church hierarchy, even though all the lay people gathered in the hall that day for the listening session had unanimously agreed and affirmed the validity and power of the team approach to transform the life of a parish. In this case, for sure, the '*Vox Populi*' (the voice of the people) was not accepted as the '*Vox Dei*' (the voice of God).

After a wonderful and enjoyable two months in this suburban parish, on the last but one day before my departure, I was invited to spend some relaxing hours at Revere Beach by Joe, one of my close parishioner friends. He asked me to dress casually in jeans because we were going to be outdoors all day. When we returned to the rectory in the late afternoon I was tired and ready to call it a day. I still had some last minute packing to do, so I thanked Joe and wished him goodbye. But Joe wasn't leaving and he asked me to come along with him because there was something he wanted to show me in the parish hall.

When he opened the door and we walked in I got the shock of my life. There, before my disbelieving panicked eyes, were at least six hundred parishioners and friends in formal dinner attire applauding my arrival. The exuberant applause could have been for a celebrity sighting but all I could do was embarrassingly look down at my tattered jeans and casual clothes. But a few moments later, I was totally at ease. My energy comes from people. That evening I had the time of my life. What a great surprise and what an awesome send-off party!

I could hardly fall asleep that night. The next day another surprise awaited me at the airport. There were at least twenty-six parishioners with bottles of champagne and cheerful smiles. In the early eighties security at the airport was not an issue as it is today. We toasted each other and imbibed the bubbly right till the moment I said: "Goodbye. I love you."

Then I boarded the plane that would take me back to India — forever. Or so I thought.

*****

I had met some international priests in the United States who either came to visit or to study. But they decided not to return to their homeland even going against the wishes and demands of their bishops and superiors. My perceptions and thoughts were different. I wanted to return home and use the new knowledge I had acquired in the past year for the good of our people in India. I felt a strong sense of responsibility and accountability.

Before the year of my study leave was finished, my Archbishop had written me a letter reminding me that it was time to come home and that everyone was eagerly awaiting my return. I did not need this reminder but I was still happy to know that my superiors were thinking about me. I was particularly excited because for the first time I realized that I had found my vocation within the vocation to the priesthood, which I had been anxiously seeking.

As soon as I landed in Bombay, I wanted to kiss the ground, so glad I was to return home.

The smile was wiped off my face very quickly. My first shock happened at the airport Customs area. India was a poor country so all returning residents who had purchased electronic equipment abroad and were bringing them back into the country were made to pay excessive fees and fines. To participate fully in the audio visual program in France, I had purchased my own Yashica camera with a variety of lenses. The duty on that camera was going to be one hundred and fifty percent of the cost. I did not have that kind of money and I gently reminded the Customs' agent that I was a trained photographer now and that the camera was part of my professional equipment. He knew from the form I had filled out and my passport that I was a priest. So, he simply laughed at me for considering myself a photographer. I couldn't convince him that I had done a course in photography and I needed the camera for my audio-visual work. It was sad that at the end I had to leave my camera behind in the big hall of confiscated goods till I could return with the exorbitant duty fees.

Although the Archbishop had reminded me to come home giving me the impression that he had some definite plans for me, the fact remained that he had absolutely no clear assignments or decisions made for me or my future. He simply wanted me to come back. A priest is an endangered species so each bishop wants to see his priests return as soon as possible if they have been sent abroad for continuing education. I had called his office right after I reached my parents home, and all I was told was to wait for further instructions from the Archdiocese. My family wondered why I was in such a hurry to start work. My sense of duty and responsibility was strong and I was becoming impatient – again.

A few days went by and nothing happened. No news, no communications. What was I going to do? One mistake a priest often makes is imagining that his superiors are frequently thinking about him and are constantly worried about him and his welfare. It has taken me many painful years to realize that very rarely authority figures have the time to care personally or directly about you because most of them are burdened by their own responsibilities.

I began to experience a return to a feeling of restlessness. Deep down I couldn't deal with my own lack of patience and what I perceived as the snail's pace of Church life in India. Not receiving an immediate parish or special assignment and not willing to wait doing nothing, I went to a pastor of a former parish of mine where I had a wonderful experience of priestly ministry and collaboration, and who was now pastor of a parish in the inner city of Bombay. I spent the next eight months there helping whenever and wherever I was needed. I was so eager to do ministry that waiting around doing nothing was not even an option.

My priestly life is nourished by parish life and I blossom and bloom when I am planted in the midst of a faith community.

Finally, the Archdiocese assigned me to the Pastoral Center in the suburbs of Bombay. This center was the headquarters of Catechetical Ministry. A section of the building was given to former alcoholics, so that with spiritual help they could overcome their addiction. I was put in charge of a non-existing Communications Center.

My living quarters and office were a small room with a bed, a small table and two chairs. And there were absolutely no resources for Multi-Media Communications. I was informed by the Archdiocese that there were international Church grants available for mission countries, but the earliest we could expect some funds, without any guarantees, was at least three years away.

Bombay was and is the financial capital of India. If Bombay had no resources to share at that time, the rest of India would have next to nothing at all to offer. I was pessimistic about implementing my audio visual goals for the Church in India. And I lacked patience.

My sojourn and studies in Europe had changed my life. For some reason I wanted to get things done right now and immediately. My world of time and space had shifted radically. Indians are generally stereotyped as being tolerant and patient with life. Was I no longer Indian in mentality, attitudes and in ways of thinking? (Even today there are parishioners and people I meet who cannot accept that I am from India). Since I went to Rome for seminary studies and then to France, Canada and the United States, I was more and more impatient with life situations and with the slowness of making decisions in the local Church of India.

When I returned from the United States less than a year after my study leave of absence, I did not allow jet lag to slow me down and right away I informed the Chancery of my return and indicated to them that I was ready to start the assignment they had planned for me. If I could not be patient for a short duration of time then, what would I do waiting at least three years before any funding (without guarantees) could be received for Communications Ministry in the Archdiocese? I was way up high on the scale of impatience and frustration.

I was also feeling emotionally cheated and blackmailed. Why was I asked to hurry back when there was absolutely nothing to return to by way of plans, assignments, resources and mission?

I approached the Archbishop several times to talk and to share my deepest emotions. I shared with him as honestly as possible my feelings of alienation and frustration. I told him how happy I had been when exercising ministry in Europe and in the United States. I told him I felt at home there. In our initial conversations, the Archbishop asked me to pray about my situation and also offered me some other options of priestly ministry, like being part of the Vatican's diplomatic corps. Perhaps I should have taken his offer but God had other plans for me.

Since I had two wonderful experiences in Boston parishes, I asked whether he would give me permission to leave the Archdiocese of Bombay and serve as a priest in the United States of America. He asked me how I could tell whether the United States would be the right place for me. All I could say was: "I don't know but I place my complete trust in the Lord."

I was at peace knowing that the Lord would provide for my future.

We said a short prayer together.

I thanked him.

And we parted ways.

The following reflection by Brian Chalker sums it up for me:

People come into your life for a *reason*, a *season* or a *lifetime*. When you know which one it is, you will know what to do for that person. When someone is in your life for a Reason, it is usually to meet a need you have expressed. They have come to assist you through a difficulty, to provide you with guidance and support, to aid you physically, emotionally or spiritually. They may seem like a Godsend and they are. They are there for the Reason you need them to be.

Then, without any wrongdoing on your part or at an inconvenient time, this person will do or say something to bring the relationship to an end. Sometimes they die. Sometimes they walk away. Sometimes they act up and force you to take a stand. What we must realize is that our need has been met, our desire fulfilled, and their work are done. The prayer you have sent up has been answered and now it is time to move on.

Some people come into your life for a Season, because your turn has come to share, grow or learn. They bring you an experience of peace or make you laugh. They may teach you something you have never done. They usually give you an unbelievable amount of joy. Believe it, it is real. But it is only for a Season.

Some people come into your life for a Lifetime. Lifetime relationships teach you lifetime lessons, things you must build upon in order to have a solid emotional and spiritual foundation. Your job is to accept the lesson, love the person and put what you have learned to use in all other relationships and areas of your life.

As I prepared to leave the shores of India for the United States of America, within me I said to all in Europe, Africa, Australia, Asia and especially, India who had crossed my path and entered my heart: *thank you* for being a part of my life and journey, whether you were there for a *reason*, a *season* or a *lifetime*.

CHAPTER 7

A FISH FINDS THE OCEAN

A S SOON AS I received permission from the Archbishop to leave India and serve as a priest in the United States of America, I wrote a letter to the Cardinal of Boston, introducing myself and expressing my intention to minister as a priest in his Archdiocese. At that time it was the second largest Archdiocese in the United States and it would be a good transition for a young priest like me who was raised in the largest Archdiocese of India. I was used to city life and to Church ministry in a big metropolis. I informed the Cardinal of Boston that his Archdiocese was the only church I was familiar with in the United States, and that my two summer experiences in the parishes near Boston, were exceptional. I also added that I had my own Archbishop's permission to leave India and serve as a priest in any part and diocese of the United States of America.

I waited for a couple of months for a reply, but there wasn't any, positive or negative. There are many modern conveniences and advantages to living in a city like Bombay but waiting is not one of them. I was getting anxious and impatient day after day, going to the mailbox and finding no response from Boston. Was God continuing to test me?

I remembered the prayer of the mother battling impatience with her children: "God, please give me patience — right now!"

I was also feeling a great deal of loneliness during this interminable waiting period. I thought the decision to leave India wasn't going to sit well with the other priests of the Archdiocese. So, I did not talk to anyone about my decision to leave India or share with anyone the plans for my future. They would not understand the inner turmoil that I had gone through for so many years since my return from Rome trying to readjust to life in India because they did not have the same unique life experience I had.

Once more my faith was being tested.

In my loneliness and in my impatience, like the Psalmist, I did not stop crying to God. A friend reminded me that our disappointments are God's appointment.

I always believed that God hears our prayers and answers them in mysterious ways. In the book of the prophet Isaiah, God reminds us: "My thoughts are not your thoughts; my ways are not your ways."

So, one day I happened to be celebrating a funeral Mass in my parish in Bombay. After Mass, the man whose mother's funeral I had just celebrated came to greet me together with his wife. They were both from California. The man was of Indian origin and his mother had continued to live in India even when he immigrated to the United States several years earlier. His wife was a native Californian. Even though it is not a normal Indian custom, Americans generally love to stop by after Mass and greet the priest, and even say, "thank you," especially if they are the ones who have offered the Mass. This is exactly what happened that day when I met this kindhearted couple from California.

When I heard their accent and found out they were from the United States, I mentioned to them my own plans to minister as a priest in their country. I told them that I was waiting daily for a response from the United States.

They asked me, "From where?"

I replied, "From Boston."

With surprised looks, they said in unison, "Why Boston?"

I told them that Boston was the only Archdiocese I had visited in the United States. I also tried to describe to them briefly the fabulous experience I had had over there. All they wanted to know was whether I had experienced life in Boston for a whole year. I asked, "Why?" They then began to describe to me the cold New England winters and the very hot and humid summers. I began picturing in my mind the East Coast of the United States being a combination of my experience of a severe winter in Ottawa, Canada, and a very hot and humid summer in Bombay, India.

Then they added: "Have you thought about coming to California?" I told them that I had never been there, and would not consider moving to an unknown place, since I was contemplating a permanent relocation.

They then invited me to their home in Santa Clara, California, and added: "If you don't like it in California after a few days with us, you can always move to Boston or anywhere else in the United States, because it is all one country." This couple was not inviting me to California because church life was better in their city than in Boston. They just believed that I would be happier and more comfortable in the Golden State.

Since no reply was forthcoming from the Archdiocese of Boston, I decided that I would fly to sunny California, and more specifically, to the Bay Area, also known as the Silicon Valley.

There is a saying: "Man proposes God disposes." I knew what I wanted when I first decided to go to Boston. But God had other plans for me.

No prayer goes unanswered. God's response to our prayer may not be what we are seeking or what we want. God's answer to prayer can be one of three responses: 'Yes,' 'No,' and 'Wait.' As an answer to my prayer, God sent a couple from California to fly me in a direction different from my original flight plans.

The excitement of leaving for California was coupled with the sadness of saying 'goodbye,' again, especially to family members. All of my siblings as well as my mother were excited about my prospects of settling abroad. The pain I felt the most was in saying 'goodbye' to my elderly dad.

As a teenager as well as a young adult, my conversations with my dad were always brief and to the point. Dad had much wisdom, but he was also a man of few words. Over the years at family birthdays and parties, he would usually say a few words in praise of his child being honored that day, sing a short song in Konkani to the delight of everyone, and then, after dinner, retire quickly for the night. He was especially proud of me and would always sing my praises at every family gathering. He wholeheartedly supported every plan I made for my life.

He was aware of becoming old and of his mortality and also the uncertainty of ever seeing me again in this life. But he never expressed these thoughts or feelings to any of us. So, as I prepared to leave for the United States, he said to me: "Son, do you *really* have to go?" I did not know what to say. I knew in my heart that my dad wanted always what was best for me and he trusted my judgment a hundred percent. But this 'goodbye' was like no other. There was some tone of finality to it. Was my dad heartbroken to see me go because he would never see me again? We hugged each other and I asked dad for his blessing. I could not look him in the eye without crying.

I heard that after my departure, my dad had felt weak and had almost passed out. But they got him home and he was fine after that. I was relieved.

When I arrived in San Francisco at the airport for the first time in my life, my hosts, the kind couple I had met after the funeral Mass in Bombay and the ones who had invited me to their home in California, were nowhere to be found. I walked around for almost an hour thinking they were delayed by traffic. When I got a hold of them by telephone, we discovered that there was a miscommunication whereby they thought I was flying in the following day. There's about twelve hours difference between San Francisco and Bombay. Anyway, my hosts asked me to stay put at the airport and they would be there to pick me up within the hour.

They had a beautiful home with a swimming pool in Santa Clara, the heart of the Silicon Valley. I enjoyed a whole week relaxing at the pool, drinking 'Mai Tais' and California wine, and watching 'Hawaii Five-O,' their favorite television police show.

The world is a big place and the United States of America is a huge country almost three times the size of the Indian sub-continent. Having never visited California before, the only cities I was familiar with in my study of world geography were Los Angeles and San Francisco.

I now began to hear about the 'Silicon Valley' where the computer, the internet and the digital technological revolution were started and was now affecting communication and information technologies all over the world. This Silicon Valley was the new name for an even prettier description for a valley that at one time was filled with orchards and fruit trees. Before this valley came to be known for computers and 'start-ups,' it was called, "The Valley of the Heart's Delight" or simply Santa Clara Valley — the Valley of Saint Clare.

Out of twenty-one Missions in California, one of the mission churches founded by the Franciscans, under the leadership of Blessed Junipero Serra, was situated in Santa Clara, a city among fifteen other cities in the Santa Clara County. At one time the Archdiocese of San Francisco covered a lot of territory from San Luis Obispo in the south to nearly touching the southern borders of Oregon. As more and more people and immigrants came west to California, especially Catholics from Central and South America, Vietnam and the Philippines, newer dioceses came to be created.

In God's mysterious plan and providence I landed in one of the newest and youngest dioceses of Northern California: the Diocese of San Jose. It was created in 1981 and includes the entire territory of Santa Clara County.

After spending a whole week relaxing with my new friends in their beautiful home, I began to get a little bit restless. It appears that restlessness has always been a way of life for me. Or is it for every human being? The reason why I came to the United States was to exercise priestly ministry, but here I was living the celebrity Hollywood lifestyle. I could take this easy going hedonistic lifestyle only for a short period of time before getting thoroughly bored by it. I wanted to do priestly work in a parish with real people.

When this new diocese was created, priests in both San Francisco and the new territory of the South County were asked to decide where they wanted to work as priests. Apparently the older priests stayed with the Mother Archdiocese while several of the younger clergy decided to join the newly formed and smaller diocese of San Jose. I arrived in this area just two years after its foundation as a diocese. So, I was warmly welcomed and immediately given a temporary parish assignment at an inner city parish of the fast growing city of San Jose. The name of this poor, largely immigrant parish was none other than 'Sacred Heart.'

Sacred Heart parish in San Jose started out as a community with largely immigrant Italians. When I arrived for my temporary assignment, it seemed to be equally divided between Italian families and a fast growing Spanish speaking population.

The number of Catholics in the United States has consistently grown because of an increase in conversions, births as well as in immigration from Mexico, Central America, South America, the Philippines, Vietnam and several other countries. Yet, the number of priests has not kept up with the demands and the needs of the Church. There are fewer priests because of deaths, retirement and a shortage of vocations to the priesthood and the religious life. More and more of the priests who are active in this country are immigrants like me from other countries. The fact of the matter is that I have never seen myself only as an immigrant priest. Wherever I go, I adapt and I feel right away at home. In this diocese of San Jose, in God's mysterious providence, I felt that I had finally come home for good.

CHANGES IN THE PRIESTHOOD IN THE USA					
U.S. Data	1965	1975	1985	1995	2005
Diocesan Priests	35925	36005	35052	32349	28702
Priests Religious	22707	22904	22265	16705	14137
Total Priests	58632	58909	57317	49054	42839
Ordinations	994	771	533	511	454
Seminarians	8325	5279	4063	3172	3308
Permanent Deacons	–	898	7204	10932	14574
Religious Brothers	12271	8625	7544	6535	5451
Religious Sisters	179954	135225	115386	90809	68634
Parishes	17637	18515	19244	19331	18891
Without Resident Priest	549	702	1051	2161	3251
Catholic Population	45.6m	48.7m	52.3m	57.4m	64.8m
% of US Population	24	23	23	23	23

CHANGES IN THE PRIESTHOOD IN THE WORLD				
World Data	1970	1980	1990	2000
Diocesan Priests	270924	257409	257696	265781
Religious Priests	148804	156191	145477	139397
Diocesan Priestly Ordinations	4622	–	5938	6814
Parishes	191438	206503	215805	218196
Without Resident Priest	–	94846	107566	105530
Catholic Population	653.5m	783.7m	928.5m	1045m

It is apparent from the statistics above that, since the Second Vatican Council that took place from 1962 to 1965, the total number of priests, religious brothers and sisters and priestly ordinations have diminished considerably in the United States of America. Yet, the Catholic population has grown tremendously, thus highlighting the shortages of vocations all across the country. Even worse, there are many parishes in the United States without a resident priest. In response to this dire situation some parishes have been merged while others have been closed.

However, according to Vatican statistics in the 'Annuario Pontificio' (yearbook containing information about every Vatican Office), the number of Catholics in the world and the number of deacons, priests and bishops all increased in 2010. At the end of 2010, the worldwide Catholic population reached 1.196 billion. The Vatican said the number of bishops in the world increased from 5,065 to 5,104; the number of priests went from 410,593 to 412,236, increasing everywhere except Europe. The number of seminarians around the world showed continued growth, from 117,978 at the end of 2009 to 118,990 at the end of 2010.

One bright spot in this ecclesial situation is the constant increase in vocations to the Permanent Diaconate. There are thousands of married deacons and their wives who are very involved in the life of their parishes. The Vatican reported that in 2010 the number of permanent deacons was 39,564, an increase of more than 1,400 over the previous year. 97.5 percent of the world's permanent deacons live in the Americas or in Europe. These permanent deacons can baptize, celebrate nuptial ceremonies, and assist and preach at Sunday liturgies. All this can be a great help where there is a shortage of ordained priests.

As yet, there are no statistics to the number of priests who have come to the Catholic Church from other Christian denominations. Blessed Pope John Paul II opened the doors to welcome this flow of conversions from other churches, and allowed the 'new' priests to remain married and to live with their families. Recently, Pope Benedict XVI has made it even easier for entire Anglican parishes and communities to join the Catholic Church as groups and not only as individuals as in the past; and for their priests to minister to them through some of their familiar Anglican prayer forms and faith traditions.

Fortunately, vocations are flourishing in many other countries other than in Europe and North America. While Poland is a good example of this growth from Eastern Europe (many young Polish seminarians and priests grew up their entire lives knowing only one Pope, their beloved hero, Blessed Pope John Paul II), in Asia, countries like the Philippines and India are awash with vocations to the priesthood and the religious life. Africa is the fastest growing continent for the Christian faith in all its forms and expressions.

When I was studying as a seminarian in Rome, about sixty percent of our college seminarians at 'Propaganda Fide' were African. Countries in Africa were flourishing in vocations but had no seminaries or houses of formation. So, African students were sent to Italy, Spain, France and every other European nation that would welcome them. Now, seminaries have been built in many parts of Africa and priests and nuns are being sent to meet the needs of the Catholic world.

No wonder I was warmly welcomed in the new Diocese of San Jose. After the split in 1981 from the Mother Archdiocese of San Francisco, priests were urgently needed here. When the Chancellor saw my Indian bishop's release letter, he assigned me temporarily to a pastor in the inner city of San Jose with a bilingual (English and Spanish) population. His two associates were on vacation and he needed the help.

I had heard some horror stories about American pastors. For instance, at meals, in the good old days, the pastors would help themselves to the best cut of meat, appropriately named, 'The Pastor's cut.' The associates were expected to do all the baptisms, funerals and weddings, while the pastors kept their share of the stipends generally without doing the work. The wine, beer and alcohol in the rectory belonged to the pastors alone, who would welcome their associates to their spacious apartments for cocktails before dinner but they would not permit the associates to entertain their own guests in the rectory. The rectory was first and foremost the pastor's home.

I knew God was watching over me because he sent me to one of the most lovable and humble pastors of this new diocese. To my surprise when I rang the doorbell the pastor himself came downstairs, picked up my suitcases and showed me to my room.

Coincidences are God's way of remaining anonymous. Such spiritual events, happenings and coincidences help one to see the hand of God in one's life. On my first visit to the United States I was welcomed to the parish of the Sacred Heart in Medford, near Boston. In this my first visit to California, I was sent to the parish of the Sacred Heart in San Jose. When I look at this mystery further into my past, the first parish I was assigned to as a deacon in Bombay, fresh from my five years of life, studies and adventure in Italy, was Sacred Heart Parish!

My significant beginnings were always situated in the loving Sacred Heart of Jesus.

I had no relatives or friends in California (except the couple that invited me to the West Coast), so this God-moment assignment and my encounter with a friendly and unassuming pastor gave me a sense of immediate peace and belonging. Since one of the two associates went on a sabbatical after his vacation, my two weeks at Sacred Heart parish got extended to five memorable months.

The pastor was an amicable priest who loved life. He played golf regularly, watched football, baseball and other games on Sundays, and played the violin at every opportunity. When he discovered that I loved music, he made me sing and play the guitar in church. Once a week, he and I would serenade the homeless who came to the parish hall, or to "Martha's Kitchen" as it was called, for a hot, decent meal. While the homeless ate, he would play the violin, while I strummed the guitar and sang. Many of the homeless were thrilled.

In most dioceses priests in the United States are given room and board and a generous stipend to live a decent, dignified life. Car and gas are a priest's personal responsibility. Other needs like clothes, travel, books and hobbies are also to be taken care of by the priest himself. Diocesan priests are allowed to keep money they receive as gifts as well as any inheritance they may have received from their families. So, there are priests who are well off and there are others who manage to survive while they take care of the needs of their families.

This pastor was in a category by himself. With whatever stipends he received he would visit the local thrift stores and buy gifts for others. He would find out what talents or future needs you had and then look for good bargains to match them. I remember he gave a family several used golf clubs so that one day they could sell them as antiques for a good price and send their kids to college. When I told him that I loved the sound of trumpets, a few days later a used trumpet from the local Goodwill store was placed as a gift outside my door.

One important way the Holy Spirit has sustained my vocation to the priesthood has been to send joyful, committed priests into my life. My first pastor in Northern California was one such priest.

"Martha's Kitchen" was founded at Sacred Heart parish by a parishioner, Louise Benson, who came to be known as Mother Teresa of San Jose. I knew her well because she was a member of my weekly Scripture Study group. She started out her outreach ministry by giving food to the hungry and the homeless from her own garage. Her neighbors in her rather well-established wealthy neighborhood were not too happy to see a long line of poor starving people lining up outside their homes. Because they complained she moved into the hall of Sacred Heart parish and that was the beginning of Martha's Kitchen and Sacred Heart Community Services.

Two reflections come to my mind when I think about Louise Benson. First of all, the study of Sacred Scripture must have influenced her and motivated her to start Martha's Kitchen. The words of Jesus in the parable of the last judgment in Matthew's Gospel are very clear and unambiguous: "Whatsoever you do to the least of my brothers and sisters, you do it for me." I have found that many Catholics in America, like Louise Benson, live out this criterion and challenge of love found in the gospels. When there are natural catastrophes like earthquakes and tsunamis, no matter where in the world, Americans always respond very generously. I am happy to think that my small effort of having a weekly Bible study may have inspired a parishioner like Louise to dedicate her life to the poor and the needy.

My second reflection does not logically follow from or connect with the first. In Palo Alto, California, the garage where Hewlett and Packard started their creative work in computers is now almost treated like a shrine. The same respect should have been given to Louise Benson's garage, from where she lived her faith with so much intensity that today Sacred Heart Community services is able to help thousands of needy and poor individuals and families. Why do we give more importance to machines and computers than to human needs and human dignity? Just as the Holy Spirit has sustained my vocation to the priesthood by sending dedicated priests into my life, so also my priestly ministry has been nurtured by the example of holy women and men and parishioners like Louise Benson.

I began to notice how everything is so much bigger in the United States. My first visit to and experience of the re-modeled East Ridge Mall was impressive and mind blowing. There were so many stores, bright lights and so much merchandise for sale. The San Jose Flea Market was another gigantic open 'shopping mall' for used and cheaper goods. It reminded me of 'Chor Bazaar' (The Thieves' Market) of Bombay, where you might find what has been stolen from you on sale to the public. Finally, the Ladies Sodality of the parish took me for my first visit to a gambling casino. In the bus, they even gave me some money to play at the slot machines. The bells and sounds of the casino were simply mind boggling. One can get easily carried away in this environment and time goes by very quickly because there are no clocks in the casino to tell you the time of day. From time to time, some of the ladies from our parish would come by while

I was trying my luck at the slots and ask me, "Father, how are you doing? Are you having any luck?" I would ask them to be quiet because I did not want anyone in the casino to know that I was a priest. What if I had the luck of winning the big jackpot?

During those initial months, my youngest sister who had become a flight attendant came to visit me at Thanksgiving with my mother. Dad stayed at home. That year, Thanksgiving Day happened to fall on my sister's birthday. It was our first Thanksgiving in the United States. Our parishioners planned a wonderful celebration, with delicious turkey and all the trimmings. While my mother and my sister sat down with all these wonderful parishioners in the parish hall, I brought out my guitar and sang several songs. One of my new friends from the Philippines videotaped the entire evening. Today their son has joined the seminary to become a priest. When my mother and sister returned to Bombay, they took the videotape with them and that turned out to be a treasure for my dad who apparently watched it over and over again, even till the day he died.

Before my mother and sister returned to India, we went to Tahoe to play in the snow. It was a new experience for my mother and my sister and it was a lot of fun. On the way we took in a guided tour of a winery. California is covered by vineyards and wineries and competes with the best wines in the world. At the end of our guided tour we stopped by for some free wine tasting. Before my sister could sip from her glass, she was asked for some identification. My sister at that time was in her twenties and felt insulted to be asked for identification. My American friends told her to consider this request for identification as a compliment to her good, youthful looks.

Parishioners at Sacred Heart were sad to see me leave their parish after only five months. In that area was a mortuary run by an Italian American family. The head of this family, in typical 'Mafia' style, asked me whether I wanted to stay at Sacred Heart and if so he would do the needful to make it happen. It was never my intention to challenge the will of God. If it was in God's plan that I move to another parish, I was ready and willing to make the transfer.

Even though it was a short period of only five months, it was a great beginning to my new phase of life of my journey of priesthood in the United States. At the end of Matthew's gospel, Jesus promises his disciples that he will be with them always till the end of time. Through the symbolism of the Sacred Heart of Jesus, my first introductory parish, I was being assured that God's love would always be with me, that I would not be abandoned so far away from home and from loved ones and that Jesus would always be watching over me every step of the way.

Even though I had to move, I was at peace. I collected all my belongings in a huge white bed sheet and in a friend's van arrived at my new assignment in a suburban parish of the diocese as a full-time Parochial Vicar.

Since I arrived at Christmas time at my new parish called the Church of the Transfiguration, I was introduced as one of the Magi, as a wise man from the East. This parish was radically different from the inner city 'immigrant' parish of the Sacred Heart. It was an all White Anglo parish and people were generally younger and well off compared with most of my previous parishioners. It was also very liberal in its approach to and model of Church.

The lay people were very involved in ministry and in the life of the parish. There was a strong sense of social justice and an equally strong sense of ownership of the Church. The Second Vatican Council had enabled the People of God here to say confidently: "*We are the Church.*" And they truly believed it and lived it.

The pastor was a strong social justice advocate. On the first morning I arrived at the parish office in my clergy suit, I was asked whether I was celebrating a funeral Mass or simply planning to get arrested that day. When I looked surprised I was told that the pastor wore his clerical clothes for precisely those two reasons: to celebrate a funeral Mass or to march in a demonstration, which would subsequently lead to his arrest and give the Church more visibility later on television in the evening news.

Back in Bombay, I was raised to be afraid of the police, whereas here the pastor showed me that marching for the rights of the people in public demonstrations makes the news and allows the world to know that the Church cares and is involved in the daily lives of the poor.

This church started out as a large parish in the suburbs of San Jose, California. It was one of the first parishes to introduce guitars and folk music in the liturgy. The church was always packed at every Mass especially with children, youth and young adults. There was a strong emphasis on social justice and community ministry. Parishioners believed strongly in the mission of the parish and of how they felt called to be Church after Vatican II.

Here in this passionate and active community, I was learning a new way to be Catholic and to be a priest. I remember reading a book by Juan Arias entitled *The God I Don't Believe In.* In one of the book's chapters he refers to the parable of the last judgment in the twenty-fifth chapter of Matthew's gospel, as the parable of the atheist. He contends that both believers and non-believers will ask the same question of Jesus at the end of time: "When did we see you thirsty, or hungry, or naked, or ill, or in prison?" And Jesus will answer both believers and non-believers alike: "Whatsoever you did to the least of my brothers and sisters, you did it for me." Thus, Arias concludes that Jesus will associate himself with anyone in need and the same criterion for salvation will apply to everyone, believers and non-believers alike: "Did you respond in love, when your love was needed the most?"

At the last judgment no one will be asked if they followed and fulfilled the usual criteria of their religious beliefs and traditions. For instance, for a Muslim, did you pray five times a day? For a Catholic, did you go to Mass on Sundays and Holy Days of obligation? For a Hindu, did you go on pilgrimage to your holy places? For a Protestant, did you study and memorize your Sacred Scriptures?

The purpose of everything we do in churches or in the mosques and the temples of the world is to be motivated and to be inspired to love when love is needed the most. That is the universal criterion by which we shall all be judged whatever our status or position in life.

Did God send me to this parish to learn and to live what was essential in my life of faith and in the teaching of Jesus? We never stop learning to be better disciples, if discipleship is our way of life.

Jesus had lived this way himself, but he had never alienated anyone through his teachings and his way of life, except those in authority and leadership positions who were challenged to change their hypocritical and false ways.

This progressive community had a unique style and structure of parish leadership. I had experienced parishes in the past where the pastor exercised leadership as a benevolent dictator or a self-sacrificing missionary or even as a team member on the East Coast with one or more priests. But here, the pastor wanted to be considered a member of a team, not just with a fellow priest but with other lay-people and staff members who were also going to share the same title with him of 'co-pastor.' It was leadership exercised as equals between clergy and laity without any hierarchy. Decisions were going to be made solely by consensus.

Among the new important experiences I had at this parish were the *Catechumenate* (Rite of the Christian Initiation of Adults, or R.C.I.A.) and RENEW.

The *Catechumenate* was the process by which the Church welcomed new adult members and older children, both those who had never been baptized as well as those baptized from other Christian traditions, into its Catholic family and apostolic tradition, through the initiation sacraments of Baptism, Confirmation and Eucharist.

Even though India is a mission land, where Catholics are a minority, I had never in all my life witnessed the baptism of an adult in parishes there.

Here at the Easter Vigil and on the Sundays of the year, I witnessed how the full signs of the Sacraments were being joyfully celebrated: a loaf of bread and plenty of wine consecrated at the Eucharist and offered to all to eat and drink as Jesus had invited his apostles to do at the Last Supper; generous amounts of oil used at Confirmations and the Anointing of the Sick; and plenty of water, not just a trickle, flowing at Baptisms, whether of infants or adults, immersing them in the life, death and resurrection of Jesus, into the profound depths of the Paschal Mystery.

The faith experience expressed through the life of the community and through liturgy and rituals in this parish was dynamic and vibrant. You felt transformed, never bored or indifferent.

RENEW was an adult faith sharing program, based on the Scriptures and people's life experiences. The basic question people asked themselves in groups and shared with each other was: "Where was God in your life this past week? Did you recognize the presence of God in the events and circumstances of your daily existence?" The Sunday Scriptures evoked other thought provoking faith sharing questions to help the group members grow spiritually. Over the years these RENEW groups had become communities, reflections of the community of the disciples of Jesus and of the early Christian Communities. They came to be called in fact: 'Small Christian Communities.'

After two thousand years of Christianity, where the Catholic Church alone is over a billion members strong and has spread all over the globe, there is sometimes a nostalgic feeling in parishes to experience the risen presence of Jesus as the early Church did. The first Christians, who were mainly Jewish converts, would meet in homes (or House Churches) and break bread together after celebrating the Word of God in synagogues.

When Christianity became the official religion of the Empire, after the conversion of Emperor Constantine, Christians worshipped openly, now no longer in homes but in huge basilicas. The sense of intimacy and community was lost even though the fear of practicing Christianity openly was gone from the lives of Christians everywhere in the Roman Empire.

That is why 'Small Christian Communities' or 'Basic Ecclesial Communities' are flourishing everywhere in the Catholic Church today. One advantage of having such faith communities in my new parish was to offer the opportunity of faith sharing for the entire parish community at Sunday gatherings of the Eucharist. At every Sunday Mass I celebrated, following the lead and example of the pastor, after the initial greeting and welcome, I would ask the assembly to be seated and then proceed to ask them a faith sharing question usually based on the Sunday Scriptures and then allow some time for spiritual insights to be shared by anyone who wanted to speak freely and personally for the benefit of the entire assembly.

Amazing reflections would come from the simple question: "Where was God in your life recently?"

These faith sharing moments provided a wonderful link with the past week and brought the experiences of the week into Sunday worship. There was a thread of continuity for the assembly. The faith life of the people was not truncated into one hour worship segments per week separated from their daily lives. Life and Liturgy truly came together as one.

I felt truly blessed as a believer and as a priest to experience the presence and the power of the Holy Spirit in this community.

After the Second Vatican Council, church buildings and structures began to go through quite a transformation. Newly constructed churches appeared to be more like community gathering multi-purpose halls. While traditional churches had the tabernacle as a symbol of reverence for the worshipping community, in the modern worship spaces a side chapel would be built for the Blessed Sacrament and the entire gathering space would be focused on the community itself.

While in older churches and cathedrals, the sacred was experienced as flowing and moving outwards and beyond the church building itself to the rising sun of the Resurrection, now the entire focus in modern churches seemed to be on the community itself. Before the Second Vatican Council, the priest had his back to the people because everyone in the assembly faced the rising sun in the east, symbolizing Resurrection. After the Council, the altar was positioned in such a way that the priest now faces the people and celebrates the sacred within the community.

This parish community mirrored the Second Vatican Council approach to Sunday worship and sacred structures. The parish itself did not have the word 'church' associated with the assembly, once the new worship center was built. Within the name of the parish the word 'Church' was changed to 'Community,' to create a shift from a cold, external structure to a warm, welcoming gathering of God's people, appropriately named: Transfiguration Catholic Community.

The altar was brought down to the level of the assembly to indicate that God, in Jesus Christ, through the Incarnation, is among the people. God was truly experienced as 'Emmanuel,' God with us.

I remember attending a Mass in another traditional wealthy parish church one day with the pastor of Transfiguration Catholic Community and he asked me to observe where the Presider's chair was placed. It was several steps above the level of the assembly and revealed in his eyes a Triumphalistic rather than an Incarnational approach to worship.

A full immersion baptismal font was constructed with steps going down into the pool and steps leading out to indicate the dying and the rising of Jesus. There were no pews, just comfortable chairs, which could be moved around to change the focus of a new liturgical season. The new worship space was in the round, thus enabling people to see and hear one another when faith sharing took place during Sunday and special liturgies. All this was done to strongly emphasize and celebrate community.

This worship space and its symbols were radically different from the churches of my childhood in India. I was now experiencing a whole new way of being church: inside and outside.

*****

In the confusion caused by radical changes in liturgy and Church life, I realized that it was only up to me to try to relax and unburden myself from all these stressors. At Sacred Heart parish I did not know what to do with my day off, so I would lock myself in my room and watch television all day. Through television the world implodes into your living room. The staff of my new parish, on the other hand, forced me to leave my television behind and helped me to move outdoors in order to explore the world on my days off.

With the pastor and another staff member I learned to play tennis. Gradually, I became part of a foursome that played tennis regularly on my day off. When my playing partners moved away from the area, I was lost for almost a year not knowing how to spend my day off fruitfully. Then I was introduced to the game of golf. I was hooked.

Now there was something I could do the whole day long on my day off. Golf took me away from work and stress. What lay men and women cannot do easily because of family related responsibilities turned out to be the right solution for me, because golf took me away from the parish for an entire day. Out on the beautiful greens and fairways, there were no phone calls, no appointments and no interruptions!

Golf taught me a great deal about life. Even though the game appears to be simple, golfers know that it is not. The book *The Road Less Traveled* begins with these three words: 'Life is difficult.' And so is golf. The goals, which are the flags and holes on the greens, are clearly set before you, yet challenging to achieve. And as in life, you play the ball wherever it lies, with honesty and integrity. Along the fairways there can be all kinds of hazards and challenges. Your personality comes through in the game of golf. You know whether you are patient or not, easy going or competitive, gentle or the cursing kind when things don't go your way. As in life, there are many angles and surprises on the golf course, but they are not insurmountable. True, life is difficult, but it can also be fun. And it's all up to you.

It is said that Golf and Prayer are alike: in both of them it's important to keep your head down.

As I settled more and more to the American way of life, I learned how to ski and to bowl. Unfortunately I went skiing only once a year with the youth group. A once a year skiing holiday makes you hurt in more places than you can imagine. Bowling was a good substitute together with movies when golf was not possible due to rain. I bought my own shoes and a bowling ball that made a huge impression on the youth of the parish.

The pastor, with some other priests, owned a house among the beautiful redwoods of California. The staff of the parish often went there for relaxation and study days. California is a huge state and there is so much to see and do in this richly blessed part of the world. Not only is the climate pleasant all year round, there are mountains, beaches, deserts, sequoias and redwoods, vineyards and lakes, Disneyland and Hollywood and much, much more. Even though California has a Mediterranean type of mild climate, if you drive up a few hours into the Sierras, you can ski to your heart's delight and then joyfully and thankfully leave the snow behind.

Since I was a relatively good photographer, on my day off, I would pack my camera, some sandwiches and set off to discover many interesting places on day trips. The more places I visited, the more suggestions for day trips came my way and very soon I had four huge albums of pictures I had taken on my one day adventures in California.

I remember vividly my visit to the Pinnacles. When I arrived there, I saw an entrance to the caves, but there was a clear warning before you entered to make sure you had a good flashlight or you were part of a larger group. Since I was alone, I checked my rechargeable flashlight, but the light appeared dim and I wasn't sure how long ago or how much it was charged.

I was very keen on going into the caves but I was afraid and I did not want to take the risk. I hiked around the perimeter of the caves and found myself on the opposite end of the Pinnacles. All the time I was wondering whether I should take the risk to go in alone. On the other side, I peeked into the darkness of the caves, not sure of myself, and then, suddenly, I heard a voice say to me: "Go on. Don't be afraid." I clearly remember that when I arrived at the other side of the Pinnacles, there was nobody there but me. Now when I looked over my shoulder, I saw an elderly man gently smiling at me. I faced the caves once again and entered boldly. I made it to the other side, happy that with the help of my Guardian Angel I had overcome my fear and conquered the Pinnacles!

Since we had no regular full-time cook at the rectory, I was invited often by families to dinner. I let the parishioners know what days were open on my calendar for meals. I enjoyed this quality interaction and found it the best way to get to know the parishioners quickly. People were happy that I knew them by name.

About six months later, since the parishioners loved to hear me sing and play the guitar, they decided that I should headline a parish concert and have a festival of songs. They thought the entry donation to the concert would help me raise some funds and make a trip to India to see my family. Americans love music and many elderly parishioners do not have the opportunity to go to concerts anymore. But a church concert sounded like a wonderful idea to attract both young and old to gather and to sing along.

We began the evening in the church to the tune of "Do you know the Way to San Jose?" In my monologue, I said that I had met someone before the concert who asked me whether this was a Catholic Church, because surprisingly all those who walked in first were seated in the front pews! This behavior was highly unusual because Catholics tend to sit in the last rows for Mass in order to make a quick exit to the parking lot. After doing a few solos, we gave out booklets with popular songs so that everyone could join in. After the intermission, I again sang some solos, including some songs by Elvis Presley. I had the whole church swinging with 'Jailhouse Rock.' As a result, later on, I was given a new name: 'Elvis Priestley!' We ended the show with more popular community songs. It was an unforgettable evening for all.

*****

A full year had gone by since I arrived in California. I woke up one morning to have breakfast and was ready to leave for my day off. I was told by the pastor that there was a long-distance call for me at the parish office next door. It was from my brother-in-law, Joe, calling from England with very sad news that my dad in India had passed away. I sobbed quietly on a staff member's shoulder. I remembered that a year earlier when I left India my father was heartbroken to see me go. Somehow, he knew that he would not see me again in this life. It was exactly a year to the day of my departure for the United States of America.

I was told that my dad had died peacefully in his sleep. It wasn't even bed time. Around seven in the evening, my mother had just returned home from the evening daily Mass and saw my dad who appeared to be peacefully resting on the sofa chair in front of the television. The program that he was watching, as he had done many, many times before, was the one I had made for him on the previous Thanksgiving Day in California when my mother and youngest sister had visited me for the first time. My dad loved to watch this video of his favorite performing son. To my mother he appeared to be soundly asleep on the sofa. When she tried to wake him up, she discovered that he had died of heart failure.

The only thing that consoled my mother was the painless way my father died. I continued to weep when I got the news. The last time I had wept bitterly was when my eldest brother had passed away and I was only seventeen years of age. I wept for my brother then because I was so confused by this major loss in our family. Now, I wept for my dad simply because I loved him and I missed him so much.

Traditional Catholics always pray for a happy death. In fact the prayer "Hail Mary" concludes with a request to Mary to pray for us "now and at the hour of our death." My dad prayed the full Rosary daily since his retirement. As a family, in India, we always prayed the Rosary every evening. God heard my dad's prayer and took him peacefully to heaven.

I could not decide whether to fly to India right away for my dad's funeral. I was faced with an immigration issue. After arriving in the United States a year before, I had applied for permanent residence in the United States, and it is stipulated that while the paperwork is in process one should not leave the country.

One of my older sisters called from India and reminded me that my presence would be much appreciated by the whole family at the funeral. According to Indian (mainly Hindu) custom, as the eldest of the living sons in the family, it was my duty to be present at my father's funeral services. I put aside the immigration issue of permanent residence, booked an emergency flight to Bombay and decided that it was more important for me to be with my family at this crucial hour of saying the final goodbye to my beloved father.

On the long journey home, there was plenty of time to reflect on my dad's life. When my brother had died I was only a seminarian, but now I was going to be not only the eldest son but also the priest at my father's funeral. My dad, who had been the voice of God for me urging me not to quit the seminary but to persevere in my vocation to the priesthood, was now going to have that same priestly son to celebrate his homecoming. I believed that my dad had lived a long and full life and so I planned a celebration of his life and waited patiently for the plane to arrive at my destination.

I remember traveling very light for my dad's funeral. After all it was an emergency flight where I had time to pack only the bare essentials. India was largely a poor country and whenever Indians returned home they would have very heavy bags filled to the brim with stuff and gifts for their families. It was an expectation and a burden on anyone who came from abroad. This time I had no suitcases or any luggage, just a small carry on.

I remembered the words of St. Francis of Assisi (in the context of my father's death): "When we die we cannot take with us anything we have received; only what we have given."

I remembered also the Zen story of the tourist who visited a monk in a remote mountainous part of the world and when he entered his tiny abode and not seeing even a chair to sit on asked the monk: "Where is your furniture?" To which the monk replied: "And where is yours?" The tourist said that he was only passing through. To which the monk added: "And so am I."

Traveling unencumbered this time made it much easier to reflect on the reality of death. My dad was going to take with him a lot, because he had given a lot to us his family in his lifetime.

I wasn't yet incardinated into my new diocese, and so my ties with Bombay still remained. An auxiliary bishop was sent to celebrate my dad's funeral Mass but I felt that I had to speak and preach and share personally the memories of my father. I did precisely that with the huge crowd that attended the funeral services. My youngest brother served the Mass and read the prayers of the faithful. While reading he broke down. My brother was the one who daily shaved my dad when he could not do this task for himself.

"He lived life to the fullest," were the words I had printed on the card below the picture of my dad. The Holy Card distributed to all was that of Our Lady of Perpetual Succor, the patron of the engineering company my dad had started with my eldest brother. The company was called PECO, the Perpetual Engineering Company.'

221

Dad had dedicated himself totally to my mother and to my many siblings. He never appeared to worry about anything. His faith was strong. He was a simple man and he lived simply. On the day before he died, he and my mother had received two halves of the same consecrated host from the local pastor. I was happy that dad was finally with the Lord and his blessed Mother, both of whom he loved so much.

Deep down in my soul I was happy that my dad was not only instrumental in my being born into this world but also in my becoming a Catholic priest.

*****

I had to restart my immigration process from Bombay right after the funeral. Once again I had to ask myself if this was the right choice I had made to leave India for good. Was God giving me another opportunity to change my mind? I cannot say for sure that this is the characteristic of all Indians, but it is definitely in my family to change our minds often and to go back and forth several times before making decisions (sometimes even after finalizing them).

But a year in the United States had already affected how I made decisions in my life. It was only a fleeting thought to want to stay behind in India. I quickly put it aside and concentrated on collecting my documents and certificates to claim permanent residence in the United States of America. It took about five months for the process to be complete and gave me a golden chance to spend quality time with my mother and my siblings.

At the American Consulate, I remember noticing that the officer, who was perusing my documents, turned to another officer behind the counter and showed him with a smile the page where all the languages I had learned over the years were listed. It looked like the Americans were glad to get my skills and talents for their country and yet upon arrival in the United States, I would still be given the grand title of 'Resident Alien.'

While I was waiting for my immigration papers to come through, I wrote to my American bishop that I was perfectly comfortable getting a new assignment upon my return to the United States, if he felt the need to appoint someone else in my place at my last parish. I was secretly hoping he would assign me to another parish so that I could have a fresh start. In his reply he told me not to worry and that I still remained assigned where I was. My dad's funeral services were held in July. Almost five months later, with formal, completed immigration documents in my hand, I landed in San Francisco and arrived at the same Transfiguration Catholic Community once again in time for Christmas. The wise men from the East never fail to arrive in our mangers for Christmas and Epiphany every year.

All the parishioners were excited to see me again. Some had stayed in touch and many had prayed for my return. My excitement was short lived because I lost my voice due to laryngitis just before the big family vigil Mass of Christmas. The wise man from the East could only smile. He had no words of wisdom. He had nothing to say!

Another year with this dynamic community made for more growth and learning. During my years in the seminary in Europe I did not get a chance to have practical parish experience. Thus, when you come to your first parish assignment you quickly forget everything you've learned in the seminary. As you go from one parish to another, you begin to see that parish communities have their own flavor and spiritualities; their own, according to Avery Dulles, model of a Church.

Life for me was becoming one continuous journey of learning and growing.

At this parish, the rectory was a four-bedroom house, a block away from the church building. The pastor and I each had two small bedrooms to ourselves. It was a cozy arrangement. There was one big adjustment we had to make to rectory living. The pastor was an extrovert while I was "half-and-half," an introvert and an extrovert straight down the middle. Whenever the pastor returned from his social justice meetings, he would love to narrate the whole story, the meeting details and all their thorny issues to me at dinner. Then he would go to bed and sleep soundly, while I would end up sleepless thinking about all the issues he had brought to the table at dinner. One day I sat him down and explained my dilemma. I told him that I was happy to listen to his stories and his justice dilemmas as long as he brought them to me at breakfast the following morning.

Then I would have all day to think about them without loosing any sleep over them.

Priests in rectories have to work on their relationship much like couples and families in homes.

One other issue that helped rectory living at this parish for me was to never again eat what the pastor had prepared from his duck hunting trips. The first time I bit into the delicious duck he had prepared, I chipped a tooth from a bullet that was still lodged in the duck's side.

The personnel policy for priests of the diocese stated that a priest seeking incardination should have the experience of at least two parishes in the first five years of ministry. After two-and-a-half years with Transfiguration Catholic Community, the personnel board recommended to the bishop that I be sent as an associate to St. Lucy Parish in a relatively small town called Campbell, also in the Silicon Valley.

*****

I was very happy to see my assignment at Transfiguration as an enriching training period of my early priesthood in the United States, but now I was also very excited to move into a more traditional Catholic parish.

After the Second Vatican Council each parish tends to have and develop its own unique personality and characteristics. An immigrant international priest has to be aware of this reality and constantly make adjustments to survive and to thrive.

The parish of St. Lucy in Campbell was large and ethnically White. The pastor was of German origin and had been at this parish for twenty-three years. In the pre-Vatican II model of the traditional hierarchical church, he made sure that everybody knew that he, and he alone, was the boss. He had no parish council, no finance committee and no lay ministry groups of any kind.

There was a full-time housekeeper at the rectory, so all meals were provided. Being of German origin, the pastor had a strict schedule for meals: breakfast, at 8:30 a.m., right after his 8:00 a.m. morning Mass; lunch at 12 noon, right after the last Angelus Bell, and finally, following cocktails at 5:30 p.m., dinner, at 6 p.m.

sharp. He had a good sense of humor. He loved to tell jokes and he enjoyed a good laugh.

Every Monday morning, he would personally take the Sunday collection bags to the bank, and while the money was being counted he had a new joke for the tellers, who looked forward to his weekly visit. He smoked cigars, had his own radio station and was known to shut the doors of the church after the opening prayer so that latecomers to Mass would learn a lesson for their souls about the consequences of tardiness.

I was ordained a deacon in Germany so the commonly shared knowledge of the German language helped us get along very well.

The sometimes grouchy pastor was getting old and feeble. He was still the canonical pastor but he allowed me to be involved in the day to day management of the parish. When he saw how active and busy I was he cautioned me to take care of myself and not to be burned out. In many ways he was a father figure to me. He even looked like my dad from a certain angle.

While my last parish claimed to be the first parish to have folk singing and guitars at Mass, this community, on the other hand, was the first parish in the diocese to have a Sunday evening Mass. It was so popular, especially with working young adults and yuppies of the Silicon Valley, that the church would be packed wall to wall every Sunday night. The music was provided by a spiritual rock band called 'Cornerstone.' People loved the music and the prayerfulness of the liturgy.

The Notre Dame research conducted in parishes has shown that people who come to church look for good music and an inspiring homily. There are many other aspects and elements of liturgy which help participation. But music and preaching are considered to be most important. 'Cornerstone' at this parish provided the kind of inspirational music young adults were seeking. When I arrived, I filled the void on Sunday night with good preaching (at least that's what parishioners told me). It was a marriage made in heaven. The crowds kept coming Sunday after Sunday from all over the Silicon Valley. Fortunately in size it was one of the largest Catholic Churches in the Bay Area.

At my previous parish I was introduced to the *Catechumenate*, the process by which adults and older children are received into the Catholic Church at the Easter Vigil. When I had the opportunity, I attended 'Beginnings and Beyond,' a workshop and practical experience of the Rites of Christian Initiation of Adults (R.C.I.A.). Since the R.C.I.A. and the *Catechumenate* were unknown at St. Lucy Parish, I announced the start of the very first journey for adult inquirers. As a pioneer I had to organize and celebrate everything. I had to form a team, advertise the process throughout the parish and eventually be the main priest celebrant at all the stages, scrutinies, and liturgies of the Church year related to the *Catechumenate*.

That first Easter Vigil at St. Lucy's I baptized twenty-one adults and received several more adults into full communion with the Catholic Church through the sacraments of Baptism, Confirmation and Eucharist. Since I knew all the candidates personally and by name, I may have sounded like the announcer of the game show "The Price is Right" shouting joyfully, "Come on down. You're the next candidate to be baptized!"

I have said before that I had never experienced the baptism of an adult in India, even though India is a mission land with under three percent of the population claiming to be baptized Christians. So, it was very interesting that here in the United States, in a largely 'Christian' nation, I was having a powerful missionary experience baptizing adults in large numbers.

The *Catechumenate* speaks for itself. Once people are welcomed into the Church in this very visible process, more and more individuals begin to seek the joy and the fulfillment of fully belonging to the Catholic Church. The Easter Vigil can become such a powerful experience of the Holy Spirit that the effects are felt for years to come. I remember advertizing for the Easter Vigil with the following words: "Come, experience the greatest night of our life of faith." At that first Easter Vigil service at St. Lucy Parish over a thousand people showed up to experience our greatest night of faith celebration.

At different times in her history, the Catholic Church has neglected the needs of certain sections of its membership. At times workers have been generally left out. At other times, women have felt excluded by male authority figures in the

Church. Recently, young adults from the ages of eighteen to thirty-five have lost their sense of belonging in parishes. With so many young adults attending Sunday evening services at St. Lucy's, I started a Young Adult Ministry.

It was not limited to the parish, because young adults are independent and will choose where they want to go. They also have the means to get around. This group was strong and the meetings were well attended. It was run by the young adults themselves with me as their spiritual guide.

I learned quickly that adults should be treated as adults in the Church. They should not be handled as babies or teenagers, where you do everything for them at every turn. In the Silicon Valley most young adults are highly skilled and are very competent and specialized in their secular, professional fields.

One of the key things I planned for this group was a three day retreat. A live in experience, away from the chores and responsibilities of daily living and work, was ideal to create a sense of camaraderie, fellowship and community among these wonderful young adults. The planning of the retreat itself and all the other details were taken over by the natural leaders in the group. The retreat became a defining event for the entire young adult ministry.

The good news is that this group became a community strong in their faith. The bad news was that the group became extinct after only four years. The best news of all was that each young adult found a church-going faith filled suitable partner for life in the group itself. What better ending could one expect?

*****

It was now ten years since I was ordained a priest and I decided to pursue my goal of obtaining a Masters degree. I had tried in vain to do a Masters program in social work in India after my return from Rome. I researched and discovered a brand new Masters program in Pastoral Ministry with emphasis on liturgy, catechetics and spirituality, offered at Santa Clara, California, at a Jesuit-run University.

The new life and fresh air blown into the Church, thanks to the Second Vatican Council, encouraged not only priests and nuns but also lay people to pursue a religious education and a master's degree in theology and ministry.

This time around I was a different kind of student. I worked full time in a parish during the day and attended lectures at Santa Clara University in the evenings. I did not have the luxury anymore of being just a full time student.

One advantage of my current situation was that my studies enriched my day-to-day ministry at the parish and I brought the issues of my pastoral work to class discussions and written assignments. Another interesting detail was the fact that for the first time, in my experience, priests and nuns were studying side by side with lay people dealing with the same pastoral problems and issues.

In the olden days, before the Second Vatican Council, a parish would be staffed solely by priests and occasionally a secretary. The parish school would be run by nuns and the rectory would have a full time live-in housekeeper. After the Second Vatican Council parish staffs began to have more lay people than clergy, and more women than men working for the church in a variety of ministries.

In the seminary we were not prepared or trained to work with lay people, especially with women.

I worked hard for two years at Santa Clara University, often using my days off to research and to write my papers. Now since we were working with women in the church, all of us were asked to be sensitive to the issue of language in our papers and in our presentations.

Language is an expression of culture and words are powerful symbols of how we see ourselves. Many societies of the world were dominated (and perhaps still are today) by men and hence even the Scriptures were written in largely male terminology. I was already made aware of this issue when I was a full time associate at Transfiguration Catholic Community. The difference was that in the parish the fight for inclusive language appeared to be a form of protest against a male-dominated hierarchical Church that refused ordination to women. At Santa Clara University, on the other hand, we were asked to be sensitive to the women of today who would be our co-workers in our parishes.

I used to car-pool to Santa Clara University with four women who worked in parish ministries. Our discussions in the car and during study sessions increased my appreciation for the role of women in the church. Jesus himself had several women disciples who followed him and ministered to his needs. Paul and some of the other apostles had the support of many women converts and some noble women who were financially well off and who shared their resources for the spread of the gospel. In Paul's letters we note that a few of them were named as co-workers and leaders of their communities.

After completing my Masters at Santa Clara University, I decided that I wanted to be part of the festive graduation ceremonies. In Rome, where I received my Bachelor Degrees *summa cum laude* in Philosophy and Theology, we would leave for our vacation soon after the final exams. Vacation travel in Europe meant getting visas and long delays at embassies. There was no time to attend graduation ceremonies or to celebrate. But this time it was going to be different. I made sure I had my cap and gown and was part of the celebratory graduation parade on the grounds of Santa Clara University.

It's so important to stop and enjoy the moment. It's so important in life to celebrate. The long hard years of study called for its own reward. It was party time and my family and friends made sure we all had fun and a memorable celebration.

I was back in the world of books and lectures. The Masters program gave me the impetus, the inspiration and the momentum to move to the next and final level: the Doctorate.

The Masters degree in Theology, with emphasis on Pastoral Liturgy, from Santa Clara University seemed to fulfill a need to update myself as a priest after ten years of ordination and to be relevant to the times. It was also my first opportunity to pursue a degree in the context of life in America. I felt the degree program helped me understand not only the theological and liturgical issues of our times, but it also opened my eyes to the reality of the Church in the United States of America.

Where we study is almost as important as what we study. Perhaps if I had done the Masters program in India, I might have adapted more easily to life in India. Only God knows for sure what could have happened.

At first I was interested in pursuing a combined doctoral program in Theology and Mass Media Communications at the Graduate Theological Union in Berkeley, California. It would have brought together my past and present interests. But God had other plans for me. I was informed about a doctoral program in the area of counseling psychology at the University of San Francisco, the oldest Jesuit University in the western United States.

I was interested in this program because there was no psychology taught either at the seminary in Bombay or at the Pontifical Urban University in Rome. One of the main tasks of a priest is to advise and counsel parishioners of all ages. While today psychology is offered in the seminary curriculum, in my seminary years one was expected to be a natural counselor without the opportunity for training or the development of special skills.

Listening is the best therapy. But effective listening is a skill and one does not automatically receive it at ordination. Many priests are poor listeners because they have been trained to tell you what the Church teaches without understanding where you come from. Moreover, they will also make the decisions for you. True listening empowers the other to own the right decision.

Many bishops and clerics in authority are poor listeners because they have degrees in Canon Law but not in psychology. They will inform you about the law but not necessarily care about how you feel.

A priest needs to have both theology and psychology in his background. Armed with these two weapons he can help people first identify their problems and then give them spiritual direction to effectively deal with them.

My Indian bishop was not happy when I told him that I would like to have open-ended discussions with people regarding faith. What I intended to do in true Socratic fashion was to dialectically help people to think for themselves, to discover their own reasons to believe and to live fully. I felt that the objective teachings of the Church were generally known by everyone, but not everyone understood why we believe what we believe. Not everyone was prepared to take ownership and to speak up for their beliefs. That is why the faith development of many adult believers today is stunted and limited.

In many organizations and institutions, members know the 'What?' and the 'How?' What's really important to retain membership and to invite new members is to ask ourselves the most important question: 'Why?' When we are able to answer the question 'Why?' then we may be also able to verbalize the inspirations, the beliefs, the causes and the purposes that motivated us from the very beginning.

In a book entitled *The Heretical Imperative*, heresy in a social context is defined as a choice. A choice is made against a known belief or practice. Therefore a heresy is committed against a particular institution when one makes choices different from the ones the institution holds to be true.

In the modern world choice is a way of life. You ask for a cup of coffee at Starbucks and you will be dazzled and puzzled by the number of coffee options and combinations. There is never a simple choice for sodas. You have to first choose a name brand and then decide whether you want regular or decaffeinated. On television you have hundreds of channels to choose from.

When I was a child I was seen and not heard. Moreover, being one of many siblings, it meant that I took seriously and without questioning whatever was given to me or decided for me. Today's children have been raised in the world of the heretical imperative. They know what they want in schools, in families, in restaurants and on playgrounds. When they grow up they will also let you know what they want from their work, their businesses, their country, and, yes, even their Church.

It has made life more complex and, at the same time, more enriching and engaging.

For almost four hundred years before the Second Vatican Council the Catholic Church was monolithic and uniform all over the world. Latin was the language of worship, and people knew when to sit, stand and kneel; when to pray, pay and obey.

Unity was founded on uniformity. The teachings of the Church were in the form of questions and answers. You were a Catholic if you knew and memorized the answers.

The Heretical Imperative today has given rise to 'Cafeteria Catholics' who pick and choose what they want to believe and practice.

Just as the Church in the fifties and sixties felt the need to dialog with the modern world because so many changes were happening all around thanks to technology and the flow of information, so also the Church today needs to dialog with her own members to help them understand what they are supposed to believe and to give them a strong and sound reason to believe.

It is unfortunate that so many Catholics today don't find a reason to stay in the Church in which they were baptized and raised. No wonder the second largest religious group in the United States is composed of former Catholics.

The United States of America is the wealthiest nation on earth. Yet, there are many poor families even here and there are many individuals and institutions that go to battle for them and for their rights. Some people are passionate about the issues of hunger and health care. Was I being called to do the same? As I looked at my own journey I realized it would be more beneficial for me to focus less on the physical well-being of parishioners and concentrate more on the mental and spiritual health of people around me.

What about the physical dimension? I have always believed in developing a sound, healthy body. I was never one to adore the body or its shape but I remained healthy by being an outdoors kind of guy, walking and hiking and playing all kinds of games and sports. The ultimate sign of health for me was the integration of the physical, the mental and the spiritual.

The Latin word for health is *salus*. The word 'salvation' is derived from the Latin for health. Even the name Jesus stands for 'the One who saves.' Jesus came to save us from our sins, from a sense of incompleteness, alienation and brokenness to lead us to heaven and to the integration of the physical, mental and the spiritual in our lives.

Education is expensive. So I wrote directly to the President of the University of San Francisco and received a generous presidential scholarship towards the doctoral program. The diocese with the consent of the bishop and the education board also agreed to partially help with the tuition.

When I started the doctoral program I was working full time as an associate. Because Counseling Psychology was a new field for me, I was obligated to complete sixty semester units, including all the core courses. This degree program was geared to active professionals from different walks of life. Working men and women came from all parts of California, Nevada and Arizona to the University of San Francisco's School of Education. This was a unique opportunity for full-time workers like me to make a living and to get, at the same time, an advanced degree. I had my own commute of about sixty miles each way. Every other week, there was a four-and-a-half hour lecture on a Friday evening and then, two lectures totaling nine hours on Saturday. When I drove back Friday night and Saturday evening, the ride home was my down time to unwind and to prepare for the busy parish weekend.

My life got busier and fuller every day. I found the blending of ongoing education and pastoral ministry to be very enlightening, enriching and stimulating. Deep down in my soul I felt intensely happy and youthful as a priest.

St. Lucy Parish gave me not only an opportunity for continuing education, but also the training and skills to become a pastor and a shepherd some day.

God calls and then sends. The Holy Spirit guides you throughout the process of calling and sending. A spiritual person is one who is aware that in God "we live and move and have our being."

CHAPTER 8

MAN ON A MISSION

R IGHT IN the middle of my doctoral program, as I settled into a rhythm of commute, study and parish work, I was approached by my bishop during a clergy recollection day, asking me whether I would be willing to become the pastor of a huge suburban parish, which included a parochial school.

I happily said "Yes," thanking him for the honor and for his trust in my ability and skills. By way of a helpful tip for my first assignment as pastor, he said to me with a twinkle in his eyes, "All you have to do is smile!" I thought to myself that that should not be too difficult and that consequently, a pastor's life must be really easy. I know how to be happy and I do have, as several people have told me, a disarming and charming smile. I thought to myself that being pastor for the first time in America would be a piece of cake.

I remembered the words of a popular song: "When you're smiling, the whole world smiles with you."

In the year 1990 the parish of St. Lucy in Campbell went through a complete clergy change. The ailing pastor retired early and was moved out of the rectory into a nursing home. The other associate was transferred, and I was sent only three miles away to start a new life as shepherd of a wealthy Anglo community of about two thousand and seven hundred families, called St.

Martin of Tours, with a parochial elementary school of about three hundred and thirty children.

At this parish I was succeeding the only Monsignor of the diocese. The Monsignor had worked for many years in Catholic charities and the hospital health care system of the Archdiocese before it was split. He was well-known as an organizer and administrator. During the eleven years of his only assignment as pastor he had divided the parish into several departments based on ministries. Each one functioned independently and had its own budget. Such a structure can work if all the parts and departments work smoothly with each other and work collaboratively. But such was not the case.

Each ministry took off on its own and made its own demands on the Monsignor, who now felt that he had created, as he called it, an uncontrollable monster.

Weeks before I moved in I met with him to discuss the status of the parish. I had to know what I was inheriting. The parish did not have any debts. Whatever construction work was done at the church, or remodeling projects undertaken for the school, were paid for by the sale of the former convent to the congregation of nuns who managed the nearby Catholic hospital.

The Monsignor was well loved by many people. He was very charismatic in his style of celebrating liturgy and the sacraments.

But the Monsignor also confessed to me that he had created a monster through this style of parish leadership where each ministry functioned almost independently. I had a dilemma. How does one smile at a monster and still manage to stay alive?

*****

The appointment letter from the bishop reminds you that at your ordination, you were given a share in Christ's ministry as shepherd of God's people. You are further told that this role of leadership in the Church is especially evident in the office of Pastor, to which is entrusted the care of a portion of the Christian Faithful, so that they may become in Christ a sign of unity and an instrument of God's peace.

A week before my fortieth birthday, I was installed as Pastor by the Bishop. The installation ceremony is quite simple and is celebrated in the context of a parish Mass. The installation ceremonies are repeated at each new Pastor assignment. The new Pastor is asked to lead the faithful in the profession of faith and then to promise loyalty and fidelity to Christ and to the '*Magisterium*' (teaching authority) of the Church.

The Mass of installation was a big event for the parish. Since my mother and some of my siblings were present, they were asked to bring up the gifts of bread and wine. My mother's presence, especially, reminded me of the day of my ordination when my parents vested me to celebrate Eucharist for the first time. How proud my dad would have been to see me installed as a spiritual leader of a large American parish. At the reception that followed there was a lot of food, seven huge cakes and plenty of champagne.

A week after my installation, friends of mine invited my family and several other friends and parishioners for my fortieth birthday party. I was not personally stressed out when the big forty came along. A diocesan priest is moved from time to time to different cities and newer assignments. Each new posting is like a fresh beginning. One does not feel age or tiredness when faced with fresh new challenges. I felt as if I was newly ordained even at forty because I was made Pastor for the first time.

My friends who hosted the party had some pretty bizarre ideas as seen through the lens of an Indian cultural point of view. They looked at forty as the age for being 'over the hill.' Scattered everywhere in the house were black balloons, a dark chocolate cake with black icing, and many scary signs of the Grim Reaper. My family was puzzled, because in India, the older you are the more respect you get for becoming a wise person. I definitely did not feel that my life was sliding 'over the hill' at forty. But I was a good sport and took everything with a grain of salt. We enjoyed ourselves and laughed the night away!

This was turning out to be a big year with many important milestones in my life. Soon after my fortieth birthday, I was informed by the Immigration and Naturalization Service that I had a date for my citizenship test. I began to prepare in earnest for the exam. I went to the local library and picked out the materials I needed to learn about United States citizenship. At the same time I asked the members of my staff and some

American parishioners whether they knew the answers to the test questions. To my surprise some of these individuals born and raised in this country could not answer quite a few of the questions. It made me realize that we can take our freedoms and our rights for granted.

One of the key advantages of citizenship is being allowed to vote. Yet, so many Americans don't go to the polling booths on election days. In sheer numbers, India is the largest democracy in the world. Since I had left India the first time for Italy when I was about nineteen years old, I never had a chance to vote in India or anywhere else. Now I was going to get my first opportunity. But did I know all the answers?

My memory rescued me. By the time I went through all the citizenship books I could find at the library, I was more up-to-date with regard to American history, civics and politics than quite a few of my American friends born in the good old U.S. of A.

So, with great confidence I went to my citizenship test which I passed with flying colors. In March, 1991, I became a naturalized citizen of the United States. I was no longer an 'alien.' At the citizenship naturalization ceremonies, there were new United States citizens from about forty seven countries. The setting in the court house reminded me of my college seminary in Rome that also drew seminarians from almost all parts of the world.

The day I became a citizen was truly a momentous catholic, universal event. The officer who had to read out our names had quite a job that morning with all the tongue-twisters from so many languages and cultures. He did a pretty good job pronouncing difficult names from Vietnam, Cameroon, India, Lebanon, Sri Lanka and so on. What I found amusing was that when he came to my first name, which is 'George,' he mangled it trying to pronounce it as if it were a foreign name, while, at that very moment, I was becoming a citizen of the country of George Washington; and the President of the United States that year was none other than George Bush Sr.

As we received our naturalization papers proclaiming us citizens, we had to throw out our 'permanent resident green cards' into a huge basket, and while taking the oath of citizenship, we had to renounce our prior citizenship. This created new emotions in me. Yes, I had decided to live in the United States, yet, being born and raised in India I still felt her roots and nurturing in my bones. Can one simply throw away the past by renouncing it?

I had thought for a while before becoming a citizen that since I had adopted the way of life of an American, it was natural for me to also seek United States' citizenship. I was definitely used to eating my dinner at 6 p.m. now in the United States, as opposed to having a big lunch (the main meal) and a late light supper at about 9 p.m. in India. There were many other cultural aspects of adaptation that motivated me to seek citizenship in my new adopted country: like language, music, educational methods, Church life, personal responsibility, communications, innovation, opportunity and the unique sense of time and space that one finds in the United States.

But all this meant letting go of my past links with India, the land of my birth. I had already noticed that my address book with names of Indian families and friends was getting smaller and smaller each year. Most of my family had also expressed their intention of eventually immigrating to the United States.

So, after the citizenship ceremonies, I did what all Americans love to and are supposed to do: I ate apple pie and ice-cream and called my mother! I truly felt one with my adopted country. When my parish's school children found out I had become an American citizen I was invited by the Principal during the school assembly to lead everyone in the Pledge of Allegiance.

After the installation ceremony and the fortieth birthday party the week after, and all the excitement of becoming an American citizen that year, work started in earnest both in the parish and in my doctoral program.

As I look back, my doctoral studies, both from an understanding of what was going on around me and a therapeutic point of view of what I was sensing within me, helped me better tackle the so-called 'Monster' of my predecessor. What I saw was not a scary or threatening nightmare, but sincere professional lay ministers who were doing their best to enliven the parish and to make it a vibrant community. .

I remember once how one of our staff members created a website for our parish without consulting me. I knew very little about the internet and websites but I was concerned because I thought, as pastor, I should be responsible for the contents of the website. Everyone was excited about the website and when I finally understood its value for the community, I gave it my full support. The important thing is to see beyond your own insecurities and to learn how to empower others, especially laypeople, who may be more knowledgeable than you are in many fields. I felt that to be a strong and effective leader I needed to understand and use the expertise and the experience of both my parishioners and staff for the good of the whole community.

I have never forgotten my first liturgy on a Saturday evening at St. Martin's parish in my new role of Pastor. After I had proclaimed the Gospel reading, I stepped down among the people to do my homily. Just then the wooden church began shaking and swaying, thanks to one of California's many earthquakes. Saturday evenings generally draw the elderly to church. I looked at the nervous faces and was glad that the earthquake had not caused any physical damage. I stepped away from my prepared homily and calmly reassured the people that this shaking and rocking caused by the earthquake was not going to be in my style of parish leadership. I saw people smiling and there was a sense of relief.

People come to church for a sense of peace, serenity and stability. Everything around them seems to be in flux. I promised them that I was not going to shake things up as a new Pastor. As the new kid on the block, I was going to spend a lot of time listening. I told the people that priests and pastors come and go, but they are the ones who will remain. They are the ones with the history and the memories. I told them that I would learn from them and acquire wisdom from their faith experiences.

I put my Masters Thesis and Practicum on presiding and preaching into practice. I added a touch of humor whenever appropriate. I told the assembly once about a priest who had these words on the back of his vestments while presiding at Mass: "How am I celebrating? Please call 1-800-555-5555."

I used my gift of storytelling whenever I had the chance. Jesus told parables to announce the Kingdom of God. I found modern day stories to share that made the good news exciting and interesting. I used humor and current events to throw the hook and capture the attention of my audience and assembly.

I visited families and dined with them whenever possible. It is very difficult to really know your parishioners simply by greeting them in the vestibule after Mass. A good shepherd knows each of his sheep by name. At meals, in their homes, one has a better opportunity of seeing the whole family together and of listening to their cares and concerns.

A social worker once said to me that every leader should spend time with families asking one direct question: "Tell me, what ails you?"

The school children, especially the kindergarteners and first graders, were ecstatic when I visited them in their classrooms and entertained them with my guitar and folk songs. Very soon I could observe a radical change in the children. Once they got to know you, instead of walking away from you, they would run to greet you, and what was even more astonishing, they would call you by name. They knew who you were because they saw you frequently. You were now family to them. You were now *their* priest.

With so many ministries and departments in the parish, there wasn't a single free evening for me. I tried to attend every group and committee meeting. That's tough to do week after week. No wonder there is a parody of the words from John 3:16 which goes like this: "for God so loved the world that he did not send a committee." Attending parish meetings meant to the people that I as their shepherd was interested in them. I did not always have to say or do much. My presence spoke volumes. They felt affirmed in their ministry and in their commitment. Almost all of them were volunteers and such individuals needed emotional and spiritual support, especially from their Pastor.

Gradually I gained the confidence of the parishioners and the staff. When I first came to the parish, a hefty, tall parishioner reminded me that I had big shoes to fill (the shoes of the tall Monsignor who preceded me). I wasn't threatened by that. I had confidence in myself and in the God who had sent me there. I remember gently saying to him: "I don't need to fill anyone's shoes. I have my own!"

I began to develop some celebrity status from presiding well at parish liturgies. Some of the celebrations were recorded and played back for other priests and staffs to observe, especially the celebrations of the rites and the stages of the *Catechumenate*.

While I was still an associate in St. Lucy's parish, I was invited to become the District Chaplain of the Italian Catholic Federation. This fraternal organization was started in 1924 in San Francisco by Fr. Bandini and Sir Luigi Providenza to help and support Italian Catholic immigrants to the United States. Because of language and unfamiliarity with life in America, most of the Italian men would not go to church. So, the Italian Catholic Federation was formed to help them practice their faith, have connections with Italy, the fatherland, do works of charity and celebrate their Italian heritage. The branches mushroomed into districts and very soon, this organization became a national federation, spread all across California, Nevada, Arizona and the city of Chicago. Annual conventions are held over the Labor Day Weekend every year in different districts and delegates from all the branches gather to discuss by-laws and other issues affecting the members.

At the annual convention, several important awards are given to selected recipients. The most important is called the Pope John XXIII award and is given to a person who makes a significant impact on the lives especially of the poor and the needy. One example that comes to my mind is that of Danny Thomas, who founded St. Jude's Hospital for Children. I was present when he received his award and acknowledged his Catholic faith. There is also a district deputy award and a family of the year award. Finally, there is the Mother Teresa award, which is given to a priest, or religious who lives according to the spirit of the Saint of the Streets and the Poor of Calcutta.

In 2006 I was honored in Sacramento, California, with the Mother Teresa Award. I was the first priest to receive such an award and, needless to say, I was deeply moved. I was honored for helping people make connections between their daily lives and their faith. My planning of 'the days of recollection,' my homilies and my memorization of the Sunday gospels had made me well known and popular with the Catholic community in Northern California and beyond. Once again, as at many important moments of my life, my mother was there together with some of my siblings to share in my joy. After expressing my gratitude to the large gathering of delegates and their families, I sang *a capella* one of my favorite songs: 'I believe.' It was my turn to move the crowds. With my mother at my side, I received a standing ovation.

St. Martin of Tours parish had one of the largest branches of the Italian Catholic Federation and one of the most active. This monthly gathering of Italian Americans at the branch, and a monthly meeting of the district where I was chaplain was my closest connections to my years in Italy. The strange thing was that very few in the branch or the district spoke Italian because these Italian Americans grew up in the United States, and their immigrant parents would not allow them to speak the Italian language or any other Italian dialect at home. They insisted on them learning and speaking only English, the language of their new home and country.

When I was in Italy I had learned some classic Italian songs, like 'Santa Lucia' and 'Arrivederci Roma.' Now I was given many opportunities in the Italian Catholic Federation to sing these classic and popular songs. Yet another opportunity to speak Italian happened at the annual Mass to celebrate 'St. Joseph's Table,' an Italian tradition to make vegetarian dishes during Lent to feed the poor.

At the parish, deanery and diocesan levels I got associated with a lot of Catholic organizations for men and women. I noticed that these groups and organizations, for instance, the Italian Catholic Federation, the Knights of Columbus, Serra Club, Young Ladies Institute, etc. did not seem to draw as many new members as they used to when they were first founded. Sometimes the problem is not getting new members but keeping the ones you already have from leaving the organization. We might say the same is true for the Catholic Church.

At every meeting there is some time set aside for the Chaplain to give a brief spiritual talk, or to say a few words for the good of the Order. I was blessed with the gift and skill of seeing connections between the Scriptures and everyday life; between 'Chronos' (regular time) and 'Kairos' (God's time or sacred time). Thus I had the inner resources to motivate and inspire these members of fraternal organizations to stay the course and to remain faithful to Christ and the Church.

When I finished all my course work for the doctoral program, I started preparing to write my dissertation. Through a popular little book, all doctoral candidates were made aware of this difficult stage and of this 'virus' called: 'ABD – All But the Dissertation.' Focus, concentration, research and hard work were all essential to complete the dissertation in good time.

When I had started my doctoral studies, I was an associate, given the responsibility of the day-to-day running of the parish but without the headaches of administration and the title of Pastor.

The elderly pastor was not in good health. Yet he was not willing or anxious to retire. Some pastors appointed for life like he was used to treat their rectories as their own private residences and generally, without having to move away, lived a retired life style, making the associates do practically all the work.

Retirement without assignment would mean giving up all control of the parish and its resources. He wasn't prepared for that.

Thus, clergy retirement was not a popular option among aging pastors. Like most priests, this pastor preferred to die someday with his boots on. A couple of priests who had retired from active ministry due only to reasons of health had died suddenly soon after retirement.

Priests associated their worth with what they did and not by who they were. In retirement, unable to maintain and carry on the constant work schedule and demands of priestly ministry, they felt they were 'useless' human beings. One example of this may be the celebration of daily Mass. Even though this is not an obligation required by Canon Law, priests would always begin their day with a celebration of Eucharist. When you retire you have no defined community or congregation. If I am simply what I do, then there is a feeling of emptiness and worthlessness when what I did daily is now taken from me. Such low self esteem and the thought of having 'nothing' (no priestly ministry) to do may have discouraged many aging priests from the idea of retirement.

To retire or not to retire was the dilemma of my pastor at St. Lucy Parish.

Having lived with someone facing such a dilemma for four years, I decided that clergy retirement would be a good topic for research. I decided to study not only the 'why' of priests' retirement issues but also the effects, both positive and negative, of retirement. I also proposed to look at retirement from a cross-cultural point of view by using the survey method with retired priests on two continents.

I was hopeful that my research would also benefit me personally, in preparing for the day when I, too, would consider the final stage of retirement.

I spent a lot of time meeting with individual retired priests in our diocese of the United States. By the time I began my research, there were quite a few priests who had to retire at the mandatory age of seventy. Next, I traveled to India and met with individual retired priests in Bombay, in the retirement place for priests called the Clergy Home. In India I had to distinguish between retired and sick clergy because they were all housed in the same building complex. In both places I found a great deal of cooperation from retired priests and a strong desire to tell their stories.

At one time these were men of power who were now weakened by age and illness. Perhaps they were older now or perhaps they were not tied anymore to strict schedules and responsibilities, for I found almost every retired priest to be very courteous, relaxed and welcoming. They loved the fact that someone was interested in listening to them and to their life story.

When you speak about your life, you begin to name your experiences and important events. These moments of grace have become your identity and made you who you are today. Life seems worthwhile when someone will honor you by listening, truly listening, to your story.

I met a retired priest who in his time was known as a benevolent dictator. He had over a thousand children in his parish religious education programs. I remember him telling me that he would take a very pastoral approach in the confessional when people were facing difficult moral issues. He knew that people agonized to do their best, so he would give them the benefit of the doubt. As long as people did their best in the circumstances they found themselves, he would show his support to them. No wonder he was liked both by his parishioners as well as the associate priests. Newly ordained priests would be sent to him for training in their first years of priestly ministry.

Another priest told me about the parish he founded which his parishioners knew tenderly as 'the barn.' The people could afford the property but there was no money to build the church and the school. So, in the beginning, the people felt that everyday was Christmas because their barn-like church was similar to the manger of Bethlehem where Jesus was born.

A very elderly priest, retired for many years, appeared to be tough and strong even in his old age. He reminded me that he was the best fundraiser in the entire diocese. He would not ask for donations or free-will offerings; rather, he would tell each family exactly how much was expected of them. People grumbled but they gave, anyway.

One feisty priest never intended to leave his parish even after retirement. According to him, when he left to go on an extended vacation, his faithful parishioners built him a retirement home on the property of the parish itself. Others who knew him claimed that he was the one who had cleverly made advance plans for his own retirement home.

A priest who preferred to dress in non-clerical clothes continued to dream of all his many travels across the globe. He was very animated as he shared memory after memory of travels to exotic places. I asked him if he would like to travel again. "If I could I would take off right now," he said. "This is the only thing that stops me", he added, pointing to his wheelchair.

Yet another cleric had no disabilities to limit travel, except the lack of money.

I met the priest who had caned my behind when I was caught with my friends taking some fruit from a tree in the school playground of my youth. He was now weakened by strokes and blindness. In talking with him and listening to his side of the story after all these years, my research led me to a moment of peace and reconciliation with my past.

On both sides of the cultural divide, the retired clergy enjoyed their retirement years for a number of reasons. The 'Clergy Home' in Bombay is a community residence for retired and sick priests. There is a full time registered nurse to take care of their immediate medical needs. Not far from this retirement facility is the Holy Family Catholic Hospital, in case any of the retired or sick priests need major care or surgeries. Priests in Bombay did not have any retirement pension or social security income. But all their needs were taken care of inside and outside of this retirement facility. Therefore, they had no tangible reason for worry or anxiety.

The only thing that bothered the retired priests was to share the facility with very sick and dying priests. Somehow the concepts of relaxing and the joy of retirement did not go smoothly or coincide with the sight of very sick, depressed or dying fellow priests.

On the other hand, since priests in the United States received both a retirement pension from the diocese as well as social security income and Medicare from the government, they had a variety of retirement lifestyles to enjoy.

Some lived in rectories without the obligation of helping regularly with priestly duties; others lived on their own and did what they wished without owing anyone an explanation; and still others, lived in a decent retirement facility (formerly a convent) where meals, laundry and basic medical support were provided. With medical insurance continued even after retirement, the priests could avail themselves of private doctors and hospitals if needed. And if urgent end of life care were needed a retired priest would be sent to a comfortable private nursing home.

Thus retired clergy who were in good health to begin with got to spend the autumn of their lives either privately or with others in similar situations. Having good financial resources they were able to have more choices. Traveling around the globe seemed to be the favorite choice of many healthy retired priests.

One retired priest told me that he was forced into retirement when he had a massive heart attack at a relatively early age. The officials at the Chancery did not expect him to live very long. Having more options, choices and opportunities for exercise and good nourishment, this priest had now been retired for almost twenty-two years and was enjoying every moment of it. On the day of retirement, he told me, he received more money from the retirement pension fund of the diocese than what he was making as salary working full time as the pastor of a large parish.

If a comparison can be made in this cross-cultural study, priests everywhere seemed to find some purpose and fulfillment in retirement. It's where they ended up after retirement that determined how they felt about the rest of their lives. The priests in Bombay did not have to worry about meals, laundry and medical care, but their happiness was diminished by having to live with sick, depressed and dying priests. The priests in the United States, on the other hand, had more options and opportunities for a happier and fuller life.

While I was in the process of researching and completing my dissertation, a huge earthquake shook Northern California. When the earthquake destroyed homes and buildings everywhere, I was making my annual clergy retreat with about seventy five other priests. Even during a spiritual retreat, members of the cloth don't miss out on the 'Happy Hour.'

That evening of the earthquake I skipped the Happy Hour and decided instead to read a book on psychology entitled *Reality Therapy – How to Take Effective Control of Your Life*. I made it to the third page of the book when the earth shook violently for a good thirty seconds. Thirty seconds is an eternity when you think of the damage major earthquakes can cause. I threw my reality therapy book on the floor and, panic-stricken, ran for the door. It was a 7.3 gigantic trembler on the Richter scale. Priests who had avoided the Happy Hour like I did and were taking a meditative walk on the grounds of the Retreat House said that the trails and paths appeared to move like live snakes. Several statues were damaged and roofs were destroyed.

What were more disconcerting were the aftershocks. People were so nervous that at times they did not know whether what they felt were aftershocks outside of themselves or panic attacks within. In a practical sense, I felt the immediate value of my doctoral studies in Counseling Psychology. One of our professors circulated an audiotape to help anxiety-prone and panic-stricken individuals to understand what was going on, to cope with the aftershocks and to learn skills and techniques to handle them.

The day I had the appointment to defend my dissertation, there was a mild earthquake in the morning. I wasn't afraid of the earthquake. When one has lived long enough in California, earthquakes become a way of life. I was more concerned that my dissertation team would cancel my defense and postpone it. Fortunately for me, everything proceeded as planned.

When making the appointment for the defense, my advisor reminded me that I was the expert on the topic of my dissertation. After I defended my dissertation and answered all the questions and challenges put before me, I was asked to leave the room for an excruciating ten minutes. Then, my chief advisor came up to me and asked with a smile, "Should we call you 'Doctor Father' or 'Father Doctor'?" I replied joyfully: "You can call me anything you like. It all sounds wonderful to me."

At the graduation ceremonies, the red of the Master's Theological Degree of Santa Clara University was now replaced with the blue of the Doctoral Degree from the School of Education of the University of San Francisco. For me it was a long educational journey that started in Bombay many years ago. I am glad I made the trip and persevered to this final milestone and destination.

What Theology and Psychology together gave me were the right skills and training for true counseling guidance and spiritual direction. With only a background in Theology or a similar religious degree, one might tend to provide answers that may be incomprehensible or irrelevant to modern times. With only a background in counseling psychology, one might tend to surface problems that leave the client more helpless than before they came into therapy.

True mental and spiritual guidance respects the whole journey of each individual. The Spiritual Director, who also has some background in counseling psychology, helps the individual to be aware of how God is working in one's life. When one becomes aware of problems and issues on the journey of life, instead of leaving you with your difficulties, the Spiritual Director empowers and enables the individual to entrust everything to the Lord.

"Lay Your Burdens Down," is the title of a popular song. Even though people can name their burdens with the help of a therapist, they still need to realize that they don't have to carry the burdens themselves. Through spiritual direction they can leave their burdens in the Lord's hands, thus experiencing true joy, peace and health.

*****

With all my experience and education, I gathered that there are eight components in the spirituality of a diocesan priest, eight important characteristics that a parish priest must have and develop: Believer, Reconciler, Celebrant, Listener, Preacher, Teacher, Administrator and Man of Prayer.

Above all, a priest must be a **Believer**. Members of the clergy at a retreat were surprised that the characteristic of 'believer' made the top of the list. This characteristic is usually taken for granted by priests. After all you consider yourself to be an automatic believer because of the indelible seals and identity that come from your Baptism, Confirmation and Ordination. But as a priest do I truly believe the mysteries I celebrate? Do I truly believe in God and in the Most Holy Trinity? Is Jesus truly my personal Lord and Savior?

A priest should also be a **Reconciler** and peace-maker. There are so many broken relationships and situations of alienation in families and in communities. Too many people wallow in guilt; and too many people don't believe that sin and evil exist in the world. There is a universal need for forgiveness, mercy and compassion. A priest needs to bring hope where there is despair, joy where there is sadness, forgiveness where there is guilt and sin.

When Blessed Pope John Paul II met with his would be assassin, the Turk Mehmet Ali Ağca, in prison and forgave him that symbol of Christ-like compassion and the picture of their encounter touched the hearts of millions of people, believers and non-believers, everywhere. It was a true gesture of spiritual reconciliation from the Pope symbolizing the presence of Christ to a Moslem who does not believe in the divinity of Christ. In the spirit of Jesus Christ, whom he represents, the priest is called in his ministry of reconciler, to reconcile heaven and earth, and to bring together human failings and divine mercy.

A priest is a **Celebrant** of divine and human mysteries. When I did my practicum in Presidential Style at the Jesuit School of Theology in Berkeley, California, I happened to arrive a little late on the first day of class, and to what I presumed to be a celebration of Eucharist already taking place in the chapel. Only at the end of the celebration, I realized that these 'concelebrants' were only seminarians and not ordained priests like myself. They were practicing how to celebrate Mass and doing it so well that I thought I was in the presence of seasoned ordained priests.

Anyone can say the words of consecration or mislead the people by being dressed or vested as priests. What makes a priest a true celebrant of divine mysteries is ordination and the faculties and commissioning the local Ordinary gives at Ordination to validate the words and actions of priesthood.

In the new Roman Missal, the people's response to 'The Lord be with you' has been changed from 'And also with you' to 'And with your spirit.' There is a theological rationale for that. 'And with your spirit' is only used in response to an ordained minister. The 'spirit' that is mentioned in the frequently occurring response refers to the spirit received in ordination. It is an affirmation by the assembly that his person has received the proper anointing with the spirit in order to lead him in sacramental ministry. It is less about the person of the priest, than the office of the priesthood, which is supported and guaranteed by the Spirit of God given in ordination.

The Second Vatican Council in its document on the Liturgy has called for full, active and conscious participation from the entire people of God. I realized in this practicum on Presidential Style that even a priest's tone could affect the level of participation. If a priest speaks softly, the assembly will respond softly; if a priest prays aloud with spiritual strength, the people, too, will respond with conviction and passion.

In the past, while celebrating the sacraments, the priest was called to be 'The Faceless Priest' in order not to draw attention to himself. Today, the celebrant speaks and proclaims with his entire body and soul because he is the Presider and Leader of the praying assembly. If he fails to do so, then he will be unable to communicate and celebrate effectively the human and divine mysteries of faith.

A priest should be a good **Listener**. In communications what is really important is not what you say, as much as what another hears you say or thinks you said. In a classroom, if you, as the teacher, have to shout the word 'Silence,' then the message given to the children is exactly the opposite of your expectation of them. Today's congregations, especially in California, but also in the rest of the country, are so diverse and mixed. There are many needs and many complex issues. A priest ought to be sensitive to people of all ages, races and preferences. By listening carefully, the priest should make everyone welcome because we are all God's children. Effective non-verbal communications and compassionate non-judgmental approaches are important in the process of listening with care.

The decree on Ministry to Priests of the Second Vatican Council says that the priest's first task is to proclaim the Word of God. The title '**Preacher**' should not be restricted to Protestants and Evangelists. Every Catholic priest is called to be a preacher. Proclamation of the Word of God, according to the decree, is the '*Primum Officium*,' or first task and responsibility of priests. People who come to church on Sundays should be fed by priests both at the table of the Word and at the table of the Eucharist.

Thus, the priest should be familiar with the Scriptures he is called to proclaim every Sunday, at every daily Mass, and on every special occasion. The Scriptures are the historical community records of their experience with God. Hence, the priest needs to enter into those community records and spiritual experiences, in their cultural and historical contexts, in order to speak, like Jesus did, with authority. As St. Jerome, who translated the Greek Septuagint Bible into Latin, the language of the people of his time, said: "Ignorance of the Scriptures is ignorance of Christ himself."

Christ is the key to opening the doors of understanding of the Bible. The priest needs to be comfortable with the key to unpacking the Word of God. The word, 'Christ,' can be an acronym for the priest to understand how the Word of God:

Challenges,

Heals,

Reveals,

Instructs,

Strengthens and

Transforms.

A priest should be a **Man of Prayer**. If prayer is conversation with God, a priest needs to spend a lot of time alone with God, deepening his relationship with the divine. Jesus often went away to be alone with His Father and invited his disciples also to do the same. Although a priest's only obligation is to pray the breviary, or the liturgy of the hours, there are many ways for the priest to pray and meditate daily. Adoration of the Blessed Sacrament, silence, nature walks, music, breathing exercises, spiritual reading, *Lectio Divina*, Ignatian contemplation, etc. are many diverse avenues for a life of prayer. There is a look of emptiness in his eyes when a priest lacks prayerfulness. When Moses conversed with the Lord on Mount Sinai, people noticed that because of this encounter his face was glowing as they saw him come down the mountain with the Tablets of the Law.

For a priest, prayer is a way to stop and be grateful. It's a moment of gratitude for what is. Often people will stop me on the street or in the vestibule after Mass and ask for prayers for themselves or for loved ones in need. In the past, I would simply say that I would remember them in my prayers and later sometimes forget to pray. Now, I pause right away when I hear the request for prayer and say a few words aloud or give a blessing so that I don't forget. There are many definitions and understandings of prayer. A popular prayerful saying which I like is: "Let Go and Let God."

One of the best prayers I heard went something like this: "Lord, help me to be the kind of person my dog thinks I am."

Jesus is often referred to in the New Testament as **Teacher** and Rabbi. The priest, too, is called to teach and educate. There is unfortunately an entire generation of Catholics that is not catechized and not educated in the ways of faith. To catechize means to instruct. To adapt to the times and to make Catholics more engaged with their faith, the Catholic Church shifted away from the Baltimore Catechism, with its Question and Answer format, before Vatican II, to a fuzzy, superficial and non-challenging approach to religious education after the Second Vatican Council. Instead of learning answers to their issues and questions of faith, children were encouraged to doodle and paint during catechism class. Content was sacrificed for process.

Many young parents are unable to teach religion to their own children because they don't know much about the faith themselves and don't want to appear before others, including their own children, as ignorant. Every invitation to speak or to celebrate sacraments can become teachable moments for a priest. Just as Jesus used every healing moment as an opportunity to teach about the kingdom of God, so too, a priest can reflect spiritually on almost every major event that takes place in the world.

After all, as Karl Rahner, a Jesuit theologian once said, "A Catholic is someone who has a Bible in one hand and a newspaper in the other."

Finally, the priest is an **Administrator**. The hierarchy of the Catholic Church, when you take out the frills and the extras, is rather simple when one considers how big this institution really is. The simple hierarchy includes the Pope, the local Bishop and the Pastor. Even companies like Lockheed Martin, IBM and others have tried to understand how this simple hierarchy of an institution which has over a billion members, works. The Pastor is the overseer of his parish. With the help of the Parish Council, a Finance Committee and a trained staff, the Pastor makes sure that everything runs smoothly. In today's church, you might think of the Pastor as a CEO of a non-profit organization. Today's administrator is challenged to create a Mission Statement for the parish, to hire, fire and evaluate personnel, to meet budgetary requirements, to raise funds and to maintain in good functioning order all the facilities, buildings and grounds of the parish.

Truly a diocesan priest, in the words of St. Paul, is called to be all things to all people.

I was the first priest from India to be made a Pastor in this region of Northern California. There was a new clergy personnel policy in place in the diocese, and I was a member of a team that helped put it together, stating that a Pastor could be assigned to a parish for only six years (not for life), after which his term could be renewed just one more time for another six years.

By smiling at the 'Monster' and making peace with it, I quickly completed my first term of six years as Pastor. When I received a letter renewing my term for another six years, the whole parish rejoiced. I was personally excited because I had my first chance as a Pastor to deepen my spiritual relationship with so many wonderful families. I was looking forward to celebrating the sacraments for many more years to come with children, youth and adults of all ages. In the olden days, my mother reminded me that the same parish priest in her birth parish gave her the sacraments of Baptism, Confirmation, Penance, Eucharist and even Marriage.

In the meanwhile, to encourage youth and eventually vocations to the priesthood and the religious life, some families were urging me to do what a previous Pastor (the one who was appointed before the Monsignor I replaced) who had died some years earlier, had done in the parish for young children. Since the parish had a school, they told me that he would invite the upper elementary grade boys into his spacious living room, offer them sodas and snacks and games to play, and make them feel at ease in his presence. These families did not know then that the now deceased Pastor had a secret, which had nothing to do with vocations to the priesthood.

Luckily for me, I keep my home life separate from my work life and ministry. In the evenings when I retire to my room, either after liturgies or meetings, I like to simply relax alone, calling my family, reading or watching television.

Over the years I have got to know my preferences and my needs well. Having a personality that is partly extrovert and partly introvert, I need people but I also feel the need to be away from people. I give and receive a great deal of energy, for instance, on Sunday mornings during and after Eucharistic celebrations with hundreds of people. After all that, my introvert side likes to get away from the crowds and from all the social chatter to unwind, relax and restore my drained and tired self. It was certain that I wasn't going to take the suggestion of these families to entertain their young children in my living quarters.

Little did we know till after the sexual child molestation scandals broke out in the Catholic Church in the United States that, as it was later alleged, this same well respected priest, who had since died, had secretly abused some of these school boys by enticing them with sodas and games in his private chambers.

They say that over ninety percent of children are molested and abused by people they know, whether in their own families, schools or even religious institutions. It may turn out to be an uncle, or a neighbor or even a priest that families have trusted over the years, and who now betrays that trust, breaks the sacred bond that exists between them and victimizes the innocent and the vulnerable by molesting little children.

God was watching over me and gave me the wisdom not to follow the well-meant suggestion of these honest, faith-filled but simple, trusting families. What a sad and painful situation this priest had created for all his victims and for the image and reputation of the Church. God was watching over me even more closely, because these scandals broke out long after I had left this particular parish. The Pastor who succeeded me had to face the turmoil and the agony created by this horrendous situation.

When I see a priest in a difficult situation I say to myself: "there go I but for the Grace of God." I am always haunted by the Last Supper painting that hung in the dining room of my parish in Bombay. When we gathered for our meals each day we were reminded of the words of Jesus, referring to Judas, below the painting: "One of you is going to betray me."

The Last Supper is also the celebration of priestly ordination. As you look around at the faces of the apostles dining with Jesus, you realize that these were not the best of the best. In God's mysterious plans, these were the men he had chosen. One of them would deny him three times; another would doubt him; a couple of brothers sought positions of power and Judas Iscariot would eventually betray him.

Talking about the last supper, a fictitious story is told about Leonardo da Vinci who was looking for real people to paint the apostles gathered in the Upper Room for the Passover meal with Jesus. He found a young man who had the look of innocence, and yet appeared to be a loving, hope-filled and determined individual. Leonardo decided to paint him as Jesus. After he found others to take the roles of the rest of the apostles, the only one missing was the face of Judas. Leonardo was looking for someone who had a look of despair and darkness.

One day while Leonardo was walking down some dark alley in Florence, he saw a very dirty and desperate looking individual with a hollow, empty gaze. At first, Leonardo wanted to run away from this scary figure. He was taken by surprise when he heard his name mentioned by this dangerous looking individual. The man said to Leonardo, "Don't you recognize me? I am the same person you chose six months ago to paint the face of Jesus." Then, he recounted his sordid life and circumstances to Leonardo. After listening to his tale of misery and sin that had so disfigured him, Leonardo invited him to sit in his studio to pose for the portrait of Judas.

The story above is not real but tries to make a point of how people can change sometimes from one extreme to the other. According to Robert Wallace who wrote *The World of Leonardo 1452-1519*, Leonardo did use live models and did look among local prisoners for someone to portray Judas, but did not choose the same person as used for Christ.

*****

After completing my seventh year as Pastor of my first parish, I was asked to consider moving again and spending a term at a parish where I used to be the associate, but this time to move in as the Pastor. The clergy personnel board thought that I would be the best person for the job, since I already knew most of the parishioners and the historical circumstances of the parish.

Even though parishioners at St. Martin of Tours parish were saddened when they heard I was leaving them, I believed in my heart that God was really taking care of me. Only later would I understand how.

Very often, in spiritual life, we do not 'see' the face of God and know for sure that God is present and active in our lives. In the book of Exodus, when Moses talks to God on Mount Sinai at the burning bush, he looks down and shuts his eyes, because he knows, like all the Jewish people were reminded, that if you look at God face to face you will certainly die. Since Moses wants to tell his people what God is like, God tells Moses, "Close your eyes as I pass by you. Then, you can look at me from behind."

This spiritual experience of Moses is strongly symbolic for the rest of us. We may not recognize the Lord or his presence when we are in the midst of an important life-changing experience. We may wonder and even doubt if God is there at all. But, often, when we look back at that same experience later on, from behind, so to speak, we might see a pattern and say to ourselves: "Aha, I knew God was there all the time."

The unexpected transfer from the parish and the separation caused by it were gut-wrenching. Yet, later on I discovered that God saved me from much agony and mental anguish. A year after I was transferred, the new pastor of the parish was confronted by the sexual child molestation scandals that broke out in the local media. He now had to face the legal, emotional and possibly financial challenges caused by the clergy sexual abuses that neither he nor I were responsible for.

Again, looking back several years, the same loving provident God had also steered me away from the Boston Archdiocese, where the sexual scandals first erupted, and brought me instead to California. In 2002 the Boston Archdiocese was accused of moving some known 'recovered' pedophile priests from one parish to another or from one diocese to another.

Even though it was reported that some priests had molested innocent children and vulnerable adults, some of the bishops, believing that the abusive priests were cured after brief treatments and therapies, had transferred them to other parishes and dioceses. Thus, the abuses continued and spread all across the country.

Even though only two percent of clergy were pedophiles similar to the ratio in all other helping professions, yet these abuses were unforgivable because of the high level of trust the clergy enjoy with children and families. The victims suppressed the painful memories of these abuses and Church authorities generally kept every communication and complaint secretly and confidentially in files, so it was not known how rampant this problem was in the Church.

As the media and lawsuits exposed this shameful issue, people began to realize that the problem went back at least fifty years in the Church. Some pedophile priests were already dead, but because of the shameful nature of the problem and the secrecy surrounding it, many of the victims had not come forward to make any accusations. Only when it became a national movement to get justice for innocent victims and to expose and arrest pedophiles, more and more molested victims came forward and legally sued institutions across the country.

The Dallas Charter was the church's response to this humongous problem. Every diocese in the United States now has a clear policy for the protection of children and vulnerable adults and the training of clergy, paid lay personnel and volunteers that work in parishes and schools. With zero tolerance, whenever there is reasonable doubt and evidence, priests, religious and lay ministers are quickly removed from office and may be criminally charged so that a situation of abuse of minors may never be repeated and spread.

*****

I spent at least three weekends of homilies sharing honestly with my parishioners how I felt about my transfer to another parish. It wasn't just about packing and moving my stuff accumulated over the years. It was really about leaving friends, making new friends and starting basically a new life in a strange new location. Everyone can relate to that. They say that the average family in California moves at least seven times in a lifetime. No wonder, moving rates way up high on the list of stressors.

The parishioners were happy to know that they were not the only ones feeling the pain of separation from their shepherd. The Pastor, too, as they understood now had feelings. He, too, was feeling lost and confused. He, too, did not want to move, if he had a choice. With this kind of honest sharing, we bonded even more; many of us became friends for life.

The title of Pastor is synonymous with Shepherd. I realized from experience that after seven years in this parish, I had a natural calling to be a Shepherd. In the gospels, Jesus reminds us that the good Shepherd knows his sheep by name and the sheep follow his voice because they recognize him and trust him. As Pastor for the first time I was entrusted with a community that I was called to shepherd in good times as well as challenging situations. I felt that I was faithful to my calling. Even more importantly, the parishioners themselves in the spirit of the Second Vatican Council empowered and enabled me to guide and lead them to greener pastures.

Getting back to the transfer from my first parish as pastor, a humorous thing happened that would color my legacy at this parish. Toward the end of my seventh year at the parish, I decided to build a nice fence as an enclosure for the priests to have some privacy. There was nothing else that I was challenged to build for the future of this parish, so a fence sounded like a simple and nice gesture for the priests to have a place to bar-b-q and relax. When my successor came to see the rectory and he saw this open space with a fence around it, the first thing he said was, "This will be great for my dog."

*****

In 1995 my mother celebrated her seventy-fifth birthday. We decided to make this event into our first family re-union, so all eight siblings gathered with our friends and relatives in Bombay to honor our dear mother. My Danish nephew, Daniel, was born in the Philippines the same day as my mother. So we had a combined birthday party, with seventy-five candles for my mother and one big candle for Daniel.

It was a great celebration despite the one hundred and ten degree humid weather of Bombay in April. The cakes and candles melted. But a new family re-union tradition was started that day.

A month later my mother returned to the United States. Even in her seventies, my mother had always been a motivated individual. She was positive in her thoughts and strong in her faith. She took care of herself, walking everyday for exercise to stay healthy.

On the Fourth of July of the same year, while exercising early in the morning on the school grounds close to our family home, two huge dogs that were unlawfully unleashed and allowed to run around the grounds by a neighbor, knocked her down. She fell and broke her right femur, her leg twisted under the weight of her body.

We rushed her to the ER. Four-and-a-half hours later she emerged with a metal pin in her leg, never to be the same again. Because of her age and the severity of her condition the prognosis was not good. We didn't know if she would ever walk again.

But with all the walking and exercising she had done in the past, her constitution was strong. It's always good to get a second opinion from doctors. Her primary doctor who had done the surgery depended more on X-rays of my mother's leg than the enthusiasm and spirit in my mother's soul. He did not want her to move till the X-rays showed some improvement in the bone structure. This was an excruciatingly slow process, so we decided to get a second opinion from a young doctor who believed in my mother and her desire to walk. Even though it took a whole year since her surgery, my mother learned to walk again.

Many elderly people who have the kind of traumatic accident my mother experienced end up languishing in bed till they die. My mother's determination, attitude and faith showed that life can go on even after major accidents and tragedies.

From my mother I have learned what it means to have hope, what it means to never give up.

A Rabbi wrote a book entitled *When Bad Things Happen to Good People*. Sometimes we misread the title and instead of "When" we read: "Why?" We ask ourselves why bad things happen to good people. The Rabbi had lost a child and was wondering in the beginning why this had happened. Did he and his family do everything right in their lives so that this tragedy could have been avoided in the first place? After much soul searching he came to the conclusion that it is not important to ask, "Why;" rather, we should ask ourselves when bad things happen by accident, what should we be doing to move on with our lives?

A few days after her surgery, I remember going to visit her at the hospital and running into a nurse acquaintance who asked if I was visiting sick parishioners. When I told her I was there to see my mother, she said, "Father, it must feel different as a priest to visit a family member rather than a parishioner you don't know so well." She was absolutely right. When you make pastoral visits to sick parishioners, the visit ends with goodbyes. But when you visit sick relatives, especially your own parents, you carry them with you even after you leave the hospital.

Today it is very common for a lot of people to have to deal with the issue of elderly or sick parents. I never had to take care of a sick parent before. Dad died without ever needing our constant long-term care or help. I'm sure he was in a lot of pain sometimes, but he never complained. By character, mom was and is the same as my dad. She was always super mom to us, hardly ever sick and never complaining about not feeling well.

In India people generally don't call before they come to visit you. So when unexpected relatives arrived at the door, when we were children, mother would sometimes not eat at all so that there would be enough food for the guests and for the rest of the family. Because long-distance guests would stay overnight, she would sacrifice her own bed and stay awake all night. Hospitality is sacred. And my mom lived the sacredness of hospitality to its core.

Although Dad was a man of few words, Mom was the social butterfly. Without exception she cared for everybody. One day my Dad was in the hospital awaiting my mother's visit. But by the time she had made it to his room, she had visited practically all the other patients in the hospital (that's what my dad had us believe).

In India she would get up very early, after all the children were grown up of course, to go for daily Mass at the local parish church. But she would end up coming home around midday, because, as the neighborhood matriarch, everybody expected a social visit from her. And she did not disappoint.

It's tough helping an elderly, sick parent. After her long surgery she had to remain in the hospital for a while. She was in intensive care for a few days, then in post-surgical care for three weeks. Thanks to my work with the Daughters of Charity (I belonged to their Outreach Board) who ran the hospital, my mother received three more weeks of important physical therapy right there at the hospital *gratis*. After that she was moved to a convalescent nursing home for three months. This was a new experience for me and my mother.

There are so many patients in a nursing home that care is sometimes superficial. Family members are urged to show up at the nursing home at odd hours so that the nursing home personnel do not get into a routine of neglect for your loved one. It's a sad state of affairs. During this convalescence and physical therapy, my mother, who was always active and busy, did not know what to do with her self, and we were not always sure of how best to help her.

I realized that priests today, like anybody else, are challenged more and more to take care of elderly parents. Sometimes married siblings live far away or have so many things to worry about in their own families that a priest ends up being the sole caretaker of his needy parent. What's even more daunting is for a priest to be the only child in the family and thus to be torn between caring for the parish and simultaneously for an elderly parent.

People are living longer. There is definitely longevity in my family tree. My grandparents on my mother's side were in their nineties when they passed away. My father's brother was almost a hundred years old when he died. Priests need to care for their own families as well as their parish families.

When serious illness comes into one's life, angels appear to help. One day mom mentioned that this woman with a heavy accent brought her coffee and cookies every morning. She did not remember her name, so she became for us the invisible coffee and cookie angel. Later on I found out that it was Tina, a delightful Italian woman from Florence, who even after living in the United States for thirty years has not shed her Tuscan accent. One good deed deserves another. She told my mother that I had done a great job with her husband's funeral and I was also able to converse with her in Italian. When she heard that my mother was in the local hospital and that I would be busy with parish work, she decided to stop by every morning and bring a smile and a cookie with coffee to my mother.

Another angel nurse at night helped my mother in a big way to relieve her of pain and discomfort, simply because of something good I had done for her in the past. Even though I had forgotten what it was, she remembered and came forward to show her gratitude by helping my mother sleep comfortably. The angels were there around my mother's bedside when she needed them and when I was busy with parish work. What would I have done without their assistance?

Even after my mother came home from the hospital, she was okay from the waist up. But she needed a wheelchair to get around the house and some help to pick things up from the floor if she dropped anything. Another angel by the name of Rick came along just at the right time and made sturdy ramps for mom to glide smoothly in the house from one room to another and from outside the front door to the inside of her bedroom.

The orthopedic surgeon who operated on my mother did a great job. But being a military doctor by training, he was limited and boxed into an attitude that was not open to new and creative ideas. We would visit him every six weeks with X-rays in our hands. He would look at them quickly and say: "She is not ready to walk. I don't see any change or improvement in the bone structure from the X-rays."

Then another angel appeared in the guise of a young doctor from the county hospital. These doctors have good training, excellent equipment but not much practical experience. He did not look at the X-rays, unless he had to, but rather he looked into my mother's determined spirit and positive attitude and saw what she was capable of doing, despite her age. He said: "I'm going to teach you to walk again. The worst thing that can happen to you is that you will break your leg – again. If that were to happen, I will fix it. Don't let that worry you or stop you from trying to walk."

He offered physical therapy and walking lessons to my mother, first with a walker, then with a cane. My mother did great. Often she did not remember the young surgeon's instructions about which foot had to come before the other. But with every step she took, her bones got stronger. In the end what mattered was not science or medicine but an inexperienced angelic doctor, like Clarence from "It's a Wonderful Life," who believed in my mother and in her capacity and determination to walk again.

As a family we decided not to hire any home-care help for my mother both because it was expensive and because my mother thought it was not necessary. As she would remind us time and again, even with hired help you may end up having to do all the work yourself. When it got difficult for my brother, who was single then, and me to take care of our mother, my sisters decided to take mom home to India.

Over there, it was much easier to find inexpensive help and treatment. Recovery, too, could be quicker in the home environment. Even though my mother understood English, Konkani was her main language of communication. My sisters found maids that spoke Konkani, which put my mother at ease and on the fast track to healing and recovery.

About a year later, I got the good news that my mother was walking again. As soon as she was able, she began traveling around the globe spending quality time with her many children and grandchildren. Many elderly people who suffer the kind of fall and injury my mother had, end up lying in bed without much movement and motivation, and soon, with atrophied muscles and limbs, they waste away and die. I was amazed at the courage my mother had to face adversity. She inspired me and all my siblings and continues to do so even today in her nineties.

There was a time in my early priesthood, when priests were assigned far away from family. The call of Christ to his disciples to give up family and all other attachments was taken literally. Now it's different. If possible, one gets assigned as close to family as possible. For celibate clergy, not having your own spouse and children, this physical closeness with immediate family members is both healthy and comforting.

As people live longer, there will be more young adults needing to take care of aging parents. Priests are no exception to this situation. I have been very fortunate that my mother has lived close by to my parishes and once even within my parish. Whether in the hospital, in the nursing home or simply in the warm loving environment of our family home, it's always comforting and reassuring to spend quality time with my mother.

The most important woman in a Catholic priest's life is his mother.

*****

After seven years at my first pastor assignment I returned to the progressive Transfiguration Catholic Community, where I used to be the associate and considered then to be one of the wise men from the East, as their third Pastor. The prior team of co-pastors had disintegrated. Only about four hundred parishioners remained. And many of those who decided to stay seemed to be emotionally exhausted by all the changes. There were hardly any committees left and no paid staff. The parish was still paying off a loan from the diocese from having built the new, modern worship facility.

It's not usually a church building that attracts most worshippers; rather, it is the community and how it is managed and how it provides spiritual nourishment that really matters.

The new church was modern and beautiful. The roofs were built to look like the hills that surrounded this beautiful valley of Santa Clara and Mount Tabor where the Transfiguration took place. There were no pews, just comfortable chairs, and a sizable full immersion baptismal font.

For the first time in my life I was the only priest in the parish. I lived alone in the four-bedroom, two-story house on one of the side streets, a block away from the church. This, too, was a new experience to live at somewhat of a distance from the worship center. Normally, rectories are built right next to a church, so people can recognize a priest's residence without any problem. Not so where I lived this time. It was a regular neighborhood tract home with a front yard and a back yard and no sign to indicate that this was a priest's home.

When the parish was founded there were three priests in residence and the fourth bedroom was used as a common meeting room. Later on, when the co-pastors were in charge, there were only two priests. Finally, the whole house ended up with only one resident.

This has been the situation in parish churches in the United States since the Second Vatican Council. Where there were three priests, there are now only two, and where there were two, you find only one. An estimated fifteen percent of parishes in the United States do not have a priest in residence today.

While the global Catholic population is increasing annually by 1.4 percent, according to the latest Vatican figures, the number of priests is increasing only by 0.18 percent.

The rectory house, though large, had very little furniture and no fresh paint. When I arrived I was told that volunteers were requested from the community to help paint the house. But most of the parishioners seemed to have little energy, desire or will to take on a major project to improve the rectory or even to grow the parish.

The most positive thing about returning to this community was recognizing former parishioners and friends and calling them by name after all these years. One of my special gifts is my memory for names and faces. They say that our names are the sweetest sounds in any language and in every culture. People smile when they are called and recognized by name.

This personal interaction was a great beginning to inject new life into these wonderful, faithful parishioners. When I spoke with them often, discussed ideas and called them by name, they would respond to almost any request I would make of them. It was not that these parishioners had lost their spirit; it was still there within them. All we needed to do was enable their hidden spirit to emerge.

I decided that socials were easy and inexpensive to organize. Four times a year, one for every season, we had pot lucks. For example, we would put together an ice-cream social in the summer, a casserole night for the fall season, a soup night in the winter and finger foods in the spring. The parish would provide the basics like bread and cookies to go with what each family brought.

Soup night was my favorite. I called it "Soup Heaven" because there were at least twenty or thirty different varieties of soup. In fact I loved soup so much, we added two more soup nights to go with our Reconciliation and Penance services in the seasons of Advent and Lent. Needless to say that many sinners of all ages flocked to these services and enjoyed the forgiveness, the fellowship and the delicious soups.

The best thing that happened was that every gathering attracted new families and the parish began to grow steadily.

Since I had no paid staff, I brought along an efficient administrative staff member from my previous parish to contact all the young families with children in the parish. I wanted to reassure them that their children's life of faith would not be abandoned with the change of leadership. This personal contact was helpful for all the families to know that somehow the religious education programs for their children would continue. Knowing that their children's spiritual and sacramental needs were taken care of, the families felt encouraged not to abandon the parish community.

As time went by I got bolder and began organizing musical concerts and day long festivals besides the seasonal pot lucks. While the pot lucks were 'fun raisers,' the concerts and festivals became 'fund raisers.' We still owed a lot of money on our loan to the diocese, and we began lowering our debt little by little, month by month. I started another Capital Campaign even though it appeared as if the monies would have to come from the same pockets.

Since I usually try to start my talks and presentations with a hook, I told the parishioners before the Capital Campaign that I had good news and bad news. The good news was that we had the money we needed to pay off the loan. The bad news was that the money was still in their pockets.

After the Capital Campaign, we tagged on a once-a-month second collection that we called 'The Building Fund.' We also revived the 'Giving Tree' and its plaques for generous donors. By the end of five years, we had lowered our parish debt to about one-tenth of the total amount.

In the meanwhile, word got around that something good was going on at this parish. There were people living close by as neighbors for many years who suddenly discovered that this community was really a Roman Catholic Parish, and not some evangelical, non-denominational congregation. In the earlier days of this parish, this community was known as the Church of the Transgressions. But now with the changes, the social gatherings and the new spirit, it came to be known as a vibrant, prayerful, socially committed Catholic Church Community.

I was golfing one day with a friend on my day off. When he made a very long putt on the first hole, we both jumped for joy as only golfers know how. Then I said to him, "Great putt." To which he replied, "Spread the word, spread the word."

He told me that since he was in sales, he would travel a lot and often stay in hotels and motels. Once an attendant had done a good job for him, and he said to the attendant, "You did a super job," to which the attendant with a great smile replied, "Spread the word."

As the news got around, largely by word of mouth, that this community was vibrant, and that good things were happening there, the numbers of parishioners starting increasing steadily. Within five years, we had an increase on Sundays amounting to nearly fifty-five percent of growth. A friend of mine who owned several businesses said that those numbers and growth, in terms of sales in the business world, would be considered phenomenal.

This reminds me of a story I once heard that throws light on our parish experience of growth. In a certain monastery there were no new vocations for many years. The few remaining monks were getting older and feebler with age. They were simply waiting for the end of their lives and of their beloved monastery.

On the monastery grounds in a tiny cottage lived an old wise Rabbi, who spent his days in prayer and meditation. One day the aging Abbott told the monks at supper that he was going to his friend the Rabbi and to seek his advice to help their sad and dying community. The Abbott was gone a while and when he returned all the monks gathered around him eagerly and asked him, "Tell us, what did the Rabbi say? What did the Rabbi say?" The Abbott reported that the Rabbi had not said much. All he did say was this: "The Messiah is among you."

After this conversation, each monk retired to his cell wondering what the Rabbi meant by those words. When they returned to the chapel for night prayer, Brother Juniper turned around and for the first time smiled at Brother Bart wondering if he could be the Messiah. The next morning Brother Peter winked at Brother Clement and secretly wondered if he might be the Messiah. While dusting the pews that afternoon, Brother Conrad was whistling, enjoying his work, and trying to figure out who among his companions might be the Messiah. He hadn't whistled in years.

Very soon there were smiles and laughter all over the monastery. The word spread into the little towns and the countryside around the monastery that something unusual and special was going on. Soon, several young men came to the monastery to find out what was happening. They liked what they saw and heard and some of them decided to join the monastery. Very soon, the monastery was filled with new recruits, and the reputation of the monastery as a joyful, vibrant place spread far and wide.

Even till today, the story goes; each monk still smiles and wonders who among them could be the Messiah.

Good News travels fast. That's how Christianity spread so rapidly in the first few centuries, despite persecution, as the joyful religion of the Resurrection, of New Life, of Salvation, of Deliverance, of Freedom, and of the Good News of Jesus Christ. People began to say about these Christians: "See how they love one another."

Very soon, this parish was brimming with activity. There were now ten paid staff members, some part time and some full time. I established the Pastoral Leadership Community, a more dynamic version of the advisory Parish Council. The Pastoral Leadership Community was a group of elected parishioners who made decisions by consensus. We now had a functioning Finance Committee, mandated by Canon Law, which provided advice and guidance to the Pastor in temporal matters. Several important committees emerged out of the new enthusiasm of the parishioners. We now had a Liturgy Board, a Design Team (for art and environment in the church for the liturgical seasons), a Catechetical Committee, a Stewardship Committee, a stronger Community Ministry Outreach, and a Festival Committee.

One of the new strengths of the parish community was the presence and activity of Small Faith Christian Communities. After several years of participation in the RENEW program, interested parishioners met in small groups to share life and faith through the Scriptures and through reflection on life events. These Small Faith Christian Communities became extended families to their members. They would care for each other and celebrate with each other when special events like birthdays, baptisms, anniversaries, weddings and funerals occurred in their families. These same communities also organized themselves to help the poor and the needy. I could always count on these wonderful Small Faith Christian Communities to help me implement ideas for the good of the entire parish.

In the prayerful gatherings of these small groups we could sense the risen presence of Jesus, who said, "Where two or three are gathered in my name, there am I in their midst."

The Scriptural foundation of these Small Faith Christian Communities led me to organize Shared Scripture Study for the parish. Our first venture was a bold one. We took on the last and most difficult book of the Bible: the Book of Revelation, and used the 'Little Rock Scripture Study' resources to understand the apocalyptic language of the book. Over sixty parishioners faithfully attended all the sessions of Scripture Study. There was definitely a hunger for the Word of God.

Having a modern church building in the round, where you could see one another easily, we also spent time at the beginning of Sunday liturgy to do some faith sharing. Very often, the faith-sharing question was a basic one: "Where was God in your life this past week?" I would always begin by modeling the sharing by reflecting on a life experience I had during the past week.

When a leader models for others what he or she expects of them, faith sharing is encouraged and participation is made easier.

The most touching and powerful faith sharing used to take place during the Thanksgiving liturgy. People loved to express their gratitude for God's gifts in their lives. I still remember vividly on that first Thanksgiving at the parish, asking people to share what they were grateful for in their lives. A young man stood up holding aloft his new-born son and said: "I am grateful for this. We were told we could not have a baby. Here's God's gift to our family." People clapped for joy and we were all moved to tears.

This faith sharing at the beginning of Sunday liturgy would help people settle into a reflective and peaceful mode of prayer and worship. When people rush into the celebration of Mass, they are usually preoccupied and distracted. The faith sharing would help them to be at peace and to understand that they were now in a sacred space in the presence of the Lord.

The Psalmist reminds us: "Be still and know that I am God."

My vision was to encourage faith sharing not only during Sunday liturgy but also at the beginning of every meeting in the parish. Thus, the discussions and deliberations would be influenced by this spirit of prayer rather than by politics or personal agendas.

The Catechumenate, which had been a strong process and program in the past, had almost vanished in the parish. A church community is considered to be alive and dynamic only when it continues to welcome new members. If there are no catechumens at the Easter Vigil liturgy to be initiated into the community, how can the parish and the Church grow?

In the new church facility, this parish was fortunate to have a full immersion baptismal font. There were steps leading down into the waters of the font and steps leading up out of the waters symbolizing the dying and the rising of the new born Christian immersed in the mystery of the dying and the rising of Jesus himself. With my past experience of the Catechumenate and the Rites of the Christian Initiation of Adults, Teens and Children, I was happy to restore these powerful celebrations and to relive the full signs of the Sacraments.

St. Basil reminds us: "We baptize only once, because there is only one death and resurrection that baptism symbolizes." Therefore baptism should be an unforgettable experience.

At the Easter Vigil, the night before Easter Sunday, as presider and baptizer, I would first enter the immersion font and then invite each Catechumen by name for baptism. There were some unusual experiences in my first two Easter Vigils.

The very first time I entered the waters of the font, I stepped in with my wallet, thus having to dry dollar bills and credit cards after the services. The following year I almost forgot to take off my wireless microphone before entering the waters. That might have been the end of me and my last Easter Vigil. It's no joke, because I read in the papers that year that a Baptist minister had been electrocuted after entering the baptismal waters still connected to the live wires of their sound system.

The beauty and the power of the baptismal font becomes the experience for the newly baptized of a full immersion in the dying and rising of Jesus. It replaces the trickle of water that has been the way of baptizing for so many centuries in the Church. Of course, both forms of pouring and immersion are valid in the Church. And the pouring of water is still a good way to baptize most babies. What is important today is that families have a choice in deciding whether they want the simple pouring of water on the head, or the full symbol of immersion in the baptismal waters. After they have attended an Easter Vigil celebrating the full sign of baptism, they want the same experience for their children and grandchildren.

When it came to anointing with Sacred Chrism, I would spread the fragrant oil all over the faces of the newly baptized, of those received into full communion with the Catholic Church from other Christian traditions, and of those Catholics who desired Confirmation as adults during the Easter Vigil. A teenager who had witnessed my way of conferring the Sacrament of Confirmation asked his mother whether I would be doing this 'face-painting' for him when he would be confirmed later that year.

Many adults have been moved to tears by this experience, where the presence of the Holy Spirit can really be felt, and have even asked whether they could be reconfirmed, which, of course like baptism, is not repeated in the Catholic Church. Members of the Catechumenate team have video-taped these moments of Confirmation at the Easter Vigil and have shared the experience with other parishes. Once again, what's important is to celebrate the full sign of the Sacrament of Confirmation; not merely to smudge the forehead of the Confirmation candidate, but to truly and fully anoint the person with the gifts and the fruits of the Holy Spirit. The Confirmation candidate is going to need this powerful sensory reminder that the Holy Spirit will always be there in his or her journey of faith for the rest of their lives.

Finally, for the climax celebration of the Eucharist, real unleavened bread (prepared by the Catechumens themselves) was used together with an abundance of wine. Since churches usually use hosts instead of unleavened bread, a bishop once said to me that it takes more faith to believe that the hosts are real bread than to believe that Jesus is really present in the consecrated bread of the Eucharist.

Again the issue here was celebrating the full sign of the Eucharist, which is eating and drinking, as Jesus asked that we do in his memory at the Last Supper. Catholics do believe that the full presence of Jesus is found even in the single species of the precious body or the precious blood. Yet, the symbol of the Eucharistic meal and the Wedding Banquet is best celebrated in both eating the body of Christ in the consecrated bread and in drinking his blood from the consecrated cup of wine.

Thus the initiation sacraments were fully celebrated for the newly baptized and the newly welcomed into the Catholic Church. The Easter Vigils were henceforth so well planned and powerfully celebrated that people flocked in great numbers and tried to grab the front seats for what was announced as the holiest nights of the Church liturgical year.

I remember visiting St. John Lateran Basilica in Rome, which has one of the most ancient baptismal fonts in the Catholic Church. Our professor of Liturgy told us that the 23rd Psalm would be recited at the Easter Vigil to prayerfully express the journey and the sacraments of initiation to the Elect. The Psalm says:

> *The Lord is my shepherd, I shall not want.*
> *He leads me to the waters (Baptism)*
> *He anoints my head with oil (Confirmation)*
> *He sets the table before me (Eucharist)*

Africa is one continent which has many converts to Catholicism. I heard that in one parish, because of drought, they had no water to symbolize the dying and the rising of baptism. So the catechumens and their sponsors dug a huge grave and one by one the catechumens stepped into the grave to understand the true meaning of baptism, an immersion, with or without water, in the death and resurrection of Jesus Christ.

After one particular Scripture Study series, during Holy Week, since Catholics don't baptize a second time, and since baptismal fonts are kept empty throughout the season of Lent until the Easter Vigil, I invited each of our Scripture Study participants to step into the empty font, pause for a few moments of silence, and then to emerge as the neophytes would after their baptism in water. All were moved by the experience.

This unusual parish gave me the unique experience of living alone as a priest in the rectory. I would jokingly say to the parishioners that living alone meant that I often had to talk to myself. But I also let them know that, in itself, that was not a huge problem until the day would come when I would answer my own questions. Then I would really have a problem.

I wasn't alone for very long. God sent a special blessing my way.

My mother came to live with me for two whole years. For the first few days she was very uncomfortable because where she was raised lay people kept a respectable distance from the clergy and the rectory. I reminded her that there were no other priests living with us. Yet, for her I was not only a son, but also a priest of God.

Once she relaxed she was able to enjoy the peace and tranquility of the rectory. My mother loved to walk in the parking lot and the surroundings of the church, and when I came home in the afternoons from the parish office, she always had a hot lunch waiting for me. Before these hot and healthy lunches, I would jokingly tell my parishioners that I was getting acquainted with my neighbors: Jack in the Box, Carl's Jr., Wendy, McDonald etc. The evenings would bring plenty of good family style conversation, which I had missed for many years. Thus, my mother and I made up for the five long years I spent away from her while living and studying in Rome.

One of the strengths of the parishioners of this community, which is also the well-known quality and mark of the Catholic Church everywhere in the world, was social consciousness and outreach to the poor. Religion is never meant to be a private affair between Jesus and me, as some evangelicals preach in their mega churches, but a commitment to feed the hungry, to clothe the naked, to visit the sick and those in prison, to shelter the homeless and to give drink to the thirsty as the twenty-fifth chapter of Matthew's Gospel reminds us to do in the parable of the last judgment. These, according to the Catholic Church's Catechism, are the corporal works of mercy. "As long as you did this to one of the least of my brothers and sisters, you did it for me," says Jesus in the conclusion of the parable.

The Catholic Church's social teachings have always been a source of inspiration and a call to action to the people of this parish. One important way these teachings were lived was through 'Community Ministry.' This ministry provided food, clothes, furniture, temporary housing and rent, employment opportunities and other forms of charity – no questions asked. One of the leaders in the community would often remind us: "If you want to live the gospel, you can't remain seated." Or, as the saying goes in Africa: "If you want to spread the Gospel, move your feet."

One day I was visiting a neighboring parish to do a wedding rehearsal. Since I had arrived early, I stayed a little bit longer in the car to collect my thoughts, and then coming out in a hurry to rush to the rehearsal, I absentmindedly left the keys in the car. While waiting in the Pastor's room for the towing company to open the door of my car, I happened to page through their parish picture directory.

They say there are no accidents and coincidences in spiritual life. I felt it was Divine Providence that made me leave my keys in the car that day, so that God would give our own parish a new key to getting to know one another. Since many new families were joining the parish, we published our first picture directory to put names and faces of parishioners together, and to see ourselves as a growing faith family.

The founding Pastor of this community had died and left the parish a sum of five thousand dollars in his will. For the first time in five years I thought I would take care of the needs of the rectory with this financial windfall. So, I decided to landscape the backyard of the rectory and install a sprinkler system.

About the time it was finished, I was approached by the clergy personnel board to consider taking a new parish assignment in a northern city of the diocese. Once again, according to the board, like a familiar refrain, I was told that I was the best person for the job and that my skills would be best suited for this unusual combined three-parishes-in-one situation. They said that I was so successful in my current parish with its multiple needs that I would also be able to do what was necessary for my next even more complex assignment.

A parishioner once said to me that I should change my name to 'Father 911' because of all the challenging parishes I was being asked to manage and fix in the diocese. I told the clergy board member that came to talk to me about the new assignment that I would think about it because I hadn't yet completed one full term of six years as Pastor of my current parish. And things were going so well here. Why leave now?

Although all I happened to say was that I was going to think about it, the personnel board proceeded to send me one of the fastest appointment letters of my priesthood. It appears they were happy that I had not objected to the transfer to a more challenging assignment.

When I stepped out into the parking lot one day after Mass, I saw three women (two of them parish staff members) weeping bitterly. I thought it was a personal matter, yet as a Pastor I stepped in to help, if I could. I knew these women really well. It happened that a few moments earlier these women had found out about my transfer and were already mourning the loss of a close priest friend and brother in me.

It is moments like these when one is surprised by the circumstances which are beyond one's control, yet in that same experience one feels very deeply loved.

There was another group I had founded and nurtured, and the members of this group were also saddened by the news of my transfer. Two years earlier, to bring together as many Indian Catholic families of the Bay Area as possible, I started an organization called: 'INFOCUS' (Indian Families of Catholics 'r' US). The 'US' referred both to our gathering of Indian families as well as to our presence in the United States.

Once a month, we would celebrate a Sunday afternoon Mass with a pot luck luncheon. The parking lot was safe for the children to play and run around. About a hundred people, including children, came to these monthly gatherings, and both the church facility and the hall with its large kitchen were ideal for this size of a group. It gave these Indian children born or brought up in the United States an opportunity to meet other Indian children like them, a chance for families away from their own loved ones to deepen their faith and their cultural heritage, and a possibility for me to find a shepherd's connection between life in India and in the United States of America. The pot luck food was excellent and always a delightful surprise (as long as there was pizza for the children), and everyone seemed to have fun.

Every month had its own theme of celebration, like the pilgrimage month of September, Christmas caroling in December, an outdoor picnic in June and so on.

Today after ten years INFOCUS has its own website and continues to inspire dispersed Indian Catholic families. Individuals on temporary work permits and new immigrant families who often feel lonely being so far from loved ones in India and from cultural traditions they grew up with find camaraderie, friendship and faith in these monthly INFOCUS gatherings.

*****

In the year 2000 I went on a four month sabbatical to Rome. It was my 25th year as a priest. I spent my sabbatical with thirty-eight priests from the United States and Canada. What was really significant was the fact that my sabbatical was taking place in the North American College of Rome, which is located right next door to the College of the Propagation of Faith where I spent my last year as a seminarian. My priestly life seemed to be completing yet another full circle.

On the way to Rome, I kept a journal in which I would write daily at least one event or experience of celebration. The question before me was very simple: "What special moment have I celebrated today?" The idea was not to fill my mind with regrets about the past twenty-five years of priestly ministry, but to acknowledge that every new day is a gift from God to be celebrated, that every moment of my life is graced.

When we arrived at the North American College, the Rector, who is currently the Archbishop of New York and a Cardinal, welcomed us. He told us that in the past year whenever he walked on the streets of Rome, he would see one recurring sign in Italian: 'Restauro.' The city of Rome was preparing for the Jubilee year of 2000. He told us, for instance, that the façade of the Basilica of St. Peter's was cleaned the previous year for the first time in about four hundred years, and that the original colors and hues that we could see now after the clean up were the same that pilgrims saw four centuries earlier as did artists like Michelangelo and Bernini.

He reminded us that we were on sabbatical for a *'Restauro,'* a restoration. We were not there to completely dismantle our many years of priesthood and to start anew. In ancient cities like Rome, people were constantly touching up older buildings and historical monuments, without destroying the past. Our past as priests was not a mistake to be changed, buried or destroyed. Instead, we needed simply a touch up, to look fresh and new in our lives as priests. What we were going to get was a face lift or vocation lift. Not a total reconstruction.

Only in places like Las Vegas, for instance, entire buildings are torn down to make room for even bigger structures. Only the future and what is bigger and spectacular are important in cities like Las Vegas; not the past. In this sabbatical we were reminded that our vocation to and experience of priesthood were not to be equated with the concept of 'destroy and rebuild' as in places of entertainment.

Being the season of Lent, we accompanied the seminarians of the North American College every day for a pilgrimage to all the *stational* churches of Rome. Some of them had remained closed for many years but now we had access to them briefly for Mass during the Jubilee year.

Like other pilgrims we also visited the four major basilicas of Rome and prayed at the Holy Doors, which are opened only once every twenty-five years.

We, priests, appreciated the sabbatical even more because we had classes during the week and we were free on weekends. This hardly ever happens in parish life because weekends are always busy for priests. So, I traveled everywhere in Italy by trains and buses on the weekends and enjoyed revisiting familiar sites. The knowledge of Italian from my seminary days was priceless.

I had many wonderful experiences during my sabbatical. On April 23rd, Easter Sunday and also the feast of St. George, my patron saint, I was invited to distribute Communion with two hundred other priests to the more than 300,000 pilgrims gathered for Mass in St. Peter's Square and beyond. Every morning, during my sabbatical, I would draw the blinds of my window and see the Dome that Michelangelo built over St. Peter's. But on the morning of Easter Sunday, the Dome was gone. It was eerie to see a familiar sight disappear completely.

There was a simple explanation. The fog had rolled in and blanketed most of the taller structures. I arrived at St. Peter's at the appointed time and we, concelebrants, were asked to hold the gold plated ciborium in our hands during Mass because there was not enough room on the altar for two hundred ciboria. During Mass we stood behind Blessed Pope John Paul II as he celebrated Mass.

During the consecration, when the Pope lifted up the host the sun came out. Our gold plated ciboria began to glisten in the rays of the sun. It was such an exhilarating moment for me, one that I will never forget.

There was a possibility for me, because of my 25th anniversary, to participate in daily Mass with the Pope in his private chapel at the Vatican. No guarantees of participation are given to any priest because the Pope may have a last minute change in travel plans and appointments. The nuns at the Vatican call you the day before to invite you for this once in a lifetime experience.

Every evening we would watch old movies. One night we saw the first 'Mission Impossible' and because it was quite late I decided to go to bed. Something made me go to my phone to check for messages. I had no message before that so it was not part of any daily routine to check for voice mail. I was pleasantly surprised to hear a nun's voice inviting me for Mass the next morning with the Pope.

Early the next day I arrived at the Vatican and with about twenty others was taken to the Pope's private chapel for Mass. Before we entered we were asked which language we would prefer for the celebration of Eucharist. The Pope was gifted with the knowledge of so many languages that his personal preference was not even considered. We decided on Italian and then we walked into the chapel. The Pope was already at his kneeler praying intensely. This Polish Pope was a giant of a man on the world stage but after the assassination attempt on his life and broken bones from falls, he appeared to be so feeble and small. After Mass, he came into the hall to shake hands with us and to give us a Rosary as a gift. The Vatican photographer took several pictures in those few seconds we individually had with the Pope, which I was later able to share with my parishioners and family in the United States.

Recently he was declared Blessed because of a miracle which happened to a nun when she prayed to him. The French sister had Parkinson's disease like the Pope when he was alive. So, her superior asked her to pray for healing through the intercession of John Paul II. She was instantly and miraculously cured.

Thus he is on track to be canonized a saint. I will always remember the once-in-a-lifetime opportunity I had to shake hands with and to kiss the hands of a saint. After my return to the United States, I showed my mother the Rosary the Pope gave me. She took it away from me and smilingly said: "You would never have got it in the first place without me." She was right and I was happy to share this precious gift and memento with my beloved mother.

During the sabbatical, thanks to the wonders of the internet, I would stay in touch with my parish in the United States by e-mail. I would send detailed reports of my adventures and experiences in Rome. These then appeared in the parish bulletin every week. This is how we stayed in touch even though I was gone for four months.

When the new Pastor arrived to take my place, the first thing he noticed and liked was the lovely landscaped backyard. The first words out of his mouth were, "This will be wonderful for my dog."

When I heard those words, I remembered what Yogi Berra once said, "It was déjà vu, all over again." I decided then and there that I would never wait too long to make improvements in living arrangements and to enjoy these extras right away with other clergy, family and friends. One is never certain of the length of one's assignment, so why make all this effort at the last minute and then let it go to the dogs???

*****

Moving to the northern most part of the diocese for my third assignment as Pastor was like moving to a new world. The beautiful city of Palo Alto was about thirty miles from San Jose.

This city of about sixty thousand residents was also known as a city with an attitude. Stanford University was close by and so this area was not only the birthplace of several computer and internet technology companies but also a university town. University Avenue was always bustling with activities and lined with exotic restaurants and outdoor cafes because of the student population of Stanford and their families and visitors.

The inhabitants of this city were well known to have strong opinions. Just as its citizens were involved in city politics and strongly voiced their agreements and disagreements about every civic issue, the same happened with regard to participation in the life of the local church. It's not that people here loved to demonstrate and challenge everything; as highly educated individuals they had sometimes opposing ideas and opinions, and as church members and ministers you were invited to join in the debate and discussions.

Very early in my assignment I was given a valuable nugget of wisdom by a parishioner on how to become an effective pastor in the city of Palo Alto. I was reminded not to consider myself a shepherd among sheep; rather, I should strive to become a leader among leaders.

Over six percent of the city's population moved around on bicycles to school, to work, or for pleasure. It was an environmentally friendly city that attracted the likes of a former Vice-President, Al Gore. There were many highly educated and very wealthy people. Entrepreneurs who come up with creative and revolutionary ideas and venture capitalists that fund many of the start-ups could be seen brainstorming ideas in some of the quaint restaurants that dotted the city's landscape.

The story is told that one day someone had a heart attack in church and the priest asked if there was a doctor in the house. At once everyone in the congregation stood up.

In the late eighties, as part of a study to pool resources and to prepare for the exodus of Catholics from the Northern areas towards the South and the South-East of the diocese, all the five parishes of Palo Alto and the Newman Center of Stanford University were merged into one parish.

At first, one of the churches, named after the saint whose name I share as my middle name, Aloysius, was closed down and sold to a new age Hindu fellowship called 'Ananda,' meaning, Happiness. The Hispanic community which was left over from the parish church of St. Aloysius was relocated to another of the five originally merged parishes, called Our Lady of the Rosary. The Hispanics walked in a grand procession and were warmly welcomed in their new surroundings.

When Stanford University permitted the celebration of Catholic Masses at the famous Memorial Church and became its own congregation, a very popular parish, named after St. Anne, was sold to a conservative Anglican community that fortunately maintained the same name. The sale created endowments and offered support for the newly created University parish of St. Dominic, which would now cater mainly to the needs of the Stanford student and faculty community.

St. Anne Parish which served also as the Newman Center for Stanford University was a very popular faith community which attracted a lot of young families. They had fond memories of watching their children sit around the altar feeling 'at home' in the church. The backyard and the Newman Center next door were popular gathering places for parish families. There was a great deal of disappointment and bitterness when this church, too, was closed down and sold.

In the end there were only three parish churches remaining that were merged into the one canonical parish of St. Thomas Aquinas, the Catholic Community of Palo Alto. This situation of three parishes in one was not only unique to the city, but also the only one of its kind in the entire diocese.

The two Catholic elementary schools associated with these three original parishes were closed down because of lack of demand for Catholic parochial schools in this area and the highly competitive quality of the local public schools. Again, this created a unique situation in this city, compared to the rest of the diocese. Everywhere else there was a strong demand for Catholic schools, except here.

One of the schools and its adjoining grounds was rented by the parish to an international language immersion school that taught French and Chinese. On the other Catholic school premises, a new ethnically inclusive elementary school was created to help poorer kids mainly from the neighboring city of East Palo Alto and other poorer areas of the region to get a good Catholic education. Over ninety per cent of the families that currently send their kids to school here cannot afford to pay any tuition. This elementary school was run by a religious order of nuns. The school became a successful outreach project of the entire parish and of the larger well-to-do community of this region. The graduation rate was a hundred percent and all the kids each and every year got into good high schools and colleges of California.

I had never been to this Northern Bay Area city before I received my formal assignment. But I had heard rumors about the challenges and the complexities of this merged parish. As a priest I was particularly concerned about the situation of the Pastors who had preceded me in Palo Alto. Two of them had died relatively young, one, while still in office. Finally, a Pastor who was young, intelligent and dynamic had left the priesthood.

There were many factors that created a challenging situation for parish leaders. Some parishioners claimed that they were not consulted in the merging process. Others were afraid that their church would be the next one to be closed.

Even though earlier research indicated the aging and the diminishing of the local population, there was in the early nineties an economic boom that drew a lot of younger families with children to this affluent area. Thus the demographics changed and created new liturgical, catechetical and pastoral needs and expectations at each church site.

Between the three remaining worship sites there were eight Masses every weekend: all in English, except one in Spanish.

When I first arrived in California, I became conscious that so many people spoke Spanish everywhere: in grocery stores, shopping malls, public transit and fast food restaurants. I was surprised by that since I did not know the history of California and especially, its association with Mexico. Having the gift of languages, I was wondering then whether I should learn Spanish for ministry purposes. But I initially resisted the thought because I said to myself that if I wanted to minister in Spanish, I should have chosen to go to Mexico or to some other Latin country as a missionary. For me, when I first arrived, there seemed to be unity among the fifty states in America mainly because of its English language that helped facilitate communications in this vast country.

India has many languages which is both a blessing and a curse. While Indian society celebrates diversity through its many languages and cultures, it also foments animosities and divisions because it lacks the unity of one language.

From the very beginning I was always assigned to parishes that had Masses only in English. So you can imagine my surprise when I got assigned to this affluent city (ironically with a Spanish name, Palo Alto) and here, of all places, I encountered my first Spanish Mass community as Pastor.

With this new Hispanic connection in my life, I finally made the decision to go to Cuernavaca in Mexico and immersed myself for three weeks in the study of the Spanish language. Thereafter, once a month I was able to celebrate the Spanish Mass, the first pastor of the merged parishes to do so, much to the delight of the Hispanic community.

One of the ways I resolved the bi-lingual issues that were causing a problem to some parishioners was to make the liturgies multi-lingual, instead. The intention was not to make the problem even bigger! We did not have in this northern city just the Anglo and the Hispanic communities. More Chinese had moved to Palo Alto in the last decade than any other ethnic, cultural or linguistic group. Moreover, the city became a melting pot as one of the important hubs of the Silicon Valley, drawing a variety of language and cultural groups like the French, the East Indian, the Korean, the Filipino and many other nationalities. So, I introduced the use of several languages to celebrate Holy Thursday and the Easter Vigil to reflect the multifaceted nature of our Catholic Community. Since we had the facility of digital projection, we put the English text of the readings on large screens for all to see, understand and participate.

In the downtown area and heart of this 'green city' there was a beautiful and historical gem of a church called St. Thomas Aquinas. The merged parish was named after this Angelic Doctor of the Church. Here there were four Mass communities, each with its own unique flavor.

One of the Masses was celebrated by a charismatic priest. People loved his stories and his personal approach. He knew his congregation well and was always called upon to celebrate their baptisms, weddings as well as funerals.

Perhaps some people liked this Mass because it was a quiet Mass. It was early on Sunday mornings with no congregational singing.

But the fact that the same people came back again and again to this style of worship seemed to indicate that they liked what they saw and were moved by the experience. They loved the preaching and the stories. And this early Mass community was also very generous to the needs of the poor, especially through the St. Vincent de Paul Society, and to the special needs of the St. Elizabeth Seton School for poor and needy families in the area around the parish.

Even though the Eucharist should be at the center of Worship, it is a fact that people are sometimes more drawn to the charismatic style of an individual priest and, if possible, they will follow him everywhere.

To be truly the shepherd of this entire parish, once a month, I would celebrate this early Sunday Mass.

When the parish church associated with the Newman Center was sold an Anglican community, it displaced a lot of loyal parishioners. Many of them had fond memories of celebrations and fellowship at St. Anne's church. Two philosophically and theologically polarized communities that met at St. Anne Church for worship moved, after it was sold, to the downtown historical church of St. Thomas Aquinas. One was the Gregorian Community, with beautiful sacred music chanted in Latin; while the other was known as the Thomas Merton Community, which had non-profit independent status, while still maintaining its connection with the larger Catholic community of the city.

Some aspects of the Thomas Merton Community reminded me of the progressive Transfiguration Catholic Community in San Jose where I was both associate and pastor in previous assignments. Again I was reminded that every life experience of our past has value and we never know when that life lesson will help us face similar situations in the future.

As stated in the TMC weekly bulletin: "The Thomas Merton Center for Catholic Spiritual Development was founded by a group of Roman Catholic lay persons in 1995, and incorporated in 1996, to offer Catholic liturgy, to augment, support and lead the development of ecumenical spirituality, and to foster new ways for Catholics and other Christians to develop a deeper spiritual relationship with Jesus Christ and, through him, with God. From its Catholic roots, it seeks to join with members of other faiths, Christian and non-Christian, to support religious education and spiritual development."

I had always found the Thomas Merton Community to be joyful and alive. They truly took participation seriously. The liturgies were well prepared and the praying and singing were loud and vibrant. There was always hospitality and fellowship that continued after Mass and lasted for a long time. People did not leave early after Communion and they truly enjoyed prayer, worship and each other.

As a bridge builder, once a month I presided regularly at the Thomas Merton Mass.

As an addendum, with another priest friend, I would sometimes make my annual clergy retreat in cloistered Trappist monasteries where visitors are welcome. One year the two of us went to the monastery in Gethsemane, Kentucky, and there visited the burial place of Thomas Merton. His conversion journey in the classic, 'The Seven Storey Mountain' has profoundly influenced my life as a Catholic priest.

Another displaced community that previously called the Newman Center 'home' was the Gregorian Community. They also moved to the historical downtown church for worship in their own unique chanting style. A professor from Stanford University led the assembly in Gregorian chant and conducted the choir. It was the only one of its kind in this area, so people came from afar to enjoy this unique traditional celebration, with its smells (of incense) and bells and sacred chant.

The professor, who was the music director, underscored the importance of Gregorian chant from the 1967 document: '*Musicam Sacram*:' saying that the treasure of sacred music is to be preserved and fostered. In his own words, from an interview in the local Palo Alto newspaper, the professor said:

"Chant adds something beautiful. A religious service should be beautiful because beauty is an attribute of God. When you sing it beautifully and when it really works, there's an absolute stillness in the church. That's the kind of silence that's fruitful; it represents a kind of self-awareness that is also aware of the wider realities. That kind of silence is where you have your best opportunity to speak to God and to listen to God."

I was familiar with Gregorian chant when I studied in Rome. Since worship was taking place more and more in the vernacular after the Second Vatican Council, modern Italian compositions were frequently used in daily and Sunday liturgies in the seminaries of Rome.

Once more, as a bridge builder, I frequently chanted the Mass in English and in Latin for a grateful Gregorian community.

*****

When I found out about the health situations of my predecessors and I gradually began to experience for myself the complexities of the different worship sites and Mass communities, I realized that this was going to be a very challenging assignment.

Before I took on this parish, I remembered a priest asking me if there was anything wrong with me for saying 'yes' to the personnel board and the bishop so quickly. I also remembered discussing this assignment with the first bishop of the diocese, who had agreed to merge the five parishes and Stanford University in 1987 (a few years after the formation of the new diocese) after accepting the advice of some experts in pastoral ministries and statistics; and since he had already retired he told me before I went to Palo Alto: "The merging of these parishes was one of the biggest mistakes we have made."

Both my predecessor and I were asked to provide the diocese with on-going evaluations. We had both made concrete suggestions and recommendations of what could be done to ease the complexity and the challenges of the Catholic Community of this beautiful city.

When life gives you lemons, you make lemonade. I can now add a new skill to my résumé: the juggler of multiple parishes.

Pastoral assignments take place on July 1. My youngest brother was expecting his first child also on July 1 of the same year. So, I told everyone that my brother was expecting a child, and I, as the new Pastor of this Catholic Community of three parishes, was expecting triplets!

Even though I have tried to make it appear humorous that the diocese tells me each time I am transferred that I am the best person for the job, the fact is that God has used me as His instrument in effective pastoral ways to bring about reconciliation, healing and unity.

At my first assignment as Pastor, after my arrival I was told that at least nine prominent families had left the parish when the church was remodeled without proper consultation with the parish community. During my seven years there, I am happy to say that all these families, without exception, returned to the parish.

At my second assignment as Pastor, several parishioners seemed to be without energy and Spirit because of past conflicts and ideologies. During my five years there, I am happy to say that the Spirit was restored to this community and a sense of belonging was offered to all. While the community had dwindled in the past, it now boasted an increase of almost fifty-five percent in Sunday attendance. When I left the parish, it was truly thriving and vibrant.

At my installation ceremony and Mass for this new assignment, the people were packed in Our Lady of the Rosary church. A lot of my friends including the Indian community and members of the Italian Catholic Federation, and former parishioners flocked to Palo Alto and joined the Catholic Community here to welcome their newest Pastor. When I saw the crowds, I remembered the first bishop of the diocese asking me during the installation Mass at my first parish: "Where did all these people come from?" The second bishop who installed me as Pastor of St. Thomas Aquinas parish introduced me to the assembly as a 'Renaissance man.' My mother and some members of my family were present to share in my joy. When my mother was introduced by the bishop to the community, she got a standing ovation.

The day before my installation as Pastor, there was an article about me in the religion section of the Palo Alto Daily, titled

'New Pastor grew up in Religious Mélange.' Among other things, the editor, after conducting phone interviews with me, mentioned in the article that one of my goals was to strengthen the unity between the three worship sites, but also to let each be unique in the expression of their style and identity. The editor also added that what I liked best about being a priest was the ability to touch people's lives at key moments, from the womb to the tomb.

In the first of my weekly bulletin messages 'From the Pastor to my Dear Parishioners,' I shared a Scripture quote indicating what being their Pastor meant to me:

"Today I hear Jesus saying: 'You have not chosen me. I have chosen you and appointed you to bear fruit that will last.' God's providence works in many interesting ways. I am a believer and I firmly believe in my heart that God brought you and me together for a purpose. Because God has chosen me (and not the other way around), I will seek to be an instrument in God's hands to bear fruit among you, fruit that will last. Thank you for accepting me and welcoming me as your new Pastor."

Even though the merging of these parishes was in hindsight a big pastoral blunder, there must have been good reasons to bring the Catholic Community of this city into canonically one worshipping parish family. Statistics had shown that there was not only a shortage of priests but also that the median age of priests had risen considerably without younger priests being available to replace them, after retirement or death. Another disturbing trend for the local diocese was the movement of people from the Northern areas to the South and the South-East of the county. Homes in the Northern areas were more expensive, thus making it prohibitive for younger families and newly married couples to start a life there. If the churches were getting emptier by the day, it made sense to pool together the resources of all the city parishes, and to ease the burden of single parishes to make ends meet. The decision before the first bishop was to have only one Pastor, and consequently, one staff, one finance board and one Parish Council. It appeared to be a very practical solution.

But practical solutions don't appeal to the parishioners who have been members of their faith communities all their lives and are now afraid that their church will be the next one to be closed or sold. In many dioceses of the country, churches have been closed or sold, adding to the discontent and anger of many long time parishioners. In some places there have been demonstrations and lock-ins.

Knowing that several parishioners were deeply hurt by this merger, I decided to bring about a spirit of reconciliation, healing and peace. Believing that you cannot undo the past, I began to focus on the present and the future. My constant theme and vision for the parish were: 'Unity in Community.'

Yes, we were called to be one canonical parish even though we belonged to different communities and parishes in the past. This meant that while we respected the diversity among us, we would try and share resources and work together for the good of all. We needed to break away from the past, its hurts and its resentments. We had to stop blaming and to start growing in faith together. What appeared to be crisis indicators in the past could be made into opportunities for growth in the future.

An entire generation seemed to be lacking in participation and the understanding of traditional Catholic practices and liturgical celebrations. For instance, the three important days of Holy Week were celebrated at three separate worship sites: The washing of the feet and the institution of Eucharist and Priesthood on Holy Thursday at one church, the celebration of the Passion and Death of Jesus on Good Friday at another, and the Easter Vigil with the welcoming of new Catholics and the Sacraments of Initiation at the third site, the largest of the three churches. Thus some children and grown-ups had never witnessed the washing of the feet for example or the baptism of adults because these events were not celebrated at the churches where their families normally attended.

So in my waking hours I kept insisting on the ideas of Unity and One parish. I constantly invited all parishioners to participate at every event even if it took place at a church site different from the one they attended. By regular rotation I served all three church sites and from time to time celebrated all the eight different Masses of the community. I realized that in the end, as Pastor and Shepherd, I had to be the visible symbol of unity.

What if some parishioners would not listen? There is a story told about a new prophet who came to a town for the first time to deliver his message. When he preached by the river, all the townspeople came to listen. As they disliked the message, they gradually began to leave. He continued to give his message to those who remained but very soon they also went away. He was left alone. Yet, he did not stop delivering his message. One day someone stopped by and asked him why he continued to preach even when no one was listening. The prophet replied: "Even if no one believes in the message I have been called to deliver, I believe in it. I will continue to proclaim the message, even if no one listens, so that the day may not come when I also stop believing in the truth of the message."

Besides the ideas of Unity and One Parish, I had also emphasized the ideas of Community and Diversity. The goal for me was always Unity, not Uniformity. Parents who have three children try to love them equally but try to also treat them uniquely and personally. I still remembered my dad who would give me a quarter after school once a week, and till the day he died I thought I was the only one getting this unique attention and gift. After his death, I found out every one of my siblings also received weekly a quarter from dad. Each one of us felt we were special in his sight. This is because each child is unique and each one is an individual blessed with special gifts and skills.

With my three 'parishes,' I felt like a parent with three children. Each church site had unique qualities and strengths. Even the physical spaces of our three churches were different. These differences needed to be respected like the unique characteristics of your children; these communities could not be treated in the same way. We hired liturgy directors, for example, who insisted that all three worship sites should celebrate identical liturgies and prayers. In the end these professionals of liturgical uniformity had to quit their jobs, unable to bend the wills of these distinct communities to a uniform robotic way of church life.

On the other hand, I personally introduced processionals and other liturgical adaptations at our Sunday Masses. However, when changes were proposed the unique space and the resources of each church site were always taken into consideration. It was always a question of Unity and not Uniformity.

You cannot build a family without respecting the uniqueness of each member. You cannot form community without respecting diversity.

Before I arrived at this parish, I was given the consultation results of the community. When there is a change of pastors, a consultation committee is sent to talk with the local Parish Council and other leaders of the community. Then, an open house is held where feedback is received from the people of the parish. This process gives the people and their leaders a chance to indicate the strengths and the challenges of the parish as they see them, and it gives the new pastor a glimpse into the life of the community he will soon inherit. An incoming pastor does not have to reinvent the wheel. He is given a bird's eye-view of the characteristics of the parish. Thus he can respect the history of the parish, make changes wherever necessary as suggested by the people, and finally, know from the report what not to fix if it isn't broken.

In my consultation report, the people had asked for greater visibility from the pastor. The eight Masses celebrated in the three churches often had guest priest-celebrants. The people were constantly kept guessing as to which priest would be the main celebrant. Moreover, by not regularly seeing the pastor, it was felt by the parishioners as if there was no Captain on the ship. After all, the pastor still symbolized the unity of the parish for everyone.

*****

In a new parish, since I am the new kid on the block, I try to spend the first six months listening and observing and not making any substantial changes. But since visibility was such a priority for this faith community, and the three church sites were at least three miles apart from each other, I had decided to make one important change very early in my assignment.

The movers and the shakers of this parish merger believed that even after all the churches were brought together into one parish community, there would still be enough priests to celebrate all the Masses. Yet, only two priests were assigned for the care of three churches.

Besides three daily Masses, some of the Sunday Masses were at the same hour and at different sites. A pastor like me would now require the skill of bi-location or even, tri-location to satisfy everyone's need for pastor-visibility. There was one Sunday Mass at 8:45 a.m. and two at 9 a.m. at three different churches. Then there were two Masses at 10:30 a.m. at churches three miles apart.

Besides the priest-celebrant, musicians and choir members were also shared between churches, which made it difficult to start Mass on time at the next church in a prayerful way. Sometimes the musicians would arrive so late that the gathering processional hymn would be eliminated. So, I asked the people of one site to change their morning Sunday Mass from 9:30 a.m. to 9 a.m., so that I could drive to the next church for a 10:30 a.m. celebration. They said that just as they come screeching into church at 9:30 a.m. with their families, they would do the same for me and the community at 9 a.m. I realized then that I was accepted by the community. And that enabled me to become more visible to the entire parish.

I had learned my lessons in the last two parishes not to wait till the end of my assignment to make any necessary changes in rectory living arrangements; otherwise, as in the past, it all went to the dogs!

When I met my predecessor the first time, he invited me out to lunch. As we drove in his old Cadillac, there were literally a hundred cigarette butts below and around the passenger seat. He was a chain smoker. Later on I found out that in his living room even the area rug was used as an ash tray. He smoked everywhere and at all times, even after he underwent quadruple bypass heart surgery.

Since I don't smoke and knowing the hazards of second hand smoke, it was going to be impossible to move into a chain smoker's suite. But this crisis was my opportunity to start with clean, new surroundings. It also helped that unlike my previous parish, this Palo Alto community was not hurting for money. I still had some time before I had to move in to start my work as pastor and thus I could make the necessary changes.

I first got the Pastor's suite freshly painted and then had the wooden floors polished. I went shopping for a new area rug and got rid of all the old smoke-filled furniture both in the living room as well as in the bedroom. I bought brand new sofas and a comfortable bedroom set. Simple thick blinds were installed on all my windows and new filters were put into the heat vents. I did the impossible, with the help of many friends of course. I got rid of all traces of smoke smell from my suite of rooms. That first night I slept peacefully like a baby.

My first year in this parish was especially challenging because both my associate and I were new to the assignment. The previous pastor retired and his associate was transferred. We had no one else in the rectory, except a retired priest, who was enjoying his retirement. The liturgy and music director had resigned so there was no one to coordinate the various liturgies and the diverse music groups in the parish. The board of our parish school decided to change the leadership of the school from a lay principal to a nun.

In situations like these you begin to experience the power of the faith community and the resilience of your own personal faith. People came out of the woodwork to help and a month later God sent us a talented religious sister, who became our liturgy and music director.

One of the big events to jump-start the new parish year in September was the annual parish picnic. Families returned from summer vacations and, at this parish fun event, new clergy, staff members as well as new families were introduced. The parish picnic drew close to four hundred or so parishioners from 11:30 in the morning to about 3 in the afternoon. The children had a lot of fun playing games and there were plenty of hamburgers and hot dogs provided by the Knights of Columbus.

A game that brought a lot of joy and laughter was tossing water filled balloons to your partner, and catching the same when thrown at you. Each time you succeeded in catching the water balloon without smashing it, you backed away a few more steps from your partner. I was doing well and was one of the few to remain standing till the end. When the balloon finally smashed into my face, the water was all over me. Our professional parish photographer captured the moment, which I claimed as my baptism into the parish community.

At the baptism of an infant, the baby cries while the people standing around are smiling. It was almost a similar scene when the water balloon smashed into my face!

*****

I believe strongly that when you bring people together socially, they form community. At my previous parish of Transfiguration I achieved this by having potluck socials, concerts and festivals during the year. The Catholic Community of Palo Alto had a special committee to organize such gatherings and was called 'Community Life.' The committee was responsible for organizing the annual parish picnic. Since two of our sites had school grounds, the parish picnic alternated between them. Some interested parishioners organized an annual St. Patrick's dinner dance, with corned beef and cabbage and Irish dancers. The evening would end with the singing of traditional Irish melodies. The Knights of Columbus would raise funds for the parish school by organizing an annual all-you-can-eat crab dinner.

I felt that there was more that needed to be done so that our three sites would have more opportunities to gather and to get to know one another. These social and religious gatherings were going to be crucial for the unity of our parish community. It is true that a family that prays together stays together. I believed that a parish that prayed and played together would strengthen its bonds of unity and community.

Having several churches, our community was blessed to have several patron saints. In the beginning I encouraged each church site and our school to have their own patron saint party and to invite the entire community to attend. I called it: the Parish Patron Party (PPP)! In November during one of the patron saint's feast day, I walked quickly into the sacristy while the assembly sang the recessional song, and changed into a costume, which I had picked up from the local theater. I came out of the sacristy and introduced myself in German, in the language of the Saint I represented. Afterwards, I narrated the story of this Saint's origins and what he was known for before being declared a Saint by the Church. The people simply loved it and I had the opportunity to mingle with them afterwards in the hospitality center still dressed in my Saint Albert the Great outfit. In celebration of the Saint's life, especially in his knowledge of science, the youth had brought their telescopes and spent the evening scouring the skies.

The story of another patron St. Thomas Aquinas, a student of St. Albert the Great, was done even more elaborately by several parishioners at the church itself. Several people remarked that they had never before heard the stories of these parish patron saints. At Our Lady of the Rosary, we narrated how the feast came about and its significance in the history of the church.

When it got to be difficult each year to repeat these patron saint stories separately on their feast days, we decided to celebrate them together on the feast of All Saints, November 1st.

Several years ago, when I was seeking a vocation within my vocation, I was drawn to the Media as a way to communicate faith. I wasn't able to do much then with my knowledge and expertise but here in Palo Alto I got several opportunities to do half hour presentations on local community television. The program was entitled: 'Spirit Talk' with Jean Ramacciotti. I was interviewed for three segments on the following topics: 1. Catholic Christians Today 2. Why Be Catholic? 3. The Year of St. Paul

When one of our families had visited a neighboring protestant church, they were amazed at the welcome they received as well as the follow up to their visit. I love to learn from the experiences of others. When I heard their story, I went to a Community Life Committee meeting and told them that we also needed to do something radical to welcome visitors and guests into our parish. There were four decisions made at that meeting. First, I began to welcome guests and spend some time for hospitality at the beginning of Mass every first Sunday of the month. Second, each church site began welcoming and registering new comers and visitors, some twice a month and some once a month either in the hall or in the vestibule of the church. Third, letters were sent to newly registered parishioners signed by the priests of the parish together with an informational booklet regarding the activities of the parish. And fourth, every few months a gathering would be held of new comers at the rectory either to have dinner with the clergy of the parish or simply to have dessert and coffee.

We had a strong Pastoral Home Ministry that took Communion to the homebound and to the nursing homes within the boundaries of the parish. The homebound would receive a copy of the parish bulletin to know what was going on in the parish. But from a story I heard, I felt the homebound had even more to offer.

The story is told of a woman who had first a heart attack, and then, stroke after stroke immobilized and paralyzed her from the waist down. When a Communion minister went to visit her, she did not know what to say to the suffering woman. Without intending to do so, she made the homebound woman regret that she could not get around anymore and live an active life-style. To which the immobilized woman said: "At least I can pray."

I composed a prayer so that the homebound could become Prayer Partners and form a prayer circle to pray for the sick of the parish. There are many parishioners and their friends and neighbors, who when they are undergoing surgery or facing long term care and painful disabilities, ask for the prayers of the priests and the parish. How wonderful for them to know that they are being remembered in their illnesses and surgeries by an entire army of homebound Prayer Partners. Through phone trees and e-mails, the list of the sick was constantly updated and then passed on to the Prayer Partners scattered all over the parish.

It is such a powerful feeling to know that when you are weak, when you are sick, or when you are having surgery, you are not alone. There are so many people supporting you and holding you up in prayer and love. The thought is so comforting and so healing.

One of the continuing ways I have tried to reach out to the sick, the elderly and those seeking emotional and spiritual strength to cope with life is to offer frequently the Sacrament of Anointing of the Sick. Around the weekend of the Feast of Our Lady of Lourdes, we celebrated the Sacrament of Anointing at all the weekend Masses. Every first Friday of the month, we prayed with the sick and the elderly and offered them the Anointing of the Sick at the daily 8:30 a.m., and at the 12:15 afternoon Mass.

One day the word got around that there was a controversial movie showing in public theaters called 'The Da Vinci Code.' Some people had already read the book by Dan Brown and now the movie was going to circulate all across the country and all over the world. Dan Brown's books are filled with symbols, thrills and Vatican intrigue. Even though he had claimed that his books were works of fiction, he also claimed that his writings were based on some random facts. The problem is that most people don't have the knowledge, the expertise or the time to separate fact from fiction. One of my parishioners came to me one day and asked: "What does the Church have to say about this book and movie?" She even gave me her personal copy to read. The first thing I did was to read the book.

After reading several reviews both from church magazines as well as secular commentaries, I decided to establish a new series for our parish called 'The Burning Bush.' On Mount Sinai, when Moses saw a bush burning and not being consumed by the fire, he realized that he was on holy ground and that this burning issue could be an opportunity for an encounter with God.

This is how I saw 'The Da Vinci Code,' as a burning issue that called for questions, discussion, reflection, prayer and fellowship in an open and safe environment. The Church does not have to be afraid of dialog with the world. Jesus was constantly challenged. But he made every question and challenge into teachable moments.

The poet Rainer Maria Rilke hoped that we can all surface our questions, so that we can learn to live with them. Someday these questions may even lead us into the answers we are seeking. I believed that if we provided a safe atmosphere to ask faith questions, then that environment could turn out to be the holy ground where we can encounter God.

Conversations and communications sometimes happen on different levels. A woman parishioner, when she heard about our plans for 'The Burning Bush' series complained that we were getting to be very political because she thought that it was our intention to burn President Bush.

The Burning Bush idea gave us another opportunity for fellowship and social interaction. For 'The Da Vinci Code' discussion we had over sixty people show up with books, ideas and questions. We concluded the evening with wine and cheese and a new ministry of hospitality emerged from these gatherings. We tacked on a variety of topics: stem cell research, Pope Benedict's Encyclical on Love, priesthood, capital punishment, Tridentine versus Gregorian liturgies, the Catholic response to teen suicide, emotions and spirituality, *et cetera*.

A parish community would be lifeless without volunteers. More than a third of our registered families were involved in some ministry or the other. Even though the Ministry of the Assembly is important on Sundays, and from time to time I will thank our people for simply taking the time to show up in church Sunday after Sunday, I do like to share my vision of ministry especially when we have Time and Talent Sundays.

My vision as a pastor is for every parishioner to come to church on Sundays and to be involved in at least one ministry in the parish. This involvement will give the individual a sense of belonging and a sense of ownership of the parish. We can proudly say then: "This is my parish family. And this is what I do to make it a vibrant community."

So every October we celebrated the Stewardship of Time, Talent and Treasure. On the first Sunday we presented an annual pictorial comprehensive parish report to all our parishioners. Previously, we would only have a four page financial report. Now we showed our parishioners in detail and with pictures how we spent our resources through all the ministries of the parish. This report also called us all to accountability. It was like the parable of the talents in the gospels, where each one of the servants needed to let the Master know how they invested the talents they were given.

In the annual pictorial report there was also a Time and Talent sheet with suggestions of ministries and ways to get involved in the parish. The next three Sundays, at each church site in turn, we had a Ministry Faire after Mass. All the ministries had an opportunity to share information with parishioners and get them to sign up in areas of parish life that interested them. I told every priest celebrant to lead the entire worshipping community at their Mass outside to the booths and tables of the Ministry Faire. We also provided food and drinks so that parishioners could spend some time in fellowship together.

Within the month of October I presented Stewardship Honors to those who had made a difference during the past year or recently in the life of the parish. By their unique involvement they had contributed to the quality of parish life. I had given awards to the woman who spearheaded our picture directory project; to the man who photographed us and prepared collages of parish events; to the team that initiated the parish archive project; to the woman who gathered funds and invited many families to redecorate the rectory and make it look like a home, *et cetera*. After providing six weeks of Stewardship education, we created banners that went up at all three church sites during the month of October:

'Stewardship: your calling. How will you respond?'

To show our appreciation to all our many volunteers, I continued to encourage 'The Volunteer Appreciation Party.' This celebration was held close to Valentine's Day in February. I had insisted that on this special day volunteers do nothing except be loved, fed and appreciated. All the work was thus done by paid staff members. The attendance at these parties was growing every year. One year all the staff members, including the clergy, were dressed in aprons. After the sumptuous dinner, I began the festivities by saying: "Hello, my name is Fr. George, and I will be your waiter." The people smiled and clapped in appreciation. Sometimes I read to them the poem about volunteers which in conclusion hoped that one day when our volunteers go to heaven, they would be able to sit back, enjoy themselves, and be served by people who never volunteered on earth.

People were hungry for the Word of God. Many Catholics, even though they come to Sunday Mass, will go to Bible based churches to study the Scriptures. At every liturgy Catholics are nourished both at the table of the Word and at the table of the Eucharist. Yet, people want more. I responded to this hunger by providing lectionary-based weekly Scripture Study. Since many did attend Bible study classes, I began to offer a brief introduction to give a context to the understanding of the first two readings on Sundays. This addition was highly appreciated. To include the nourishment that came from the Word of God, I ordered musical editions that also included all the Sunday readings in their entirety. This way if people showed up early for Mass, they could prepare themselves by looking at the readings ahead of time. The Sunday Scripture references were also given in our weekly paper bulletin and our weekly e-bulletin.

I continued to offer free of cost the 'Little Books' to all our parishioners: the 'Little Blue Books' in preparation for Advent and the Christmas season; the 'Little Black Books' in preparation for Lent and for Holy Week; and finally, the 'Little White Books' for the fifty days of the season of Easter that reach their climax on Pentecost Sunday.

Even though we were in the heartland of digital and technological advances, when I first came to the parish, there was no official parish website. I contacted a retired Stanford professor and he got together with his son and they put together a wonderful website for the parish. The Communications Committee made some good moves to increase awareness of our parish in the neighborhood. They had cards with basic information and directions to all our church sites that were then given to the hotels and motels in the area to be passed out to visitors who wanted to find a Catholic church.

I worked with different ministries to come up with a Mission statement for the parish. We finally agreed on a version that was comprehensive, yet simple enough to be remembered:

> *St. Thomas Aquinas Parish is a Roman Catholic community of disciples working together for the glory of God and our spiritual growth in Jesus Christ. With the guidance of the Holy Spirit, we live and share the Gospel through Worship, Education and Service.*

We also encouraged every ministry and committee in the parish to come up with their own Mission statement. In the annual parish report a ministry would be expected first to state its mission, and then, show the community how it had fulfilled that mission during the year.

For a long time I sought to create a logo for the parish. A logo can capture the essence of a community and its mission. It also adds life and color to letterheads, business cards, annual reports, invitations, *et cetera*. I contacted a former parishioner of mine, who does computer graphics, and asked her to create a logo for us. She wanted to know what was truly important for us in our parish life that we wished to communicate to the outside world with our logo. So I shared my vision for the parish and what I considered to be essential elements for our logo.

Our new parish logo was comprised of three circles that were interdependent. Each of the circles had an image of one of our three church sites. These three interdependent circles were situated within an image of the heart, recalling Jesus' invitation to love one another. The heart was superimposed on a Cross to remind us that it is not an easy task to love and that only through the Cross we can come to life and community.

From my past experience I have always believed that a retreat can strengthen one's faith. I often wondered how best to offer this possibility to families who are always busy, and yet, are truly in need of a retreat experience. We finally came up with a day's experience of prayer, reflection and faith sharing. It was a format that was offered by a group called the Mystical Humanity of Jesus. We had two parish-wide retreat experiences; one, in celebration of the 'Year of St. Paul,' and two, in celebration of the 'Year of the Priest.' Both were well received and large crowds of parishioners participated actively.

One reason why the faith-sharing model worked so well in our parish was because I had encouraged it at every level of the community. Whenever we gathered for meetings, instead of a quick formal opening prayer, we would take a Scripture reading or a spiritual reflection, and then, individuals would share how God had been working in their lives and how they had sensed the presence of the Holy Spirit.

I believed that these minutes of prayer and sharing could truly affect the outcome of our meetings and would help us understand that we were doing God's work, and not simply taking care of our personal agendas. Even Finance Committee members who get excited about numbers and little else, and Buildings and Maintenance Committee members, who dream mainly of projects and expansion plans, began their monthly meetings with faith-sharing.

I had established two kinds of staff meetings: general and ministry. Every staff member was expected to attend the general meeting where reports were given by all, so that everyone knew what was going on in the entire parish. The general meetings began with faith-sharing and ended with a celebration of birthdays for that particular month.

The ministry staff meeting was restricted to those staff members who were in charge of their ministries. We began with faith-sharing; then, we brought to the table the ministry projects for the month, so that everyone was informed and we could also see how our ministries were inter-related. In this way we could also support one another's ministries for the good of the entire parish.

When I first came to the parish there was a Parish Council with elected members from the community. Individuals were nominated and if they agreed to participate, their photos and their bios would be posted in the church vestibules. The candidates would also be given an opportunity to state their case from the pulpit a week before elections. Those elected would then begin a three year term in the Parish Council. The problem was finding enough candidates interested in holding leadership offices.

Several years earlier I had attended a stewardship convention in Fort Lauderdale, Florida. With the help of interested parishioners, I formed a stewardship committee and began educating the entire community on the benefits of Stewardship.

We are all blessed by God in unique ways. The gifts we are given are not meant to be hoarded or used selfishly; rather, we are called by our baptism to share these gifts in order to build up the community. We are called to put aside a portion of our blessings; to return them in thanksgiving for the good of all, especially for those in need.

As part of the education on Stewardship, I took ten apples to the pulpit. The first three apples symbolized our personal gifts and talents and the gifts of creation given to us generously by God. The next three apples represented our meals, our work, and our homes, gifts of survival and sustenance from a caring God. The last three apples mirrored our family, our education, our church and faith – all showered upon us by God.

Finally, there was only one apple left. God said, "I gave you an abundance of nine apples because I love you. Since I don't want you to forget who gave them to you, I want you to return the last apple to me in thanksgiving." In the pulpit, I would hold up the last apple to the light of the sun and describe to everyone how juicy it looked to me. I really did not want to part with it. In the sight of everyone, I would then bring the apple to my mouth and take a big bite out of it.

This practical theology of Stewardship truly appealed to our parishioners. Since we had such highly educated people in the community, we organized a Strategic Planning meeting. More than fifty leaders of the parish attended. Out of this strategic planning we came up with a representative leadership model that we called 'The Pastoral Stewardship Council.' This new council had as many members as the ministries in our parish.

Each ministry was asked to send a representative to the council, who would bring the concerns of the ministry to the general body and then take the deliberations of the council and communicate them to the other members of their ministry. When a representative could not attend a council meeting they were expected to send an alternate. Thus attendance at these council meetings was perfect almost all the time and all ministries got equal time to be heard and affirmed. We were a living testimony to what St. Paul expected of churches and communities of faith. As he says in the First letter to the Corinthians: "We are many parts, yet we are one body, united in one Spirit." The symbol of the circular 'MANDALA' was used to show what ministries were represented in the council and how we were all inter-dependent.

The year before my assignment to this parish was the centennial celebration of the historic downtown Catholic Church of St. Thomas Aquinas. In 2004, I reminded the community of Our Lady of the Rosary, another of our three sites, that it was the 50th anniversary of the church's foundation. Pictures were gathered of all the priests who served at this parish community, and significant events were remembered. Fortunately, many of the founding members of this worship site were still living. They made the festivities come alive by sharing their memories with all the new parishioners. Alumni and alumnae were also invited from the first graduating class of the parish school.

The beauty of this anniversary celebration was that everyone in the parish was invited, not only those who had connections with the anniversary celebrating church. The Hispanic community, too, added to the festivities through song and dance and plenty of mouth watering delicious foods.

In every way we were becoming one parish, one community of faith. I remembered when two of the stained glass windows in the historic downtown church were damaged; I informed the whole community and invited everyone to be part of a fund-raiser to restore the beauty of the stained glass. Each church site was the patrimony of the whole parish. It was wonderful to see donations coming from all over, not just from those attending services at the site in need of repairs. The same thing happened when we decided to remodel the interior of Our Lady of the Rosary church site in preparation for its 50th anniversary. I am happy to say that some of the bigger contributors to this remodel project were from the other two church sites.

If in real estate, the three key words are *location, location, location*; then, the three key words for me for this merged multi-parish Catholic community were *Unity, Unity, and Unity.*

As pastor I always kept in mind that my main task was the spiritual growth of the parish community. Thus I introduced 'Spirituality Tuesdays' to the parish. My goal was to dedicate one evening when spirituality events would be offered to the whole parish. The purpose of choosing the same evening of the week was to make it easier for people to remember. With an 'Adult Spirituality Development' committee, we planned the sessions for the four Tuesdays of every month.

Usually, the first Tuesday was dedicated to a topic that included information, formation and transformation. The second Tuesday was for Scripture Study and Faith-Sharing. On the third Tuesday we focused on different forms of Prayer. Finally, the fourth Tuesday was kept aside for 'Burning Bush' current issues.

The very first Spirituality Tuesday Assembly began with a difficult and sensitive topic: 'Teen Suicide: A Catholic Response.' In a local public high school of our city five teenagers had committed suicide by throwing themselves in front of fast moving trains. As a community we gathered to mourn but also to take action and to express our Catholic belief that we choose life. A psychologist mentioned to us that according to statistics, the fewest suicides happen among Catholics. Yet, we agreed that even one suicide was one too many. It was a fruitful evening of information, formation and transformation. We came away enriched and strengthened in our faith and spirituality.

I always enjoy vacations by myself. I never imagined going on vacation with a large group. But my parishioners in my previous parishes repeatedly told me that if I ever organized a trip to Italy, they would love to travel with me.

Through a travel agency, I finally arranged for a trip to 'The Shrines of Italy and the Vatican.' About fifty of my friends and former parishioners decided to join the trip and by the time the word got around in my Palo Alto parish, I ended taking seventy-three pilgrims to the Vatican and to major cities in Italy like Rome, Assisi, Florence, Pisa, Siena, Padua and Venice. I celebrated Mass at all the major basilicas in these historical cities. Because it was a large group and we were traveling in two buses, I called one group, 'The Saints' and the other, 'The Angels.' Our fun trip and pilgrimage included an audience with Pope Benedict XVI.

Since this first adventure was so successful, I decided the following year, which was declared as the Year of St. Paul, to follow in the footsteps of St. Paul in Greece and Turkey. I was unwilling to take a huge group like the first time, but still we had forty four pilgrims on a fabulous trip that also included a three day cruise to the islands of Rhodes, Mykonos and Patmos, in the Mediterranean. During this trip we read significant passages from the letters of St. Paul. I also decided to divide the whole group into smaller ones, giving each one the name of St. Paul's churches: Corinthians, Romans, Ephesians, Thessalonians, and Colossians, *et cetera*.

Now we were getting really bold and adventuresome. People would constantly ask me where I was going on my next trip and they would also offer suggestions. We decided that our next tour would be in the footsteps of Jesus in the Holy Land. As we came close to our departure date, the news reported daily the fighting and the bombing taking place between Israel and the Palestinians of the Gaza strip. Thus, our group in the end was relatively small, only twenty one pilgrims. Some canceled because they did not agree with the politics of Israel and thus did not want to support the Israeli government with their dollars. They missed a memorable and moving pilgrimage to all the Holy sites of our faith. Our trips have always combined fun with faith.

In the Holy Land for fun I sat on the back of a camel for the first time in my life and joyfully floated on my back on the extremely salty waters of the Dead Sea.

Our next big adventure was to witness the Passion Play of Oberammergau, in Germany. This play takes place every ten years and the townspeople have been reenacting the final week in the life of Jesus continuously for the last four hundred years in gratitude for being saved from the plague.

Several parishioners had seen all these efforts of mine as bricks to build the strong spiritual and social edifice of community. When there is a sense of growth, togetherness, fun, learning and fellowship, people tend to stick together and to feel like family. When I came to this city, I sensed that the people were torn apart by 'mergers' and 'perceived conspiracies;' the inhabitants of this great city seemed to have been like a people in darkness; now, after a long journey, they had finally experienced the light of faith and the joy of community.

My role of Pastor and Shepherd had truly been appreciated by this resurrected community.

The mission of Jesus in our world, as enunciated in the tenth chapter of John's Gospel verse 10, has also been my desire and dream for all my parishes. Jesus said: "I came that you may have life and have it in abundance."

When we produced our latest Parish Picture Directory, I introduced the pictorial book with this reflection:

"Thank you for your participation in this new picture directory. I started my journey with you emphasizing the theme of 'Unity in Community.' This mosaic of parishioners and parish families helps us to express our Unity as one parish, while celebrating our uniqueness and diversity. One of the common features we have in our three churches is the beauty of our stained glass windows.

"Our oldest church, St. Thomas Aquinas, highlights the presence of the Blessed Virgin Mary and the Sacred Heart of Jesus, while bringing us the wisdom of many saints. Our Lady of the Rosary church teaches us the Seven Sacraments and invites us to meditate on the mysteries of our Catholic faith. Finally, St. Albert the Great church makes us fly to the heavens with the four evangelists and the many parables and stories of the Bible.

"We are a community because we are like a stained glass window. The primary purpose in making stained glass windows was to provide an expression of faith, a desire to beautify the house of God.

"With our three churches and a variety of liturgical celebrations, we, too, express our faith in a unique way, and each of us contributes to the beauty of the house and the people of God in this parish.

"A true stained glass window, as distinct from an enameled one, is essentially a mosaic of colored pieces. Each of us is important to the beauty and the unique expression of this parish mosaic. From earliest times, it was a source of wonder that the basest of natural materials, earth or sand, could, in conjunction with alkali and with the application of heat, be transformed into a wonderful translucent substance, capable of repelling the weather and yet admitting light.

"Sometimes, our gifts appear to be as insignificant as earth or sand, and our words, as so much heat, yet look at the results in a truly beautiful stained glass window.

"Glass, like a community, can be shattered, even beyond repair. But shattered glass can be collected, re-crafted with colored fragments from other sources, and with an artist's hands and a vision, built into a work of art that brings not just light and illumination but connects us to the source of light and helps us to uncover the hidden beauty of life and people.

"May this picture directory continue to inspire us to believe in the resurrected power and beauty of our Savior who continues to be present in our one community of faith and within our three churches of this beautiful city. Let us always rejoice in and celebrate our Unity in Community."

*****

The daily dying and rising of the Paschal Mystery has been part of my body, my mind, my soul and my priestly ministry. Recently I have experienced a sense of dying and resurrection in the sudden illness and recovery of my mother.

In April of 2007, my mother was going to celebrate her eighty-seventh birthday. Instead of keeping it just a private family affair, something urged me to make this event a big celebration. After consulting the rest of the family, we booked a hall with dining facilities and invited more than sixty people who had known my mother over the last several years. Our bishop, who has always shown concern for my mother, also showed up and surprised us all. My siblings are wonderful and we are all comfortable with crowds. So, the six of us entertained our guests, and shared very personal stories and funny moments of our relationship with our mother. As each sibling spoke, we gave Mother a rose. She sat quietly collecting roses and memories from us.

She was unusually quiet, yet alert during her birthday celebration. When we got home she opened her presents (the Indian custom, however, is not to open gifts in front of guests; this shows how far my mother had come to adapting to Western ways) and then went to bed. After that she simply closed her eyes all the time, even though she was attentive to the conversations around her.

None of us were familiar with what was happening to her or within her.

My mother has always been a talkative person. She loves company and is a wonderful host. So, to see her so quiet made us wonder if we had done something wrong. Some of us went on a guilt trip and asked her time and again if we had inadvertently hurt her or if she was remembering a painful incident from the past. Every time we talked with her about the past or about us, she quietly repeated that she was okay and that none of us had harmed her in any way. This regressive behavior went on for a month.

Finally, a psychotherapist friend of mine suggested that it could be geriatric depression. He recommended that we take her to a psychiatrist. The medication she received helped her open her eyes. We were relieved. But this did not last for very long.

She reacted to the medication and now she was unwilling to close her eyes. She wanted to stay awake all day and night and began to hallucinate. Some of her normal behaviors changed radically. She was not the mother we knew. One of the consequences of the depression was that she refused to eat or drink. This led to severe bouts of dehydration and several days in the hospital. In one of the hospitals we visited, we were told that the only way they could keep my mother alive was to force feed her.

Each time she was hydrated and appeared to get better we thought everything was fine. Then she would be back to square one. Caring, misguided people offered all kinds of labels: dementia, Alzheimer's, body shutting down, and even dying woman. I used to get upset because I sensed that something else was going on in her mind, and not knowing what it was left me simply baffled and helpless.

Throughout this ordeal, I shared my painful journey in my homilies. I was amazed at how many people resonated with my experience and my mother's situation. My eyes were open to the fact that there are many families which have elderly parents to take care of and to worry about. Caring for an elderly parent was no longer an exception. What also intrigued me and consoled me at the same time was to know that other elderly people were going through similar problems, almost identical to my mother's.

Eventually, we learned that what my mother had was simply a temporary chemical imbalance that she could not control and that happens with aging. There was nothing wrong with her or with any of us. No one can be blamed for the chemical imbalance that happens with aging. After much prayer and consultation, we found the right woman psychiatrist for our mother. She gave her the proper medication and my mother was quickly on the road to recovery.

Thanksgiving Day in November that year was indeed a celebration of gratitude for the health and the healing of our beloved mother, as well as our own healing and growth in the Spirit.

Whenever I felt most helpless, I put my full trust in God. Through this process of dying and carrying the Cross, I felt the resurrected healing power of the Lord come into my life.

At a priest's ordination, his hands are anointed with the sweet balsamic oil of Chrism. Then, with those same hands, the priest returns the sweet fragrance of the Holy Spirit into the lives of the people he touches through the Sacraments and through daily ministry. As we read in the poem: 'The Beautiful Hands of a Priest:'

> *When we are tempted and wander*
> *To pathways of shame and sin;*
> *'Tis the hand of a priest that absolves us*
> *Not once but again and again.*
> *And when we are taking life's partner,*
> *Other hands may prepare us a feast;*
> *But the hands that will bless and unite us*
> *Are the beautiful hands of a priest.*
> *When the death dews on our lids are falling*
> *May our courage and strength be increased;*
> *By seeing raised o'er us in blessing*
> *The beautiful hands of a priest.*

When Albrecht Dürer painted the Hands of the Priest, in the fragility and weakness of those hands he placed the power to heal the broken-hearted, to bless humanity and to bring comfort, peace and life wherever his path would lead him. Wherever I find myself as a priest, I know with certainty that I am where God wants me to be, and I hope that I will always reach out and do with my hands what God intends from 'the beautiful hands of His priest.'

The hands of the priest remind me of a story from an unknown author entitled 'My Grandma's Hands.'

Grandma, some ninety plus years, sat feebly on the front porch bench. She didn't move, just sat with her head down staring at her hands. When I sat down beside her, she didn't acknowledge my presence, and the longer I sat, I wondered if she was okay.

Finally, not really wanting to disturb her but wanting to check on her, I asked her if she was okay. She raised her head and looked at me and smiled. "Yes, I'm fine, thank you for asking," she said in a clear, strong voice. "I didn't mean to disturb you, Grandma, but you were just sitting here staring at your hands and I wanted to make sure you were okay."

"Have you looked at your hands?" she asked. "I mean really looked at your hands?" I slowly opened my hands and stared down at them. I turned them over, palms up and then palms down. "No, I guess I had never looked at my hands," I said to her as I tried to figure out the point she was making.

She smiled and said: "Stop and think for a moment about the hands you have, how they have served you well throughout your years. These hands, though wrinkled, shriveled and weak have been the tools I have used all my life to reach out, grab and embrace life. They braced and caught my fall when as a toddler I crashed upon the floor. They put food in my mouth and clothes on my back. As a child, my mother taught me to fold them in prayer. They tied my shoes and pulled on my boots. They held my husband and wiped my tears when he went off to war. They have been dirty, scraped and raw, swollen and bent. They were uneasy and clumsy when I tried to hold my newborn son. Decorated with my wedding band my hand showed the world that I was married and loved someone special. They wrote my letters to him and trembled and shook when I buried my parents and spouse. They have held my children and grandchildren, consoled neighbors and shook fists in anger when I didn't understand. They have covered my face, combed my hair and washed and cleansed the rest of my body. They have been sticky and wet, bent and broken, dried and raw. And to this day, when not much of anything else of me works real well, these hands hold me up, lay me down, and again continue to fold in prayer. These hands are the mark of where I've been and the ruggedness of life. But more importantly, it will be these hands that God will reach out and take when He leads me home. And with my hands He will lift me to His side and there I will use these hands to touch the face of Christ."

One day I, too, want to touch the face of God, who called me by name, and to feel His hands upon my face.

CHAPTER 9

LEGACY

W HEN I was preparing for ordination to the priesthood, I was asked to make a silent directed retreat. My Spiritual Director was a Spanish Jesuit professor. He asked me to meditate on the story of the rich young man of the Gospel, who follows all the commandments, yet he remains attached to his riches and does not want to let go. We are told that Jesus loved him and wanted him to be a disciple. But in the end the rich young man goes his own separate way because attachment to riches becomes an obstacle to discipleship.

I was asked to reflect on this story and apply it to my own life. Were there attachments in my life that would prevent me from being a faithful and dedicated priest?

After thirty-five years of priesthood I recently made my second silent directed retreat. The Church has changed a lot since I was first ordained. This time my Spiritual Director appointed by the diocese and trained by the Jesuits was going to be a woman. She was sensitive to the movements of the Holy Spirit, which made the retreat a fabulous experience for me.

I told her that I did not know how to prepare for this form of retreat. She asked me: "What do you want from this retreat?" I said: "I want what God wants. I want to do the Will of God." Then, I quickly added another question: "How will I know what God wants for me?" She said: "Ask God."

This time I was not limited to just one Gospel story for my meditations. The first meditation was from the beginning of John's Gospel when John the Baptist and two of his disciples are following Jesus. Since I was making my retreat in a Jesuit retreat house and the Spiritual Director was trained in the exercises of St. Ignatius of Loyola, I began to enter into the practice of Ignatian contemplation. After reading a Gospel text slowly, you are asked to close your eyes and place yourself in the scene.

Among the disciples of John the Baptist who are following Jesus, one of them is named Andrew, but the other does not have a name. So, it was simple for me to be part of the scene by becoming Andrew's companion. Jesus turns around and says to me: "What are you looking for?" My Spiritual Director had said that whenever a question came my way from God, I should ask God for the answer. My first response was to ask Jesus: "What do you want me to look for?" Instead, nervous and excited at being found out, I asked Jesus: "Where do you live?" And Jesus said: "Come and see."

With my eyes still closed in meditation and yet fully awake to the scene, I saw Andrew and me walking on either side of Jesus. I felt that we were companions and close friends of Jesus. We also held hands and I could feel the strong hand of Jesus, a carpenter's son. In the Middle East and in some Asian countries like India, men who are friends will hold hands in public, while women almost never hold hands with other women in public. I felt a deep sense of joy as I walked along with Jesus and Andrew.

It was a long walk but it never felt tiring with Jesus. Finally, we approached his house and guess who came to meet us at the door? Yes, it was Mary and Joseph who bent down to wash first the feet of Jesus and then our feet, too. My eyes were closed but I was weeping at this tender, humble gesture from Mary and Joseph. Then, they gave Jesus a big hug and said: "Welcome home, son." Then, guess what? Mary and Joseph also gave Andrew and me big hugs and said sweetly to each of us: "Welcome home, son." Then Joseph had us all sit down on a sturdy wooden bench.

Like a proud father, he told us that it was Jesus who had made the bench; and then he pointed out to the dining table and the chairs and added that they, too, were made by Jesus.

There was a look of simple beauty to this furniture. Somehow, Joseph reminded me of my dad and how when we had visitors he would always say something affirming to them about me. Historically, Joseph may have already been dead by the time Jesus began his public ministry, but historical facts did not matter in this Ignatian contemplation. What truly mattered was what God was doing for me in this scene. I was weeping bitterly by now as I remembered my wonderful dad and how I received so much love from Mary and Joseph. I observed that Jesus' family was holy because it was a loving and caring family. In my meditation I continued to be grateful that God had blessed me with a loving and caring family.

The Gospel text simply states that the two disciples spent the afternoon with Jesus. I was always curious as to what happened that afternoon. I found out more in my meditation. Mary brought some snacks and tea for us, which is also a custom in Far Eastern countries. Andrew and I sat on either side of Jesus and continued to feel this strong sense of companionship and friendship. Joseph excused himself to continue his work at his carpenter's shop next door, while Mary went to prepare the evening meal.

I had visited the Holy Land some months earlier, so I could visualize exactly where Joseph went when he bade us goodbye.

Then, Jesus asked Andrew about his family. Andrew told him about Simon, his brother. Jesus indicated that he knew him and wanted so much to meet him later, because he had plans for his future. I realized at that moment that I should not worry about the future because I am not there yet and the future is in the hands of Jesus.

Then, Jesus asked me about my family. I really felt he was interested and not rushed or making small talk. I have a large family so I had much sharing to do with Jesus.

The afternoon went by quickly.

As I was returning home, the question of Jesus was still haunting me: "What are you looking for?" There are no coincidences or accidents in the Spiritual life, because at that very moment, I remembered a thin book I had just begun to read in the morning. It was a gift given to me for Christmas. It was written by St.

Albert the Great, titled *Union with God.* On the very first page and reflection, there was a quote from the Song of Songs, Chapter 3, Verse 4:

"I found him whom my heart loves."

My inner eyes were opened. I had found the answer to the question of Jesus: "What are you looking for?" My answer: "I found Him whom my heart loves."

I was in love with Jesus all over again and even more deeply than I could ever imagine. Why do I still love being a priest? I love being a priest because I found Him again whom my heart loves.

In the garden by the empty tomb, the risen Jesus (although he appears to be the gardener) asks Mary Magdalene and me: "Who are you looking for?" The answer is the same.

When you find Him again whom your heart loves, your life will never be the same. I love being a priest and I love priestly ministry even more intensely than I did before. I pray the breviary and there is passion in my preaching and in the celebration of the Sacraments. I have more patience with difficult people and with situations that cannot be resolved. I trust more in God and I feel I now have a greater capacity to love. I am forever grateful that I found Him whom my heart loves.

So where do I go from here?

One day, during an earlier annual clergy retreat (though not a silent, directed one), I went to confess my sins to one of the Spiritual Directors of the retreat house. More than a specific list of sins, I was acknowledging the confusion and the chaotic feeling of doing ministry at my parish. I was not able to pray because of the distress I was experiencing. I was being impatient with others and I was feeling lost and lonely. The confessor listened to me lovingly and patiently.

Then he told me that when I die, I will find myself in a very large, festively decorated and spacious hall. I will be alone for a few moments and even wonder why I'm there and what's really going on. Then, from a side door, Jesus will enter and walk toward me. With a kind smile, he will put his arm around me.

With the other hand he will shift my attention to the front door which will be opened by two angels.

Through the open doors several women, men and children of all ages will come pouring in. For a moment I am unable to recognize anyone. As they come closer I realize they are headed toward Jesus and me.

Now they are really close and I seem to recognize some familiar faces. But most of them are still unknown to me. As they come closer to Jesus they smile at him and he gently smiles at them. Then, one after the other, they walk up to me, shake my hands warmly and hug me tenderly. They also stop to tell me who they are and express their gratitude for what I have done for them. As I listen to them, most of the time I don't remember the events and incidents they are referring to. But their words are filled with gratitude and love for me, and they keep reminding me of how I have touched their lives. There are literally hundreds and thousands of people walking through those doors and forming a long line to get a chance to thank me for being the priest in their lives.

The last person to walk up to me is Mary, our blessed Mother. I cannot believe my eyes. She hugs her Son, Jesus, first and then tenderly hugs me. I want to go down on my knees to touch her feet, but she holds me up. She thanks me for saying "Yes" to the priesthood and to following Jesus faithfully. And I thank her for guarding me and guiding my journey.

I knew that Mary was always the silent partner in my life helping me to constantly seek and to do the Will of God. The words of the *Memorare* came to me: "Remember, O most gracious Virgin Mary that never was it known that anyone who fled to thy protection was left unaided."

Mary, the mother of priests, had led me to the One from whom priesthood flows, her own Son, Jesus, and my Lord and Savior. I was in heaven.

Conclusions

M Y VOCATION journey has finally brought me back full circle to a parish in the Mission City of Santa Clara. This is where I first stepped foot in California several years ago. It is one of many significant circles in my life's journey.

I never traveled from place to place simply to explore possibilities or to seek the thrill of adventure.

As I look back at my life, I sense that the Holy Spirit has been constantly guiding and inspiring me and leading the way.

With the experiences and lessons that travels and transitions have brought me I have learned to live life to the fullest — whatever life brings me.

Every parish community with its positives and its challenges provided the experience and the spiritual growth for me to become a more rounded and grounded shepherd of God's people.

For this reason I am convinced that I am where God wants me to be. Like the women and men of the Scriptures, I, too, have entrusted my life to God. There have been times when I have been very impatient with the unfolding of life. But God can write straight even with crooked lines.

Sometimes I would have preferred to remove those individuals and events that entered my life and put a bitter taste in my mouth. But one's life is like a tapestry where every thread has a rightful place in its overall beauty. If you forcefully remove one or more of the threads, you might end up unraveling and ruining the entire tapestry.

I don't blame others for anything that has happened to me on my journey. Rather I am grateful for all those who came into my life, because they have made me who I am today. They have been important catalysts in the direction my life has taken.

Life is like a mosaic where every piece is important, even the ones that seem insignificant to the whole picture.

A man who found out that he had not very long to live started drawing concentric circles on a piece of paper. Within these circles he inserted the names of family, friends, business partners and co-workers. Next to these names he indicated approximately how much time he had spent with them during his life that was now soon going to end. He discovered that most of his life had been spent with business partners and co-workers and very few moments with family and friends. With the limited time at his disposal, he started to reorganize his priorities.

The Jesuit priest, Fr. Pierre Teilhard de Chardin, who was both a scientist and a cosmologist, after the maturity that came to him with age and experience, once wrote the following to a young priest struggling with life and ministry:

"Above all, trust in the slow work of God. We are quite naturally impatient in everything to reach the end without delay. We should like to skip the intermediate stages. We are impatient of being on the way to something unknown, something new. And yet it is the law of all progress that it is made by passing through some stages of instability — and that it may take a very long time.

"And so I think it is with you; your ideas mature gradually — let them grow and let them shape themselves, without undue haste. Don't try to force them as though you could be today what time (that is to say, grace and circumstances acting on your own good will) will make of you tomorrow.

"Only God could say what this new spirit gradually forming within you will be. Give our Lord the benefit of believing that His hand is leading you, and accept the anxiety of feeling yourself in suspense and incomplete."

God has given me good health and good genes. He has blessed me abundantly. In reviewing my life, I don't have any regrets about the past. My entire family has moved close to me and now we have family gatherings as if we never left the shores of Bombay and India. And whenever I lost old friends, I constantly made many more new ones. I have balanced my work and ministry with rest, relaxation, travel and healthy relationships. God has been part of and in my journey at all times. I am forever grateful. Despite some setbacks and disappointments, which are part of the essence and journey of life, I am still truly happy to be a priest.

Father Pedro Arrupe, a former Superior General of the Jesuits, provided for me an understanding of where my life is today:

> "More than ever I find myself in the hands of God.
> This is what I have wanted all my life from my youth.
>
> But now there is a difference;
> The initiative is entirely with God.
>
> It is indeed a profound spiritual experience
> To know and feel myself so totally in God's hands."

Everything is Grace!

Epilogue

F ROM THE heart of an unknown author, I was reminded that the word '*guidance*' has '*dance*' as the second syllable. Doing God's Will in your daily life and in priestly ministry is a lot like dancing. I love to dance, as I did often in our family gatherings and parties. After all, I had five partners to choose from, my five sisters like the five fingers of a hand, who also loved to dance.

When both individuals try to lead, nothing feels right. What one person needs to do is to give gentle cues; perhaps with a nudge to the back, or by pressing lightly in one direction or another.

Then the two become one body, moving beautifully in a mesmerizing way across the dance floor of life. Each of the two has an important role to play in the dance.

The dance takes surrender, willingness and attentiveness from one person; and gentle guidance, timely promptings and skill from the other.

When I reflected again on the word '*guidance*,' I looked closely at the three letters that preceded the ones that form the word '*dance*.' The letter '*G*' could stand for *God*, followed by '*U*' and '*I*.'

Then the word '*guidance*' came alive for me because I saw '*God*,' '*You*' and '*I*' dancing together throughout my life.

Let the dance of Grace continue....